# Creation

"Dr. Kneip, an Anglican lay theologian, makes a convincing case for recovery of the biblical doctrine of creation as key to understanding the uniqueness of the whole of the biblical narrative from Genesis 1 to Revelation 21. The unified purpose of the Creator God—Father, Son and Holy Spirit—consistently plays out in the re-creation, redemption, and salvation of mankind until it reaches its ultimate conclusion in its fulfilment at the end of time."

—Robert Duncan, Archbishop Emeritus,
Anglican Church in North America

"This book is a remarkable call to know the biblical history of creation, its implications in history, and how important it is today as we seek to live our lives according to the moral and ethical standards of the Creator."

—Major B. Harding, Retired Justice, Supreme Court of Florida

"Robert Kneip reminds us that creation is not a discarded notion of a prescientific age, but the gospel itself. With pastoral clarity and theological depth, he draws readers into Scripture's unified story. In an age of false divides between faith and science, this book calls the church to deeper reflection, back to the coherence, authority, and beauty of the biblical narrative, and to a renewed confidence in the truth we proclaim."

—Marcus Kaiser, Dean, St. Peter's Anglican Cathedral,
Tallahassee

"What does it mean to be human and to behave humanly? Robert Kneip argues persuasively that an ultimate answer cannot be found apart from a comprehensive understanding of reality rooted in the biblical narrative of Genesis. That narrative grounds and encompasses the entire canon of Scripture, framing God's purposes for a redeemed humanity within the bounds of his good creation. We are not lost in the cosmos; we are of the earth and made to serve and keep it!"

—Joel Scandrett, Associate Professor of Historical Theology,
Trinity Anglican Seminary

"Well-reasoned, thoroughly researched, accessible, biblically grounded, and refreshingly unapologetic, Robert Kneip's *Creation* explores man's place in the cosmos and the wondrous God that made it all for his glory. He's right: the Bible's account of creation is not just one of many origin myths. It is God's inerrant and infallible record of the first event in history. Man will never know his chief end—'to glorify God and enjoy him forever'—without first knowing his beginning."

—Jim McCarthy, Pastor of Trinity Presbyterian Church, Statesboro, Georgia, author *The Two Prophets to Nineveh*

"Too often Christians in today's world are not sufficiently equipped to defend the faith. Finally, here is an accessible tool that will help you better understand and defend the truth so that we as believers can step boldly into today's culture and 'make disciples of all nations.'"

—J. Robert McClure III, President, The James Madison Institute

# Creation

## Ancient Myth or Living History

ROBERT C. KNEIP

WIPF & STOCK · Eugene, Oregon

CREATION
Ancient Myth or Living History



Wipf & Stock
An Imprint of Wipf and Stock Publishers
199 W. 8th Ave., Suite 3
Eugene, OR 97401

www.wipfandstock.com

PAPERBACK ISBN: 979-8-3852-7562-5
HARDCOVER ISBN: 979-8-3852-7563-2
EBOOK ISBN: 979-8-3852-7564-9

To my wife Cindy, who is a constant reminder of God's saving grace and enduring love;
To our daughters, Katie and Courtney, who are constant reminders of the joys and blessings of a faithful marriage; and
To our grandchildren, Colton, Delaney, Hayden, and Parker, who are constant reminders that innocent charm, unceasing curiosity, laughter, and silliness are His gifts as well.

# Contents

# Acknowledgments

THE THINKING BEHIND THIS project had been germinating for years, but it was during the pandemic of 2019–2021 that I began to put my thoughts on paper. There wasn't much to do with everything shut down or restricted, so I simply read and wrote, then wrote some more. The outcome was a draft of roughly four hundred pages.

As is generally the case, a project of this nature does not come to fruition without the support and assistance of many people. The Most Rev. Robert Duncan has been instrumental throughout the process. Archbishop Duncan has earned a place in the history of the church as one of the first to courageously speak out against the secular excesses of liberal theology and became the first archbishop of the newly founded Anglican Church in North America. He has been instrumental in the growth and development of orthodox Anglicanism across the globe and has been critical to the emergence of Trinity Anglican Seminary as the foremost source of orthodox Anglican education and thought in the United States. This worldwide renewal in traditional orthodox theology was of inestimable value to me as I developed my thesis. The archbishop has also been a consistent and cheerful supporter of this project from the outset, including a willingness to look at various sections of the manuscript and offer wise counsel. We went over drafts together and had many delightful conversations that shaped the research and the theology of this book. I am not sure this project would have made it this far without his involvement.

Early in the process, Archbishop Duncan introduced me to the Rev. Dr. Joel Scandrett, associate professor of historical theology at Trinity Anglican Seminary. I had attempted to create a coherent narrative out of loosely related topics that, in the isolation of the pandemic, seemed to make sense. Professor Scandrett was willing to dive into a four-hundred-page draft and dealt very kindly with me in his critical analysis. Among other things, he suggested that this was more appropriately two projects, and I would be better served treating the topics separately. I wisely chose to listen. The result is not only this book but material sufficient for another manuscript. His kindness and graciousness in wading through that early material was a critical inflexion point in my thought process.

Two other individuals were supportive in ways they probably did not recognize at the time. The Very Rev. Marcus Kaiser, Dean of St. Peter's Anglican Cathedral in Tallahassee, assumed his position in the middle of COVID and during a very difficult period in the Cathedral's history. As Senior Warden of the Cathedral, I spent a great deal of time with Fr. Marcus. He is an engaging and intelligent individual as well as an exceptional preacher. More often than not, our conversations moved from church management to matters of a larger theological nature. Fr. Marcus was instrumental in returning the *Book of Common Prayer* to the language and substance of its original composer, Thomas Cranmer. The 2019 revision is a great source of information on the formative theology of the Anglican church and reflects a joy and beauty in its language that is both faithful and uplifting.

The other individual is Fr. Michael Petty, recently retired Canon for adult formation, also with St. Peter's. Fr. Michael founded The Charles Simeon Institute and the Lay School of Theology. Both of these organizations have become very successful in developing seminarians looking for a career in the church, and laypeople seeking to develop stronger leadership skills within faith communities. Fr. Petty is a true scholar and a wealth of information. I've gone to that well on many occasions. Jennifer Webster is the Executive Director of The Simeon Institute and a PhD candidate at the University of Cambridge. Under her leadership, the Institute has grown dramatically in scope and quality. She has also been very helpful and supportive.

My sincere thanks to all these individuals. Any errors, controversial opinions, or theological gaffes are mine alone.

I also benefitted from the involvement of two other gentlemen. The first is Dr. Robert McClure, President and CEO of the James Madison Institute. Bob not only read through the manuscript and offered his perspectives but, more importantly, he introduced me to two of his staff writers who develop scholarly documents for the institute. Jill Mattox, senior director of grants and editing, and Adelyn Valencia, grant writer, agreed to work with me on the manuscript in their off-time. They meticulously went through every page, making suggestions and asking questions. Their comments and recommendations were immensely helpful. They cannot know how valuable their assistance was to me and the final draft of the book.

The other individual of note is Jeff Atwater, former President of the Florida Senate and the state's Chief Financial Officer from 2010–2018. Jeff has been a close friend for many years, and I served as his chief of staff in both roles after I retired. He read through many iterations of the project, offering thoughts and perspectives I might have missed. In fact, he saw the manuscript in its earliest, and least coherent, stages. Jeff has been a consistent and encouraging supporter from the beginning, frequently checking on my progress. For the contributions of both Bob and Jeff, I am eternally grateful.

The folks at Wipf & Stock are consummate professionals and have been a pleasure to work with. Among their many skills is patience, which was essential in guiding me through the publishing process. Matt Wimer and George Callihan in particular have helped to shape the outcome.

Finally, special thanks to Devin Galetta, who, drawing from his wide experience in the public sector press arena, offered sound advice on planning and managing social media. Meredith Hunter is a well respected professional who helped polish my social media skills and remains an important source of knowledge and perspective. Jon Yeaton assisted me for years in the Department of Financial Services and continues to bail me out of technology jams, which occur far too frequently. Alison Dudley tirelessly assisted me in validating and updating contact information. Jesse Romimora was able to take time from his busy schedule to take the photographs that I have used for the book jacket and social media platforms. While seemingly small details, they make a world of difference, and each one has earned my respect and gratitude.

Of course, I cannot close without mentioning Cindy, my wife of over forty years. She knew exactly when to encourage me to push forward and when to summon me from my office to rejoin the outside world. She even ran out one rainy Sunday afternoon to find a couple of books that suddenly became critical in the final stages. She has always been, and will forever be, my greatest blessing.

# List of Abbreviations

ESV: English Standard Version Study Bible
RSV: The New Oxford Annotated Bible, Revised Standard Version
BCP: Book of Common Prayer

Books of the Bible:

| | | |
|---|---|---|
| Gen | Song | Matt |
| Exod | Isa | Mark |
| Lev | Jer | Luke |
| Num | Lam | John |
| Deut | Ezek | Acts |
| Josh | Dan | Rom |
| Judg | Hos | 1–2 Cor |
| Ruth | Joel | Gal |
| 1–2 Sam | Amos | Eph |
| 1–2 Kgs | Obad | Phil |
| 1–2 Chr | Jonah | Col |
| Ezra | Mic | 1–2 Thess |
| Neh | Nah | 1–2 Tim |
| Esth | Hab | Titus |
| Job | Zeph | Phlm |
| Ps | Hag | Heb |
| Prov | Zech | Jas |
| Eccl | Mal | 1–2 Pet |
| | | 1–3 John |
| | | Jude |
| | | Rev |

# Introduction

"For we did not follow cleverly devised myths when we made known to you the power and coming of our Lord Jesus Christ, but we were eyewitnesses of his majesty."[1] Very early in the development of Christianity, St. Peter identified a challenge that has become common currency in the twenty-first century. Myths have become a preferred source for insights into the deep relationship between humanity and the cosmos, between human existence and the mysteries of the universe. This study is designed to refocus attention on the centrality, veracity, and indisputable role of the biblical creation story—a story that deepens our understanding of the essential nature of humanity and offers profound insights into the greater purposes of a cosmic journey. It also seeks to recover, for ordinary believers, cultural apologists, and philosophical thinkers alike, the full importance of acknowledging and embracing Creation[2] as the key to God's plan for the re-creation, redemption, and salvation of humanity. Along the way, critical distinctions between mythological origin stories and biblical Creation are examined, particularly God's unique and inestimable gift of language and speech.

The tensions between the Creation story found in Genesis and the creation stories of other cultures have been a fixture since the scriptural narrative began. The Old Testament Jews were constantly tempted by the robust and lively myth traditions of neighboring gods and remained frustratingly committed to family idols. Tales of gods and demigods are deeply ensconced in ancient traditions and retain some measure of cultural influence to this day. Through newly discovered artifacts and documents, these stories are constantly renewed and refreshed. God's presence across

1. 2 Pet 1:16.

2. For purposes of simplicity, the capitalized "Creation" will be used throughout the text to distinguish the Genesis narrative from other creation myths.

the ages has been framed by His engagement with competing origin stories and the allure of other gods.

While myths have created challenges to Christian faith from the very beginning, during the mid to late twentieth century mythological narratives began to pose a far more damaging threat to Christianity. Mythology had become a social science, an acceptable framework for evaluating and understanding the very deep-seated behaviors that define and govern human relationships. The philosophical and psychological explanations for how humans react to one another, the cosmic and the mysterious, are embedded in a broader definition of mythology and are now commonplace even within many Christian circles.

Over the past decades, the story of Creation, indeed the very idea of Creation, has grown increasingly irrelevant. Anyone suggesting that Creation is either historical or cohesive is generally met with skepticism or contempt. At best, the story is viewed as a prologue to something much more profound—an allegorical morality play, if you will, meant as a purely instructional device. Even when the Creation story is introduced as groundwork for a broader ethical conversation, it is a conversation stripped of any divinity. In its stead there lives a flimsy shadow of Creation's reality, carefully built around culturally derived values and socially useful rationalizations. The Creation is viewed as a chimerical idyll, beautiful and comforting but ultimately unattainable.

Contemporary culture has become dismissive of everything that has been foundational for the Judeo-Christian ethos. For thousands of years, ethics and values associated with the Bible were the core around which vigorous intellectual and philosophical issues were debated and shaped. As the influence of critical theory in the 1920s and mid-century postmodernism began to erode traditional value systems, an intellectual and ethical vacuum was created. The inhumanity of two global wars had shaken centuries-old assumptions. Vigorous debates on economic, political, and social development increasingly looked to sources of intellectual authority that elbowed Scriptures out of the picture. Cynicism and pessimism became the new language of education, arts, and the sciences. As the gap between faith and community widened, opinion elites no longer felt the need to intellectually engage Christianity, as had been the case in the past. All that is necessary in this self-absorbed, self-justified wasteland of secular presumption is to simply co-opt Creation as one of many forms of mythology that may, or may not, be useful in understanding the human condition. It has become much easier to kill with kindness.

Except in narrow theological circles, less and less time is committed to studying and understanding the purpose of Creation and the part Creation values and ethics play in developing and sustaining the physical and psychological nature of humanity. As this has become more calculated and scientific, the idea of redemption and salvation have become secular concepts. They are viewed as achievable through human endeavor alone, and what constitutes redemption and salvation are characterized by selfish objectives and cultural pressures.

Creation is not a myth. It is not a fable that conveniently ends after a couple of chapters, with tragic undertones of murder and alienation. Creation is the living and ongoing process of recentering God's value proposition within the human experience. God's desire to reestablish the initial eternal relationship with mankind, as presented in Genesis, is the theme that animates all of history. Redemption and salvation are processes by which God delivers humanity to a specifically determined end state of human experience.

Creation is more than prehistorical oral tradition, an introduction to the wisdom of following good and avoiding evil. But its complexity must be acknowledged and embraced. It is the history of a people set apart. It is not only the beginning of time but a journey of redemption and salvation which cannot be cohesive without a deeper understanding of what God had in mind when He created heaven and earth in the first place. It is not an event but a process. Absent that understanding, nothing of Scripture makes any sense. The idea of redemption and salvation have become cultural devices, not godly imperatives.

What should emerge from the Creation story is a dominant narrative with characteristics so distinct that its fullness is self-evident, not diluted, ignored, or set aside. It is not sufficient to treat Creation as a useful tale designed to keep small children engaged during Sunday school. After all, buying the idea of a universe spoken into existence by a supernatural being, populated by two seemingly indolent characters that squander a perfectly good deal because of a snake, strikes the sophisticated and learned as rather puerile. If reduced to that level, it is easy to accept the notion that Creation is just one of many examples of equally entertaining creation stories. The challenge is not simply a matter of guarding against sloppy teaching or heresy. Even heresy requires an orthodox theological baseline.[3] St. Peter's declaratory statement, issued over two thousand

3. McGrath, *Heresy*.

years ago, is a resounding call to confront a prevailing cultural premise that, if not vigorously challenged, dooms Christianity by a respectful benevolence to quaint irrelevance.

In fact, that irrelevance is on full display in many academic circles, where the Genesis story is classified and studied as just one of a number of mythical traditions. There is a seductive tendency, even among those professing a Christian faith, to accept the idea that the ancients who recorded history in the Scriptures were simply not very sophisticated. They had to rely on the literary devices of myths and fables to rationalize the ethical basis for how the universe was formed and functions. There had to be a satisfying beginning somewhere, and a fable performed that task perfectly well. This seems a woefully inadequate way to launch a magnificent story of redemption, salvation, and the re-creation of a perfected relationship with God.

Mythology is fascinating and entertaining, and I fully acknowledge that myths, fables, folklore, legends, and sagas have an important role in defining cultures and values. A recently published book on American politics entitled *A Great Disorder: National Myth and the Battle for America* is premised on the contention that current social, political, and economic tensions are driven by competing versions of our own origin myth.[4] As uneven as such an approach to American history may be, it is an example of just how pervasive the idea of founding myths can be. However, it is just as unsatisfactory to assume that Creation can be best understood by simply forcing it into mythological patterns that have been fashioned by the disciplines of modern social science.

Dusting off some collections of creation myths I have had in my library for years, I began to look for critical differences that might set the Genesis Creation apart from other origin narratives. There are three distinct traits that clearly distinguish Creation from other origin stories.

First is the monotheistic framework introduced in Genesis and developed through the remainder of Scripture. The Genesis Creation is the only origin narrative that insists on the recognition and adoration of one God for all of history to the end of time. It is not only His oneness but His uniqueness that differentiates the Creation God. All other creation myths speak to a very busy collection of gods and demigods, most of whom are engaged to greater or lesser degrees in the business of mankind. They

4. Slotkin, *Great Disorder.*

are distinguishable from one another only to the extent that they may assume differing roles within the cosmos.

The second distinction is the manner in which God is invested in His Creation through all of human history, from its beginning until its end. God wants His Creation to succeed, whereas other gods of other narratives demonstrate only sporadic and seemingly random interest in humanity. They will respond to requests under certain circumstances and may adopt a distant concern about the fate of humanity, but they are not constantly and consistently engaged in perfecting the relationship with that which they created, and certainly not throughout human history, past, present, and future. The God of Creation made covenantal agreements, contracts with obligations on all parties, that were aimed at salvation, resurrection, and a place in His kingdom. Eventually, the "Almighty and everlasting God, who in the Paschal mystery established the new covenant of reconciliation"[5] anointed the incarnate Word,[6] His Son, as the new high priest.[7] The gods of other creation myths demonstrate nowhere near this level of commitment to delivering humanity to a perfected conclusion.

Finally, the third distinction is the role of language and speech, not only within the Creation narrative itself but as a part of a living legacy. It is a legacy that requires humanity to act as stewards, implementing God's value proposition and managing Creation and re-creation as God's representatives on earth. Not only are language and speech the tools by which God created but the use of language and speech have been, and continue to be, the very same tools that define and protect the integrity of God's Creation as it moves through time to its final re-creation at the end of time. They were a gift God gave to humanity to share in the ordering of His universe according to His moral and ethical standards. Such a gift is without parallel in the catalogue of creator gods of other myths.

Language and speech grant a unique authority to mankind and, with it, extraordinary power to operate in partnership with the Creator. If we are to order society in accordance with His moral and ethical standards, as God charged humans in the first and second chapters of Genesis, it can only be done by maintaining the accuracy and integrity of the Creation narrative. Not only are the gifts of language and speech unique to

5. BCP, 612.

6. "Word" is capitalized throughout when it refers to the Word of God or His manifested Word as used by John in John 1:1.

7. Heb 8:1–7.

Creation, they are the ongoing tools by which humanity is to serve God as He redeems the universe. It is the authority of language and speech as both Creative and re-creative that is so unique. Prometheus's gift of fire cannot compare with the gift of language and speech.

Psalm 51:15, which reads in part, "O Lord, open my lips, and my mouth shall show forth your praise," is but one of many verses in Scripture that identify and define human responsibilities growing out of the act of Creation. I began to wonder, after years of reading this as part of morning prayer, whether this is just a plea for help with improving behavior or if there is something more insistent in the verse. After all, it does not read "open my lips and once in a while let me slip in a nice phrase on your behalf." Are we simply meant to pray that somewhere in the day's conversations we acknowledge the Lord's influence, or is it one of many reminders that we are to protect the integrity of the Creation narrative and ensure that the narrative is passed down through the generations both accurately and powerfully? Not that we are constantly called to preach but that we remain sensitive to speech that either reinforces or diminishes the language and symbols of salvation.

More importantly, are language and speech being used to most effectively move the redemption and salvation of Creation forward? This is a pivotal question. Given the uniqueness of the Creator and His covenantal relationship with humanity, the willingness to accept the responsibilities attendant to the gift of language and speech determines whether we can, in the words of Paul, "abound in the work of the Lord, knowing that in the Lord your labor is not in vain."[8]

Once started down this path, it became increasingly apparent that the Scriptures deal with the issues of speech and the use of words constantly, not only for the purposes of maintaining the integrity of the scriptural narrative but also to reinforce the uniqueness of God and fulfill His covenantal agreements. I began noting every reference to speech, words, lips, mouth, and tongue that I came across. I consulted my concordance,[9] and counting the references to speech, words, lips, mouth, and tongue, with all their appropriate variations, there are nearly three thousand citations (2,797 to be precise). This far outpaces much more profound subject matters such as prayer (545), love (532), praise (287), and worship

8. 1 Cor 15:58.

9. Strong, *Concordance.*

(198), again, with all their associated variations. Hardly an empirically derived analysis, but informative nonetheless.

It is clear that language and speech reflect the speakers' core values and that our conversations can be just as purposeful and powerful as those in the Scriptures. "Let no corrupting talk come out of your mouths, but only such as is good for building up, as fits the occasion, that it may give grace to those who hear."[10] These instructions, given by Paul to the Ephesians, came directly from the teachings of Jesus as recorded in Matthew and Luke.[11]

This is not a call to strict asceticism. Just as the Scriptures are full of language of love, beauty, laughter, and joy, so should our language. No gift of God has ever been intended for pain and discomfort, and language and speech are no different. Holy language is not empty, mechanical, or desiccated. It is not merely an encoded set of symbols, useful for positioning humans in their cosmic environment. It is meant to convey the rich fullness of a godly life, and it can do so across a wide range of topics and emotions.

The act of re-creating is just as profound a mystery as the original Creation itself. The words of Creation, and the language we choose to protect the narrative, are the same words that became incarnate in the form of the Christ. There is a direct line from the words of Creation, through the incarnate Word, to the everlasting Word, the Holy Spirit. This leads to three conclusions. First, to the original question, this is clearly a qualitative distinction between Creation and myth. Secondly, the word has retained its initial creative power to govern humanity and drive history, and finally, the faithful use of language and speech affords us the opportunity to participate, as God's partners, in re-creating the universe according to His purposes.

Language and speech are much more than tools for sharing information. God's vested interest in our salvation is reflected, in part, not only by His ardent desire that we continually communicate with Him through prayer but that we continually communicate with others through worship and the uplifting language of faith. We participate in the communion of saints through the language of prayer, and those who have gone before continue to speak to us through the Holy Spirit. The entire Creation story, from the garden to the new kingdom, is one of building

10. Eph 4:29.

11. Matt 13:48; Luke 6:43.

divine and human relationships by protecting, securing, and spreading the faith. Language and speech attest to the uniqueness of a monotheistic God, and are the tools for satisfying the terms of His covenants with humanity while faithfully documenting the authenticity of the narrative.

Creation is also a story of the failure to use the gifts of language and speech to support our own witness or reinforce the witness of others. The Scriptures are replete with examples of the spoken word undermining faith rather than building it up. Hence the constant admonitions, warnings, cautions, and guidance throughout Scripture on the use and application of speech. Nearly every chapter of Scripture has something instructive to say about matters of language and speech.

In response to criticism from the Pharisees and scribes about some of His sayings, Christ addressed the question in this way:

> Hear and understand: it is not what goes into the mouth that defiles a person, but what comes out of the mouth; this defiles a person. . . . Do you not see that whatever goes into the mouth passes into the stomach and is expelled? But what comes out of the mouth proceeds from the heart, and this defiles a person. For out of the heart come evil thoughts, murder, adultery, sexual immorality, theft, false witness, slander. These are what defile a person.[12]

That which defiles a person also creates threats to faith and the narrative of salvation. An individual can put things into his or her mouth that produce bad outcomes, whether it is overeating, excessive drink, drug abuse, or even poison. The impact, while potentially horrific, is somewhat limited. Obviously, the individual is harmed, and his or her immediate circle is damaged but, in the scheme of things, the scope is relatively local. On the other hand, we see every day the scope of the devastation caused by what comes out of one's mouth, be it insensitive, intemperate comments, or malicious, intentional speech.

In the secular arena, language and word choice can incite terrorism, violence, suicide, and hate. From the Christian standpoint, what one says can undermine another's faith or the quality of the speaker's witness. While physical behavior is somewhat constrained by the limits of contact and natural laws of time and space, the spoken word can carry on well beyond the speaker and over a great span of time. The psalmist pleaded with God, "O God, you know my folly; the wrongs I have done are not

12. Matt 15:10–11, 17–20.

hidden from you. Let not those who hope in you be put to shame through me, O Lord God of hosts; let not those who seek you be brought to dishonor through me, O God of Israel."[13]

As Paul is offering guidance to Timothy, he says to his young coworker, "Charge them before God not to quarrel about words, which does no good, but only ruins the hearers . . . avoid irreverent babble, for it will lead people into more and more ungodliness, and their talk will spread like gangrene."[14] The fact that the Scriptures contain so many references to language and word usage simply underscores how corrosive speech can be and how critical it is to our spiritual and temporal relationships.

The purpose here is, first, to recognize and acknowledge the unique and powerful story of a Creation with a beginning and an end, and the ongoing relationship of a loving God with His creation. There is one, true God, worthy of worship, the author of transcendent, absolute truths. These truths do not morph and change because of social or cultural pressures but remain constant throughout all of history. God's value proposition is the substance around which the human experience is to be built.

Secondly, while there may be elements in the Creation story that are similar to a wide variety of other creation myths, the narrative that begins with Genesis and ends with the Revelation is unique precisely *because* of its totality. No other creation myth is built upon the Creator's desire for an immediate and intimate relationship with all of Creation, which He then nurtures and guides across history. It is a narrative that describes both the beginning and the end of time. It is a relationship that is covenanted between Him and humanity until the objective of living within the fullness of faith is achieved.

Finally, communication, language, and speech are vital and distinct elements of the scriptural Creation. They are the gifts of God to His Creation for the express purpose of assisting God in the reclamation and completion of Creation.

> When I look at your heavens, the work of your fingers, the moon and the stars, which you have set in place, what is man that you are mindful of him, and the son of man that you care for him? Yet you have made him a little lower than the heavenly beings and crowned him with glory and honor. You have given him

13. Ps 69:5–6.
14. 2 Tim 2:14–17.

> dominion over the works of your hands; you have put all things under his feet.[15]

The role of stewards, the correct ordering of the universe, are essential to our successful participation with God, as well as a necessary component of personal redemption and salvation.

The Christian narrative is superior to any transitory cultural narrative, and speech is the mechanism through which this authenticity is conveyed. Philosophical and psychological constructs, with their symbolism and semiotics, cannot co-opt the symbolism and semiotics of a cross-cultural, historical, and scripturally based faith.

From a purely argumentative standpoint, the traits that separate Creation from other origin myths (monotheism, covenantal relationships, and the gift of language and speech) are sufficient in their own right to make the case that the Creation narrative is unique. But they also form the foundations of faith. The Scriptures continue to reinforce these three characteristics and caution that there are certain behaviors that pose specific threats to their standing. These behaviors are obvious in key themes that carry through the whole of Scripture. For example, idolatry, false prophets, false teaching, social justice, and cultural syncretism challenge the standing of a monotheistic and covenantal God. Instructions on language and speech remind the reader and the hearer that redemption and salvation are only possible in an atmosphere of a carefully preserved and protected narrative faithfully recounted from generation to generation. "We will not hide them from their children, but tell to the coming generations the glorious deed of the Lord, and his might, and the wonders he has done."[16] The unique characteristics of Creation, and those behaviors most threatening to their integrity, are the dominant themes of the scriptural narrative. The fact that they have been at the core of scriptural truth and teaching since the beginning of time proves the point that St. Peter made: we do not follow cleverly devised myths.

The urgency of this discussion does not rest simply in its intellectual appeal. Paul, writing from prison, reminds the Ephesians (and us) that they are engaged in a battle for their very souls:

> Finally, be strong in the Lord and in the strength of his might. Put on the whole armor of God, that you may be able to stand against the schemes of the devil. For we do not wrestle against

15. Ps 8:3–6.
16. Ps 78:4.

> flesh and blood, but against the rulers, against the authorities, against the cosmic powers over this present darkness, against the spiritual forces of evil in the heavenly places.

Paul goes on to address the preparations in military terms: "the belt of truth," "the breastplate of righteousness," "the shield of faith," "the helmet of salvation," and "the sword of the Spirit."[17] What Paul emphasizes is that we are not engaged in a cultural tug of war for the supremacy of one mythical ethos over another. We are engaged in spiritual warfare, and the stakes are eternal life or eternal damnation. We must hold fast to the ethical qualities of truth, faith, righteousness, salvation, and the Word of God upon which Creation was formed. Its narrative, which Paul demands be protected, is the only path to redemption and building the kingdom.

It remains our obligation to hold these truths close, to protect the integrity of Creation, and to fully embrace an authentic narrative that leads through the crucified and risen Christ to the establishment of a new kingdom at the end of time. The recognition of my own sloppiness in this respect has been humbling, but the awareness has brought reflection and, hopefully, some reform. "Whoever restrains his words has knowledge. . . . Even a fool who keeps silent is considered wise; when he closes his lips, he is deemed intelligent."[18]

This is not intended to be an academic treatise. It is not a study in history, archeology, anthropology, theology, philosophy, or linguistics. It has not been written for an audience of learned scholars and theologians. At the same time, the subtleties, nuances, and fullness of the Creation story cannot be reduced to a "Creation for Dummies" approach. Instead, this study is meant to offer a defense of our faith in readily accessible terms for those who may be discouraged by the erosion of Christianity, by the incessant bombardment of arguments that faith is an outmoded remnant of an earlier, less sophisticated time, or worse yet, useless, weak, and destructive for modern purposes. It is time to look at our faith in a new way, accepting and appreciating its vitality while acknowledging its powerful impact on both past, present, and future—recognizing that Creation is a living, immediate journey with real, eternal consequences. It cannot remain the exclusive purview of abstract, theological debate. This is not to reject the generations of scholarship and prayer that have shaped our faith but to conceptually embrace explanations of the majesty

17. Eph 6:10–16.

18. Prov 17:27–28.

of faith in terms that are more relevant to those coming of age in a post-modern, heavily secular environment. Christianity is built on hope and promise. It is my hope that the following is encouraging, and my promise is that I have approached this task with humility and joy.

# Chapter 1

# Genesis: A Purposeful Creation

Determining, with any certainty, what God had in mind with the Creation is a bit presumptuous, since no one can know the mind of God. Paul, citing Isaiah, questioned the capacity of humans to discern God's purposes when he declared to the Romans, "For who has known the mind of the Lord?"[1] When faced with such mysteries, Paul's response was to simply accept God's wisdom and rest in His glory.

Nevertheless, God has made no secret about what His ultimate intentions are for mankind, and the Scriptures continually provide insights into what these original intentions were. Unlike other origin stories, where the focus is entirely on beginnings, the Creation journey's end is the most important element. The Revelation to John settles the matter. God's purpose was, and continues to be, the creation of a completed universe that is in perfect alignment with His moral and ethical nature.

At the outset, it was meant to be eternal, never ending and never changing. To be eternal is to eclipse past, present, and future, so in that sense, there was no history in the beginning since the relationship between God and Creation was never intended to move or change through time. Only the occasion of original sin made the narrative historical. Therefore, man's history becomes, in part, the story of reestablishing Creation and will end with the inauguration of the new kingdom. This history documents a universe governed by God's perfect love and humanity's struggle to reconnect with His core values. Human history did not begin with the Creation. It began after the fall, with God's willingness to intervene and guide the journey to redemption and salvation.

1. Rom 11:34.

This perspective would seem to clearly conflict with historical, biological, and archeological evidence. If debated at a purely scientific level, the argument devolves into the question of whether protohominids, such as Australopithecus or Homo Erectus, knew God. Certainly, as the Creator, God knew them. The real question is at what point in human development did a consciousness of God emerge. Even purely secular scholars wrestle with the issue of free will and moral awareness and when that capacity emerged. The resolution hinges on the point at which the ability to discern moral and ethical distinctions became impactful—when such matters began to influence decisions—not at a point in which humanity developed empathy or self-consciousness. It also involves the ability of humans to begin the process of examining and recording their past. I would argue that the latter is impossible without the former. History can never be morally or ethically neutral.

This is not the same as early humans drawing on the walls of caves. That is certainly evidence of an awareness of their surroundings and circumstances, but it is not evidence of any moral imperatives or ethical considerations surrounding their actions.

These considerations are critical to understanding the Creation story. The fall is the moment when mankind made moral decisions that fell outside the perimeter of God's intentions, not the purely atavistic reactions of hunting for food or protecting the tribe. That is when human history as we know it, examine it, and discuss it in its social, economic, and political contexts begins. The ethical tensions of human history are vastly different from the mere matter of biological existence or evolution. That is indeed what separates mankind from every other species, notwithstanding the somewhat tortured efforts to describe the ethics or politics of a troop of great apes or a pod of whales. The idea of the prehistorical is a secular convention, not theological.

The image of God, within which mankind was created and will be discussed in greater detail later, is the moral and ethical nature of God, not any physical similarities or behavioral characteristics. Therefore, humanity cannot be considered to have been fully created until it could comprehend and act upon God's image. That was, and remains, the principal distinction between humans and other living things. It is a distinction clearly drawn in the first two chapters of Genesis. And it is, in the second chapter of Genesis, the basis for setting humans above all living things and designating them as God's stewards, meant to oversee the universe on His behalf.

Thus, there is nothing in the foregoing conversation that is inconsistent with the idea of a garden of Eden experience. God frequently refers to a chosen people or a people set apart. It is not inconceivable that with the moral and ethical emergence of mankind, those who began to grasp the significance of memorializing the past would identify a point at which two moral individuals, as opposed to two simply biological individuals, were identified by God to be His stewards of Creation. After all, the first chapter of Genesis quite clearly distinguishes the amoral qualities of the rest of Creation from the moral qualities of mankind. Such an approach is no more or less legitimate than a modern historian rationalizing the images and impacts of the past against its realities. To those expressing concern that this flies in the face of the Genesis seven-day timeline, I will leave the matter to Moses. "For a thousand years in your sight are but as yesterday when it is past, or as a watch in the night."[2]

The fall from grace is nothing less than humanity's decision to chart its own moral course, which is at the core of the serpent's temptation. Under those circumstances, God could have moved in two different directions. Denying humanity free will would certainly have eliminated disobedience, but the sincere worship and adoration that God expects requires a choice. Rather than take that approach, God chose to remain committed to Creation and offer a path towards the ultimate reclamation of His original intentions. So it follows that human history is intended to be purposeful and intentional, focused on the re-creation of the original, perfected state of the initial Creation. While the relationship between God and man had changed, it became a matter of process, not purpose, and tools were needed to steer the course of this history until the end of time.

Unfortunately, too often this historical sense of Creation is ignored. Frequently there is a hard stop after the second chapter of Genesis that looks something like this: heaven and earth had been created, all manner of living creatures populated the earth, and man and woman were, at least for the moment, living in perfect harmony with all of Creation. After the fall, what followed was a new, distinct phase. Creation was done and what was left was a catalogue of sin, despair, pain, and suffering.

If viewed from this perspective, God's involvement is reduced to simply protecting humanity from becoming a victim of its own corrupted excesses. There is no sense that God is continuing to create, to reshape,

2. Ps 90:4, a Psalm attributed to Moses.

and redeem the detritus of disobedience and separation. It may seem like a fine point of distinction, but none of the qualities of redemption and salvation, heaven and hell, or a new kingdom on earth make any sense if Creation is simply a one-off event and God started over. Human history is a continuum, a record of re-creation, not a new beginning. The power, the majesty, the mystery of God and Creation was not a holy mulligan

There are thirty-nine books in the Old Testament and twenty-seven in the New, a total of sixty-six, not including the books of the Apocrypha. There are 1,189 chapters in those sixty-six books, including the one hundred fifty psalms. From a purely internal perspective, a piece of literature that begins with the creation of the earth and all living things, and ends with a new Creation, could hardly be defended as a thoroughly integrated work if the idea of Creation is not understood to be the foundation for an ongoing, unifying theme. The tendency, however well intentioned, to present the Bible as a series of vignettes that impart moral wisdom without acknowledging its robust thematic strains only reinforces a patchwork approach to scriptural understanding. One could simply recount individual tales of heroism and tribal travails as standalone narratives if the redemption and recovery of Creation did not provide context for all these components. The news of Christ's appearance in the New Testament, and His message of salvation, would be of much less significance without first understanding the intentions of Creation and redemption in the first place.

The growth of what is referred to as redaction analysis only compounds the problem. Redaction analysis is the process of breaking down a segment of prose or poetry, in this case, the chapters of the Bible, and studying any linguistic, grammatical, philosophical, historical, or stylistic elements of that segment that do not seem to fit. An effort is then made to identify who or what might have been the source of the outlier. While perhaps not intentional, redaction tends to undermine the integrity of the work, again, in this case, the Bible.

That is why it is so important to not lose track of the integrity of the message or the arc of the narrative as a whole. All of Scripture deals with the idea of creation and re-creation, the redemption and salvation of a fallen people, and the completion of heaven and earth at the end of time. Most importantly, it is the restoration of the relationship humanity initially shared with the Creator in the beginning. A careful reading of the Creation story provides insights into what is to come and, more importantly, what the purpose of Creation was. It does not really matter for our purposes if Isaiah is a compilation of two, four, or forty-two different contributors. It may be relevant under other circumstances, but the divinely inspired writings that make up the Bible present a cohesive and fully integrated narrative. The conclusions that can be drawn from Isaiah or any other element of Scripture remain unchanged: Creation is a process of redemption and salvation that will ultimately end with the re-creation of a new kingdom built around the ethical and moral image of God. That point will become clear as this conversation continues.

As the processes of science increasingly altered the approach to non-physical subjects, such as art, history, literature, and theology, and the concept of social science gained ascendency in the twentieth century, traditional understandings of structured religion began to erode.[3] The idea that an omnipotent and omniscient God created the universe became far easier to undermine using the tools of physical science. Under those circumstances, Creation, as either a verifiable event or a unified narrative of history, was harder to accept. To fill the void, secularists were able to argue that there were no revealed or absolute truths governing behavior, only atavistic reactions built into human experience. Absent the unimpeachable moral and ethical value proposition of God and Creation as a shared framework for governing behavior, a morally relative environment emerged, within which a whole series of competing theories of human experience were able to thrive: functionalism, structuralism, Freudianism, critical theory, analytical psychology, postmodernism, nihilism, existentialism, deconstructionism, and so on. Untethered to the idea of absolute truth or transcendent values, individuals, societies, and cultures were free to adjust their value systems to rationalize self-gratifying and self-serving objectives. This approach to social order is totally at odds with Creation and the salvation narrative. The role of humans as stewards of the Creation and partners in covenantal relationships with God demands order, not chaos.

Unless we are satisfied with Creation as a mere morality play (an Aesop fable on steroids), we must go one step further. We must demonstrate that Creation is a unique historical narrative, with subthemes that set it apart from any other mythical creation narrative.

Myths are part of the fabric of every culture. They play an important role in reinforcing the values of social and cultural groups. Myths may, as

3. See appendix, "Who Owns History?"

Euhemerus[4] suggested, be based on the legitimate contributions of a real individual, whose accomplishments were so important in reinforcing the culture's value structure that his or her exploits warranted deification. Similarly, seminal events in any nation's history become magnified over time and celebrated as examples of the best that a people can be. In the United States, the heroics of Bunker Hill, the Alamo, Omaha Beach, or the struggle for civil rights are real, and if they become burnished over time in the retelling, that is fine. Their importance lies in the values they impart, not simply their outcomes. Historians carefully sort through the realities, and despite frequent disagreements on specifics, in the end, a largely integrated truth is discovered that is just as remarkable as the myth. Its mythological status largely serves the role of firmly cementing the visceral attachment to the factual circumstances. For these reasons, myths are vitally important and should be cherished. And that is why every culture has a mythos and works to protect it.

It is when such myths began to subsume the important realities that constitute Christian faith that problems arose. One way to confront this challenge is to identify characteristics that depart so substantially from the patterns of myths that any suggestion that Creation is not a unique, fully integrated narrative must be rejected. Fortunately, the Creation story presented in Genesis can be distinguished from other creation myths in three fundamental and powerful ways.

First, the concept of monotheism separates the biblical Creation from all others. While other creation myths may focus on the unique activities of a particular deity, the god at the center of the tale is always part of a larger contingent. There may be struggles within the pantheon for supremacy, and jealousies were frequently evident among competing gods. That which was created may be broken into various component parts, with different gods taking ownership of specific components. Gods competed for the attention of individual humans and tribes, and their adherents ascribed good and bad outcomes to godly behavior according to culturally derived assumptions. With Creation, however, there is one supreme God who alone is accorded the status of Creator. He is unique in His power and knowledge, and He is exalted in worship above all others and to the exclusion of all others. Everything that occurs falls at His feet, and He takes responsibility for both the good and the bad. This Creator

4. Euhemerus was a fourth century BCE Greek philosopher.

is relevant and active throughout the narrative, and He is there at the end of time.

In the second instance, the God of Creation remains heavily invested in His Creation. He owns history and He takes an active part in directing events toward a conclusion that is not mysterious or unknowable. While judgment and punishment remain His exclusive purview, it is not capricious. The rules are unequivocal and consistent. Not only is God invested in the outcome of Creation, He demonstrates an unwavering love for His Creation. Other creation myths offer pictures of gods who may create, then disappear. Some may be disinterested bystanders, others may pop in and out of human history, but none display the consistent and unconditional love that God has for that which He created. God's love for His Creation throughout all of history is not only palpable, but it binds the Creator and created through obedience in a way that is also unique and compelling. He alone, among the many gods who populate various creation myths, established covenants between Himself and His created. The created are invited to be part of something that is beyond human history. They are invited to be active participants in a carefully constructed and purposefully designed reclamation of the initial Creation, one that has been corrupted by the willfulness of a fallen people. The introduction into human history of God Himself—not just in form but in substance, both human and divine, subject to real suffering and pain—demonstrates an ongoing commitment to the created that cannot be found in any other creation myth.

Finally, the agency by which the Creator created is very different from other stories. God spoke the universe into existence. That same language and speech, complete with all its powerful properties, was bequeathed to humanity. He gave mankind the power to name the rest of Creation, a power that imparts authority, identity, and ownership. God's Word at Creation was imbued with a power and authority that remains beyond comprehension. It has the ability to create the physical, not simply relate the physical. This language of Creation is the vehicle through which He physically, emotionally, and authoritatively moves events and people. It defies natural law and is not bound by its own rules. Language and speech link God to His Creation at every level and order the relationships among the created. Language and speech are not simply platforms for informing and describing; they are outcomes in and of themselves. They convey holy obligations to further Creation and uphold one another. Even in the hands of fallen humanity, they are imbued with a power to lift up and tear down, and the use of these tools is the subject of scrutiny and caution throughout all of Scripture. It is this creational quality that makes the signifiers, symbols, and rituals of Christianity, the foundational semiotics of Creation, so different from those of other origin stories. No matter the culture, the speech patterns, the geography or the historical era, the language and speech of Creation are known and recognized immediately. They do not have to first be interpreted by anthropologists, psychologists, or mythologists to be understood.

In combination, these three characteristics create the foundation for a Creation story unlike any other. They uniquely establish a platform for the Creator and the created to strive for an anticipated and preordained outcome: the inauguration of the renewed Creation. Creation is not the result of an idle whim, a narcissistic indulgence, mean-spirited mischief, competition between gods, or any other prosaic urge. It is purposeful, intentional, intelligent, and carefully designed. It is a story of grace, love, and mercy that is unparalleled, with the result that the created can share time, space, and, ultimately, matter[5] with the Creator throughout history and at the close of history.

These three characteristics can certainly be analyzed in their individual capacities and on their own merits make the case for the singularity of the Creation story. But they also work in an extraordinary way with one another. Each characteristic reinforces the significance of the others and, in doing so, only strengthens the case that Creation is not a myth as commonly perceived in contemporary treatments of the subject. Language and speech are tools for binding the entire Creation narrative into a unified whole without the necessity of reinterpreting symbols and signifiers over time. But that could only happen if the Creator is monotheistic, evidencing a consistency and coherency absent in myth. With respect to the covenantal relationships between God and His Creation, the idea of a covenant takes on special meaning with a God who jealously protects His relationship with humanity. Again, if the circumstances of creation are not monotheistic, a covenant is of no value since no one is in charge to see the terms of the agreement through. In addition, for covenants to remain binding over time, language must maintain a consistent usage and understanding. It is designed to order Creation along the lines of God's value proposition.

5. References to the idea of time, space, and matter as a unified structure are based on N. T. Wright's remarkable scholarship on the questions of heaven and the resurrection, particularly the one-volume study *Surprised by Hope*.

Despite the interconnectedness of the three, it is useful to take a closer look at each of these characteristics individually, beginning with the covenantal relationship between God and humanity. The covenants are a good place to start, inasmuch as they form the foundation of the earthly relationships that allow mankind to participate in the work of the new kingdom. The questions of monotheism and language and speech will be addressed in succeeding chapters.

## *COVENANTAL RELATIONSHIPS*

The provenance of the word "covenant" itself only goes back as far as Middle English and Old French, while its Latin roots lay in the term "convene" or "gather." Since the scriptural applications derive from much earlier applications, the Hebrew and Greek antecedents are more useful for locating the idea of covenant in its theological sense. Covenant in Hebrew (*berit* or *berith*) conveys the sense of a bond or pledge, often between a master and his servants. It is a deeply seated moral commitment by the lord or master to protect and provide for those who are bound to him. While not necessarily a legal commitment, the underlying assumption behind a *berith* is based on a broadly accepted recognition that there is a binding ethical relationship between a master and servant. The master has the obligation to act ethically towards his servants and they, in turn, are bound to obey. The bond holds as long as both parties honor the underlying moral and ethical guidelines.

Greek translators, wrestling with properly capturing the meaning of *berith*, moved between *syntheke* and *diatheke*. They eventually settled on the latter because the former conveyed a sense of an agreement between equals, which clearly is not the case. God's covenant could not be cancelled by the created. It is an everlasting promise. A *diatheke* establishes the intent of the author of the agreement to dispose of his goods and property upon his death. God is, in this sense, a sort of divine testator. Given the fact that God cannot die, and we cannot cancel the agreement, the covenant relationships are everlasting.[6]

It can be argued that the tone of this covenantal relationship was set very early in the Creation narrative, beginning with Adam and Eve. The

6. The foregoing references in Hebrew and Greek are transliterations from Strong, *Concordance*. Any following references in Hebrew or Greek are also transliterated and come from Strong.

two were given a place of eternal peace and comfort, a personal relationship with God that depended simply upon obeying a few rules.

But whether this was a covenant in the traditional sense or not, clearly a covenant was in place with God's commitment to Noah. Noah was to gather two of every living thing, as well as his immediate household, and shepherd them through the flood. When the waters receded, God would honor His agreement to nurture the remainder of humanity and never again cause such destruction on the earth. Despite eliminating virtually every living member of His chosen people, God never cancelled His covenant.

He renewed it again with Abraham, Moses, and David. These covenants express God's faithful commitment to His Creation. In two instances, the Abrahamic and Davidic covenants, the emphasis is on the fullness of God's grace. In Gen 12, God promised Abram, "I will make of you a great nation, and I will bless you and make your name great,"[7] and in chapter 15, "The Lord made a covenant with Abram" that his offspring would people the earth and comprise a great nation.[8] The Abrahamic covenant was a promissory covenant without any restrictions. With David, He promised, "Your house and your kingdom shall be made sure forever before me."[9] As subsequent events would bear out, unfaithful kings would be subject to divine punishment, but the covenant with David would not be abrogated. While there was an expectation of obedience in both covenants, the emphasis is on God's free gift of grace to those He had chosen.

On the other hand, in the case of both Noah and Moses, the emphasis is on God's merciful judgment in the face of a recalcitrant people. After the flood, God reasserted the basic ethical premise of Creation, reminding Noah that "God made man in his own image," and that He will "require a reckoning: from every beast I will require it and from man. From his fellow man I will require a reckoning for the life of a man."[10] With Moses and the book of the covenant, the Law was given to shape the behaviors of a fallen people. This was a covenant contingent upon obligations assented to by the people, with punishments associated with

7. Gen 12:2.
8. Gen 15:18.
9. 2 Sam 7:16.
10. Gen 9: 1–17.

disobedience. All four covenants were freely given, but with Noah and Moses, the importance of obedience is more pronounced.[11]

With Christ's appearance on this earth, and His subsequent death, resurrection, and ascension, the Old Testament covenants were refreshed and renewed as the Prophets had proclaimed. Isaiah foretold his listeners that God has chosen a servant who will be "as a covenant for the people."[12] Jeremiah reminded the people of the covenant they had broken but prophesied that "the days are coming, declares the Lord, when I will make a new covenant with the house of Israel and the house of Judah."[13] At the Last Supper, Jesus said, "This cup that is poured out for you is the new covenant in my blood."[14] The new kingdom had begun. Even the Holy Spirit has covenantal overtones, as it is promised to be with us always. The Creation narrative continued unabated, and the covenant was fulfilled in Christ. At the second coming, with the completion of Creation, He who offered His covenants to His people will redeem His promises of salvation and redemption. His people will live in an eternal relationship of joy with the Creator.

There is simply no parallel to this fully invested Creator in mythology. No myth carries the narrative of creation to a conclusion. The universe is simply created and wanders on without any consistent guidance from the creating agencies. The covenant theme of Creation and the Creator's promises bind the entire tale together and describe both the journey and the outcome. The God of Creation is not content to simply create and then step back. He created for the purpose of building a lasting and loving relationship with His created. He made covenants with His people as a sign of His divine partnership with mankind. These covenants were renewed repeatedly as evidence of His enduring living presence, love, and commitment.

Not only are there no instances of an invested creator in any other creation myth, but the opposite is more often the case. The myth of the Barotse in Zambia tells of an environment much like the garden of Eden, in which the creator and his wife live in harmony with all of creation. When a murder occurs, the creator initially bans the murderer from the sacred realm, only to later pardon the man and let him return. There was no repentance, the man killed again, and the creator simply

11. Metzger and Coogan, *Oxford Companion*, 138–9.

12. Isa 42:6; also the servant songs in chapters 49, 50, 52–53.

13. Jer 11; 31:31.

14. Luke 22:20.

withdrew from the world in disgust.[15] In the aboriginal Kakadu myth of Imberombera and Wuraka, the male of the two co-creators simply tires of the process and wishes to retire and rest with the sun in the east.[16] In another African myth, the Yao people of northern Mozambique come to realize that there is a disconnect between the natural harmony of creation and the human capacity for destruction and cruelty. In this case, the created simply forced their god to retreat to the sky.[17] More commonly, the pattern follows that of the Creed of the Celts, where semi-divine heroes go to battle against the gods to obtain benefits for humanity; or the Soothsaying of the Vala, where various gods, fates, and giants are in a constant state of warfare with little concern for humans.[18] In the creation myth of the Minyong, a tribal group in northeastern India, the problem is the oppressive weight of the father on the survival of his children. Younger gods conspire to drive the father away, only to leave a state of utter chaos. Other creatures are called upon to regain some order.[19] In many North American creation myths, the gods assume characteristics of animals and move in and out of human endeavors.[20]

The Enuma Elish, an ancient Babylonian myth with Sumerian antecedents, warrants more specific comment. This myth, in particular, is often presented as a source of the biblical Creation narrative because of its physical, chronological, and cultural proximity to the events catalogued in Scripture. It is a long and complex story, with a vast number of characters moving in and out of the tale. Since it deals with matters pertaining to the structure of the cosmos, it is viewed in some quarters as an origin myth. But it is not the story of creation; it is the story of the rise in supremacy of one god, Marduk.[21] Unlike Creation, all the components of the cosmos are already in place when the narrative begins. Each component is associated with a particular god who is responsible for overseeing the unique properties of his or her piece of the universe.

The purpose of the Enuma Elish is to describe how all these components became structured and ordered, not how, why, and by whom they were created. Marduk was tasked with eliminating competing gods and

15. Sproul, *Primal Myths*, 35.

16. Sproul, *Primal Myths*, 323.

17. Sproul, *Primal Myths*, 36.

18. Sproul, *Primal Myths*, 172–3.

19. Sproul, *Primal Myths*, 196.

20. Sproul, *Primal Myths*, 232–87.

21. Sproul, *Primal Myths*, 91.

putting the existing pieces of creation in order. In return, he demanded the role of chief god of the pantheon. He became the principal god of Babylon, so the Enuma Elish also serves to justify and celebrate Babylon as the most significant city in the known world. The myth ends with a recitation of the fifty names of Marduk, each one specifying a particular worldly responsibility. There is no mention of ordering the cosmos for the purposes of guiding humanity to any particular conclusion, nor are there any rules associated with governing a divine-human relationship. The only apparent obligation is an annual ceremony where the king prostrates himself before the throne of Marduk to celebrate the ordering of the universe and humanity's place in that structure. There is no description of the end of time. There is no indication that Marduk gifted humanity any special authority or skills to act on his behalf, and nothing approaching the incarnation of Marduk's essential nature into the world.

There may indeed be many areas where the Enuma Elish and the Bible seem to share characteristics, but that cannot be surprising when all the players were operating under the same conditions and sharing similar experiences. There are only so many ways in which those shared experiences can be described. In a later chapter, more detail is given to this question of cultural appropriation, but, for our purposes, the Enuma Elish falls short. Biblical Creation remains unique.

The gods of myth are baked into origin narratives without any interest in proving their existence. They were merely accepted by adherents of any given myth as participants in the story and called upon to satisfy some need or resolve some problem. But when one moves to the position of defining a creation narrative as the basis for subconscious human and cultural truths, as contemporary anthropologists and psychologists do, they must, of necessity, assign some meaning and authority to a myth's creator that was never intended. Ancient followers of myth never asked deep, probing, psychological justification of their gods. Those who preserved various origin narratives made no attempt to position their gods in this sort of alignment with the universe. This unwillingness, or lack of necessity, by followers of myth to place a single god in the center of the universe resulted in competition among gods, encouraging chaos, moral relevance, and cultural instability. This is the polar opposite of what God intended at Creation and as reflected in the Law. Identifying anything even remotely resembling a covenantal commitment is impossible in a traditional mythological pattern. Mythology forecloses that opportunity, even for those who are prepared to elevate myths to a formative or foundational role in the establishment of cultural value systems.

Scriptural history documents the commitments of Creation's covenantal relationships. The covenants, along with the Law, defined the terms under which humanity was to order society. They set forth the responsibilities of mankind's stewardship, given at the Creation. They form the basis and rationale for both blessings and punishment. Daniel acknowledged the central role of these covenants when he prayed, "O Lord, the great and awesome God, who keeps covenant and steadfast love with those who love him and keep his commandments, we have sinned and done wrong and acted wickedly and rebelled, turning aside from your commandments and rules."[22] As history continues to be recorded, personal journeys of redemption and salvation provide evidence to countless millions of God's ongoing commitment to His covenantal agreements. The fact that Judaism, Christianity, and Islam all grew out of the same scriptural narrative is testimony to the ongoing impact of this sense of a covenantal relationship, no matter how dysfunctional the relationships between the three faith traditions have become. For better or worse, no one battles over the truths of Marduk, El, Baal or Dagon.

It would be overly simplistic to say that the gods of other creation myths merely abandoned what had been created or left humanity to its own devices. Certainly, there were various deities who tried to be helpful, may have been inclined to assist mankind, or worked to thwart the impact of evil gods and spirits. But that is a far cry from a God who stays engaged from Creation until the end of time and who entered into binding arrangements with His creation. A God, furthermore, whose stated intent is to forge an eternal relationship with His people. No matter how cleverly the question is parsed, there is nothing close to the invested God of Creation in any other myth.

22. Dan 9:4–5.

# Chapter 2

# The Challenge of Monotheism

At its most basic level, monotheism seems pretty straightforward: a doctrine or belief that there is only one God. For most purposes, this simple dictionary definition is sufficient. But in fact, the idea of monotheism in the context of Creation is a bit more complicated. The challenge begins with the common misunderstanding that monotheism is merely a function of one god versus multiple gods. But a careful reading of Scripture reveals a God that is not simply operating as one God in lieu of a number of gods. It is His uniqueness as the source of all divine power and majesty that sets Him apart. The distinction is important because if there are multiple sources of divinity, there will be multiple sources of authority. That, in turn, leads to a moral relevancy that relies more upon human understanding and satisfaction than divine wisdom. Moral relevancy has given way to chaos far more than order.

A monotheistic God is the exclusive creator of the universe. There is no other agency involved. The ramifications of acknowledging and accepting this exclusivity are far reaching. Monotheism fundamentally challenges a prevailing assumption that transcendent narratives cannot exist and absolute values are impossible to identify or define. Simply stated, Creation through a single source cannot produce multiple, competing truths. One can argue about what that truth may look like, but they cannot argue that there is more than one truth. The tensions are unsustainable. Either individuals and institutions accede to the nature of truth in a monotheism environment, or they must adjust their principles and embrace alternative narratives that reject such truth. In so doing, whether consciously or not, they have rejected monotheism as well. Contemporary secular thought has already chosen to move on. The question remains whether faith communities will do so as well.

More importantly, moral relativity cannot exist within a monotheistic structure unless one can accept the sophistry that a monotheistic god can act outside of his or her own nature. What a creator creates is a reflection of what the creator is. By definition, creation must reflect the moral nature of the creator, since there can be no other ethical source available prior to creation. Thus, the created can only be created to act in a way that is consistent with the creator's value proposition. With the scriptural Creation and its God, the truly faithful must adhere to Creation's moral and ethical posture because operating outside those standards, deviating from the value proposition, must be considered a sin.

The idea of sin, as opposed to the idea of doing wrong, has fallen out of fashion in contemporary society. Doing wrong is to act outside of culturally derived patterns. It is not a matter of being held accountable to absolute, created truths. Culturally derived values are inherently unstable and subject to radical change over relatively short periods of time. Not so with the absolute, transcendent truths of Creation reflected in the Scriptures. Our understanding of Creation truths and values may be illuminated by prayerful consideration, the thoughtful application of Scripture, and the collective wisdom of church fathers and faith leaders, but they do not change. Idolatry, false teaching, and false prophets, or anything else that puts human understanding on an equal footing with God, is anathema. Anything outside of scriptural truth becomes heretical or idolatrous, concepts that contemporary culture pointedly reject.

Another problematic issue associated with a monotheistic god is, simply put, that as the source of all things, the creator is responsible for all that follows. This is the conundrum of theodicy, a term used to describe the seeming contradictions of a benevolent, omnipotent God who also allows evil to exist. Since a monotheistic theology can only admit to one God, that God must be responsible for both good and evil. In those instances where there are multiple gods, alternatives to God, or simply a denial of God altogether, causation can be explained by any number of reasons. Polytheists have a much easier path. There is no compulsion to embrace the uncompromising nature of one God's moral and ethical standards. It sidesteps the uncomfortable realities of personal responsibility and accountability.

In fact, many myths adopt patterns of pluralism in creation to avoid the logical consequences of a monotheistic theodicy. Creation by means of a cosmic egg, often accompanied by twins operating in some creative capacity, is a recurring pattern. The god of the Mande people of Mali, as an example, failed to achieve his goal of creating a single seed from which the world would grow and was forced to resort to an "egg of the world in two twin parts."[1] In this case, as in many others, the problem inherent in monotheism, that of sorting out the existence of both good and evil, is overcome by merely assigning the qualities of good and evil to one or the other of the twins. Gods may also be assigned responsibility for specific spheres of influence in the universe. The contradictions of daily life are then ascribed to the activities of these various gods in competition with one another.

Such is not the case with a monotheistic Creator. When God created man in His own image, He was not simply creating the physical universe but the moral and ethical structure of that universe as well. God's image is not an expression of physical similarities, but a reflection of His value system, one that He intended as the model for human social behavior. In a universe with a monotheistic Creator, matters such as ethics and a properly oriented social structure are ordered from the outset by the values revealed in the beginning and that maintain their vibrance and relevancy for all time. For example, God's condemnation of the nations of Israel and Judah, delivered through the words of the prophet Amos, begins with a litany of cruelty and brutality that utterly perverts the ethical standards of the Creator. For Amos, there was no avoiding the consequences of ignoring or distorting God's ethical system. And Amos was not the only prophet to acknowledge the logical conclusions of upending the ethical model of a godly society. One cannot dodge from god to god, putting the blame on some other deity. Likewise, seeking self-serving ends by appealing to different gods is not an option. One is bound to the values of a single creator in a monotheistic universe. You cannot ask for things outside of that moral structure and expect a pass by reference to some other god's dictates. How, why, and what was created establishes an unyielding and inescapable pattern. Fully embracing a monotheistic creator demands personal responsibility and accountability, both individually and communally.

1. Germaine Dieterlen, "The Mande Creation Myth," quoted in Sproul, *Primal Myth*, 67.

This lack of duality or multiplicity leads to another unique characteristic of monotheism. As the source of all things good and evil, the creator God will logically be both loved and feared. There are simply no other options. The one created cannot run from parent to parent like a spoiled child. That which is warm, loving, joyful, and positive in life, as well as that which is dark, cold, foreboding, and fearful, land at the feet of the same supreme being. If one fully embraces this aspect of monotheism, in the end, He becomes a very personal God. In the Chronicles of Narnia, C. S. Lewis captured this quite well when Susan finds out Aslan is a lion. "'Ooh,' said Susan. 'I'd thought he was a man. Is he—quite safe? I shall feel rather nervous about meeting a lion.' . . , 'Safe?' said Mr. Beaver . . . 'Who said anything about safe? Course he isn't safe. But he's good. He's the King, I tell you.'"[2]

There is nowhere else to turn for both praise and protection. This is not the case in any other environment where the individual is free to select which god[3] to praise and thank, and which one to blame for pain and suffering. One just picks the most convenient set of values as an excuse for ignoring a more accountable path. It is even worse in an atheistic environment. One simply ignores the questions of a larger moral accountability altogether and creates his or her own moral universe.

A monotheistic god is both loving and jealous, the author of both good and evil. If forced to choose one of the binaries, loving becomes the favorite since it is equated with good. Jealousy, by default, assumes the nature of selfishness, meanness, and spite. This would be true with God but for one undeniable characteristic. God continually acts out of the welfare of humanity as a whole. His efforts to redeem those who have strayed is the antithesis of selfishness and became demonstrably clear with the sacrifice of His Son. When viewed with the ultimate objective of Creation in mind, the motivation of a jealous God becomes clear. Like a parent, who fiercely defends and protects her child so that she can grow and develop into a productive and accomplished individual, God is to be praised for His enduring commitment to insisting on an obedience that assures acceptance into a perfected relationship with Him. A polytheistic system cannot offer complete salvation or promise eternal life. There can

2. Lewis, *Lion, the Witch*, 89.

3. God, in this context, refers to anything secular or divine that an individual may choose to worship. While the discussion focuses on monotheism versus polytheism, the observations are relevant in either agnostic or atheistic circumstances as well.

be no ultimate authority with multiple gods projecting competing images of the universe.

Mythology is rife with symbols and symbolic language. This leads to another quality of monotheism. Interestingly, it has no exclusive language or terminology. Except for the process of translating from one language to another, encoded symbols do not have to be realigned and renegotiated from culture to culture. The semiotics and symbolism of monotheism are commonly understood. This cannot be said for the language of other creation myths. No matter the translation, each set of unique, encoded symbols has to be interpreted and explained to have any meaning. An entire cottage industry has arisen in academic circles dedicated to interpreting the semiotics of various cultures and myths. The symbolism of competing origin myths is truly foreign outside of one's own cultural experiences. Monotheistic language and symbols are constant and consistent from place to place and time to time. The symbols and signifiers within the Passover liturgy or the sacraments of Baptism and the Eucharist are immediately recognized, known, and understood at the very deepest level from language to language.

There are no shades of meaning or subtlety of understanding. One does not need to tiptoe around conceptual signs, hoping they have not changed. Examples abound in the academy, culture, politics, and corporations of twenty-first century America. No one knows what is acceptable from one day to the next. The implications of words and actions that were commonplace and not controversial can change in literally a matter of months. The consequences for misreading the signs are significant. Jobs are lost, relationships severed, and public condemnation is severe to the point of elimination. Sources of authority shift and evolve in never-ending cycles. Monotheism, on the other hand, creates one source of authority that is consistent and never changing. There is no confusion in what a monotheistic God means or expects, and judgment is consistent. Faith in a monotheistic God does not require the faithful to constantly read and interpret social signals or, as they are referred to currently, triggers. The faithful know what the Creator's value proposition is, and it never changes.

While the question of monotheism in Judaism is clearly settled today, it was not quite as clear or as linear a development in the early history of the Jewish people. By the time the prophecies of Isaiah were recorded, the Scriptures unequivocally proclaim the idea of one true omnipotent and omniscient God as the God of Israel.[4] But prior to that time, the scriptural narrative speaks to gods and deities other than Yahweh operating at some level in Jewish life. The fact that Israel needed to be purged of idolatry on a regular basis is evidence that there were other gods, known to the Israeli people, to whom they would turn with frustrating frequency. While Moses spoke to Pharaoh in the name of the God of Israel, it is not clear that the Jews in Egypt shared the same understanding of Yahweh that Moses and the other patriarchs did. If they had, the revelation of God at Sinai and the delivery of the Ten Commandments might have been very different and far less dramatic.

Indeed, the distinctions of polytheism and monotheism would not have been recognized or understood during the period of the patriarchs and the early history of Israel. The idea of a preeminent god within a pantheon of other gods was well accepted. It was commonplace to acknowledge a first among equals, but to strip all gods but one of their divinity was unheard of. Had you asked an ancient Mesopotamian whether they were polytheistic, as Mark Smith noted, they would have no idea what you were talking about. Polytheism has no meaning apart from monotheism. The reverse holds true as well.

> If you asked ancient Israelites around the Exilic period (587–538) if they were monotheists, they would not have understood the question. If you asked them if there is any deity apart from Yahweh then that's also another question, because for them what mattered was the exclusive claim and relationship of the Israelite people and their deity.[5]

It was the exclusivity of the claim that is novel.

And that is really the point for our purposes. Whether Israelites were practicing some form of polytheism or strict monotheism early on, Yahweh was still a unique God, with authority and values distinct within the Creation context from other creation myths. Issues of idolatry and other gods remained a constant cause for concern, and competing forms of theism presented real threats to a fragile and developing faith tradition. Confronting these issues, as monotheism became centered in Jewish theology, is also unique to the Creation story. No other creation narrative is built around a unique God defining, defending, and reclaiming the original purposes of His Creation. Monotheism is more than a

4. Isa 40. See also, Smith, *Biblical Monotheism*, 179–94.

5. Smith, *Biblical Monotheism*, 11.

theological distinction. It demands a lifestyle and worldview that rejects other standards and demands complete, unwavering adherence.

The difficulties of establishing a hegemonic, national god were not limited to the Jews. While Judaism was ultimately and uniquely successful, such was not the case with other ancient Middle Eastern societies. There were frequent attempts among the Egyptians, Mesopotamians, Assyrians, Hittites, and others to solidify support around one primary god who governed the pantheon and, by extension, granted his favor and authority to the ruler. For example, in Egypt, around the time of Pharaoh Menes, c. 3000 BCE, as the new city of Memphis was being constructed, it became necessary to address the cult centers of older but still important Egyptian cities. The royal theologians were assigned the specific task of renegotiating the position of various gods to satisfy this new reality demanded by the Pharaoh. They were able to successfully demonstrate the superiority of the new cult by assigning significant but lesser roles to the gods of other cult centers. This was a rather tricky task, worthy of any modern-day diplomat, since each god attracted groups of rather fervent followers. As the god Osiris became increasingly popular, he had to be assimilated into the new mythic structure as well.[6] The fact that Osiris was eventually replaced shows how difficult, and ultimately unsuccessful, the task was.

Again, the problem was exclusivity. As regimes and regime change occurred throughout the ancient Middle East, the process of displacing one national god with another was doomed to fail precisely because lesser gods were permitted to retain their divinity. The book of Daniel illustrates the futility of this exercise, as Nebuchadnezzar constructs a ninety-foot, solid-gold god, which all his vassal states were expected to worship. He nonetheless continues to acknowledge the power of Daniel's God and insists that this God be honored. The first dream, which Daniel interpreted, foretold the result. These state-sponsored efforts routinely failed under the weight of social and community practices. Despite the repeated attempts of rulers and reformers to create a preeminent state god, individuals and families continued to call upon and worship deities with which they had strong personal attachments because no one was willing to revoke their divinity. In no instance, other than Judaism, did a supreme god emerge around which the community willingly coalesced, despite the often heavy-handed efforts of powerful leaders to demand

6. Sproul, *Primal Myth*, 77.

otherwise. In other words, monotheism could not simply be imposed by fiat. Its legitimacy is derived from a divine, not temporal, order.

As noted earlier, monotheism demands an ordered and ethical society since there can be no other social or cultural practices that fall outside the Creator's standards and values. Hence, the matter of an ethically ordered society for the early Israeli communities became a practical question as well as a theological one. Living among those outside of their faith system, intermarrying and socializing with them provided an opportunity to dilute the faith and fold in other behaviors. Moses laid this out quite clearly in Deuteronomy. "You shall not intermarry with them, giving your daughters to their sons or taking their daughters for your sons, for they would turn away your sons from following me, to serve other gods."[7] One can clearly understand prohibitions on intermarriage under these circumstances.

Intermarriage and the convenience of idols posed no threats to faith within a non-monotheistic structure. The idea of a false god simply cannot exist in a polytheistic environment. Monotheism requires two components: not only is there one God in charge, but other gods must be acknowledged as false. In other words, it is not the existence of idols that should be used to test the purity of monotheism but the wholesale acknowledgement and recognition that idols cannot exercise authority over creation, and that they are indeed false gods for that reason. Understandably, intermarriage and cultural acclimation within the early Israeli community posed a very real threat because it required the parties to at least not directly challenge competing divinities if the relationship was to survive. Historically, the vibrancy of Old Testament Judaism waxed and waned in a direct relationship to the enforcement of strictures regarding marriage outside of Judaism.

This process of acclimation is not merely theoretical, as one noted historian of religion acknowledged:

> Myths and mythological structures have been discarded by man throughout human history whenever new revelations of being and sacredness have been manifested, but it is precisely the mode of apprehension which we have called mythic which allows man to respond to the new and novel manifestation.[8]

7. Duet 7:3.

8. Long, *Alpha*, 16.

Numerous examples of this conscious cultural negotiation are evident in the study of myths. The Maori peoples maintain sacred colleges for religious instruction, called *whare wananga*, designed just for the purpose of maintaining the relevance of their creation myths. In the case of the myth of Io, the East Coast Maori introduced a new creation myth in the mid-nineteenth century.[9] The Bulu people of the Cameroons adjusted their myths to accommodate the fact that the "white man" (German, French, and British), who assumed dominion over them in the early twentieth century, had displaced the hegemony of the native black man. In a story not unlike the tree of the knowledge of good and evil in the garden of Eden, the black man becomes subservient to the white man because the black man threw away the book entrusted to him by the creator Zambe, while the white man cared for that which Zambe had given him. "Therefore we now perceive that the white men are men of understanding, but the black people are ignorant; moreover, also the black men go and serve them."[10] It is an example of one of many tragic consequences of colonization but is also indicative of the process by which creation myths are renegotiated to accommodate changed circumstances. Similar instances can be seen in Native American tribes in North America, such the Okanagon, who were forced to adjust their original creation myths to account for events that evolved as a result of the pressures of white settlement.[11] J. MacLean studied the Blackfoot Confederacy in the 1880s and had difficulty in even finding the original myths. He is quoted as saying:

> The separation of the tribes, the rapid settlement of the country by the white people, the death of many of the old chiefs, and the depressed spirits of the people have seriously impaired the purity of the folk-lore of the natives. The following fragments were gathered from the lips of Blood Indians as I sat in their lodges with note-books in hand. The younger members of the tribe could not be relied on to relate those myths accurately. Those I have given have been repeatedly verified by the aged members of the tribe.[12]

All such examples cannot be entirely dismissed as purely cultural power plays, although there are certainly elements of such pressures

9. Hare Hongi, "A Maori Cosmology," quoted in Sproul, *Primal Myths*, 346.

10. Adolf N. Krug, "Bulu Tales from Kamerun, West Africa," quoted in Sproul, *Primal Myths*, 46.

11. Sproul, *Primal Myths*, 243.

12. J. Maclean, "Blackfoot Mythology," quoted in Sproul, *Primal Myths*, 244.

involved. Part of the overall creation narrative of the Assiniboine tribe of Native Americans, for instance, attributes the creation of horses to their god Inktonmi, even though horses did not become a factor in Assiniboine culture until the eighteenth century.[13] The evolution of Apache creation myths is as much a result of the unforced migration of the tribe from what is now Canada around 1000 CE as it is pressure from eighteenth- and nineteenth-century European colonization.[14] There are no evidences of such a mythological replacement process in the Creation narrative.

All the essential characteristics of monotheism are evident in the Creation narrative. They have not been extracted and catalogued after the fact. Creation was not a group exercise. We also know from the Scriptures that the God of Creation is both loved and feared, as the patterns of monotheism require, and that He is also a personal God, invested in our well-being. He seeks to order society according to His absolute and unchanging values and demands obedience.

The core principles of monotheism were made clear shortly after the exodus from Egypt when God set forth the rules governing the relationships between humans and between humans and Himself. When Moses blessed the book of the covenant, the people, gathered as the entire nation of Israel, confirmed their obedience.[15] The first two commandments affirm the exclusivity and singularity of God. They confirm the unique authority of God over all Creation, as well as the risk of following false gods:

> I am the Lord your God, who brought you out of the land of Egypt, out of the house of slavery. You shall have no other gods before me. You shall not make for yourself a carved image, or any likeness of anything that is in heaven above, or that is in the earth beneath, or that is in the water under the earth. You shall not bow down to them or serve them, for I the Lord your God am a jealous God, visiting the iniquity of fathers on the children to the third and the fourth generation of those who hate me, but showing steadfast love to thousands of those who love me and keep my commandments.[16]

These are sharp distinctions from the narratives of other creation myths. In other myths, creation is limited to simply rationalizing

13. R. H. Lowie, "The Assiniboine," quoted in Sproul, *Primal Myths*, 253.
14. Sproul, *Primal Myths*, 257.
15. Exod 24:3–8.
16. Exod 20:2–6.

beginnings, with no interest in sustained narratives. Under those circumstances, an exclusively monotheistic god is not only unnecessary, it is dangerous to the myth itself. Other creation myths cannot rationalize the tensions and contradictions necessary for a sustainable plot line. That is why all other creation myths default to multiple gods. These myths deal only with the beginning of creation when, in reality, Creation is ongoing.

On some occasions, students of mythology make an attempt to classify a myth as monotheistic by forcing the story through the narrow funnel of a principal creator. As an example, the creation story of the Native American Joshua people, who lived in what is now Oregon, has one creator, Xowalaci (The Giver). But Xowalaci failed twice in his attempts to create humans. While he is credited with creating the remainder of the physical universe, he had to rely on an outside agency to create human life. He is not a god jealous of his relationship with mankind; in fact, he enlists the aid of a human to complete creation. He does not in any way remain invested in the outcome of creation, and he was not feared as omnipotent and all-knowing. In the Fon tradition from West Africa, the world was created by one god Nana-Buluku, who was both male and female. Eventually, Nana-Buluku spontaneously gave birth to twins, one wholly male, the other wholly female, who were given dominion over night and day. It was the twins who eventually populated the earth and Nana-Buluku retired from the world completely. In neither case does the attempt to position these myths within the category of a single creator meet the criteria of monotheism, nor does that of any other creation myth.[17]

While monotheism represents a unique platform for a creation narrative, more importantly it is the only platform that can support a complete creation narrative from the beginning to the end of time. It is the very constancy of God, and the transcendent and never-changing truths of Creation, that keep the narrative consistent and cohesive through history. If other creative agencies moved in and out of time, or if there were constant squabbling and infighting amongst the gods, there would be a similar contest for the ownership of the narrative and its outcomes. False gods, idolatry, and the ongoing struggle for control of the language of creation results in continual cultural renegotiation of the myth itself and eliminates any possibility that absolute values or ethical standards can

17. Sproul, *Primal Myths*, 232–36; 75–76.

exist. That is not sustainable and it requires a constant reevaluation of ethical and social guidelines as evidenced in other myth traditions.

Even within a cohesive, monotheistic creation narrative, the tensions inherent in "good vs. evil" remain. It is precisely the internal integrity of the process of creation, redemption, and re-creation that provides insights into these tensions. The Creation narrative covers all of history, not just the span of time in which an individual human exists. Contemporary humans are largely driven by such a consuming sense of self-importance that they cannot understand how they are not the center of the universe. Returning once again to Moses, he provided the correct perspective, the Creation perspective:

> Before the mountains were brought forth;
> or ever you had formed the earth and the world,
> from everlasting to everlasting you are God.
> You return man to dust
> and say "Oh return O children of man!"
> For a thousand years in your sight
> are but as yesterday when it is past,
> or as a watch in the night. . . .
> So teach us to number our days
> that we may get a heart of wisdom. . . .
> Let the favor of the Lord our God be upon us,
> and establish the work of our hands upon us;
> yes, establish the work of our hands.[18]

This is not the empty cry of a fatalistic psalmist. It is an acknowledgment of the center point of Creation. The psalm is a recognition of the joy of having a God to call upon who is eternal and who can guide the work of our hands in a direction that accomplishes His objectives for our salvation. It is a call to wisdom, which leads to knowing God better. He guides the work of our hands, not so that we can complete our time on this earth with some sense of accomplishment but so that we can join Him in completing the Creation that He began in us, which will come to fulfillment at the end of time. Immanuel Kant restated this in a more modern form in his *Critique of Practical Reason* when he said, "Hence also morality is not properly the doctrine how we should make ourselves happy, but how we should become worthy of happiness."[19]

18. Ps 90:2–4, 12, 17.

19. Kant, *Practical Reason*, 122.

God did not give up on His Creation after the fall from grace. Once the narrative of Creation is fully understood and appreciated, philosophical impositions and binary oppositions cease to govern. The tensions of monotheism are erased at the completion of the new Creation.

We know how the narrative begins and we know how it has progressed to date. We know that the new kingdom is at hand; we know we are working on the new Creation; and we know what the outcome will be. There should be no tensions or fears except for those still shackled to an incomplete story or seeking options to a monotheistic God.

Having addressed the covenantal nature of God and the significance of monotheism in our argument that Creation is not a myth, the third and, in many ways, the most critical distinguishing characteristic is the creative agency of speech. The covenants create the basis for mankind's participation in the re-creation and the building of the new kingdom. They do not exist simply to assure success during an ephemeral lifespan. Monotheism demands adherence to one God whose truths are absolute and enduring. No other agency can successfully replicate the dynamic acts of re-creation and redemption; there are no substitutes for God. Language and speech are matters of vital concern to the entire process. They are the living, active ingredients of Creation, and their significance has not diminished since Creation itself.

Language and speech continue to animate the journey to salvation and redemption. They are the sanctified tools for reclaiming Creation and building the new Jerusalem. Language and speech carry God's history, and they have been bequeathed to us as participants in His re-creation. This is the focus of the following chapter.

# Chapter 3

# Protecting the Narrative

The use of powerful and highly charged words in the act of creation is not uncommon in other myths. In the Enuma Elish, although not a creation myth, certain creative acts are attributed to the spoken word, much in the same way God commanded, "Let there be light."[1] The Dogons of Western Africa assign each of the stages of creation to the speaking of sacred words. The myth also refers to "the Word, which is indispensable to all beings as well as to the system of the universe."[2] So, too, the various phases of Zuni creation begin with "Behold," and it is accomplished.[3]

But because Creation as an active, ongoing process continues to flow through time, the qualities of the language and speech used by the Creator to create remain decidedly singular and distinctive. Since the scriptural narrative describes the process of returning the universe to its moral and ethical beginnings, it follows that the Creator's language and speech must continue to reflect His intentions, both in the beginning and throughout the re-creation process. As stewards, the language and speech of stewardship must be infused with the original power and authority of Creation. This is unique to Genesis inasmuch as all other creation myths move and evolve through time. With other origin stories, there is no clearly anticipated end state for creation, and clearly no effort by the gods to guide humanity to a perfected end state. There is no effort to identify

1. Sproul, *Primal Myths*, 91–114; Long, *Alpha*, 80–91.
2. Long, *Alpha*, 112.
3. Long, *Alpha*, 101–5; Sproul, *Primal Myths*, 284.

the value proposition of the mythical gods of creation because any such proposition is subject to cultural renegotiation.

In the first chapter of Genesis, God stated that He created mankind in His own image.[4] The Hebrew word used here is *tselem,* meaning reflecting the essential nature of God, mirroring His own perfections in knowledge, righteousness, and holiness, and with dominion over all other living things.[5] Not only is the value proposition of God unequivocally clear in Genesis, God makes equally clear throughout the remainder of Scripture that His objective is to realign the universe with His values and ethics. Creation is a consistent, never-ending journey of re-creation and redemption. As stewards of this Creation, designated to govern the universe as God's representatives, maintaining the accuracy and authenticity of the narrative is crucial.

All this is captured quite nicely by David in Ps 19. The song "directs attention to divine speech that goes out to all humanity."[6] The power of speech reflects God's perfection. "Day to day pours out speech, and night to night reveals knowledge."[7] But this knowledge must be heard to be of any value. If not shared, "There is no speech, nor are there words."[8] The reward for sharing and hearing is the perfection of the soul, "enduring forever."[9]

Myths, once the creative process is completed, move forward under their own power. The creator gods, if they remain relevant at all, do so in entirely different capacities. Their essential nature and role changes. They may become part of nature; they may inhabit the sky, the earth, or the waters. They may be enigmas to be worshiped or feared, or take on the form of plants or animals. In some cases, the gods create so that they have places to reside or to satisfy their own needs. Some may serve to adjudicate disputes among the other gods, between gods and humans, or between groups of humans.

The multiplicity of gods in other origin stories required some sort of structure to rationalize the complexity of their relationships with mankind. Relying upon patterns their followers would find familiar,

4. Gen 1:26.

5. Strong, *Concordance*, 238, of the expanded dictionary of Hebrew words in the Bible.

6. ESV, 960.

7. Ps 19:2.

8. Ps 19:3.

9. Ps 19:9.

other creation myths developed frameworks within which the gods lived and operated. These mirrored family structures or royal governing structures[10] that would be recognizable to those worshiping mythological gods. These arrangements were meant to take some of the mystery out of the process of worship. Genesis occasionally hints at similar formalities, suggesting Yahweh might govern a council of some sort, but it has limited relevance in the overall Genesis narrative. God makes no mystery out of His purpose, and the clarity of a monotheistic God does not require organizational gymnastics to define His relationship with the universe. In order to redeem and save, God simply continues the process of Creation so it can fulfill its initial purpose, which is humanity existing in a perfected relationship with Him. A necessary requirement is a narrative that remains accurate and consistent from generation to generation. As Ps 89 declares, "I will sing of the mercies of the Lord forever: with my mouth will I make known thy faithfulness to all generations."[11]

The Word, the animating agency of Creation, was passed on to mankind as both a gift and a responsibility. Humanity was created in the image of God, given the authority to name all living things, and charged with dominion over all of Creation. It must therefore follow that the Word, embedded in the language of the original, perfected relationship between God and man, must continue to retain the same power and authority during the process of reclaiming and redeeming Creation as well. Despite the sinful, fallen nature of man and the ensuing separation from God, the Word lost none of its power and authority. Paul acknowledged as much when he wrote to the faithful in Rome, "What if some were unfaithful? Does their faithlessness nullify the faithfulness of God? By no means."[12] Paul confirms the vitality of witness as vehicles for spreading the Word. Human language and speech have been endowed with the qualities of the Creator for the purposes of moving re-creation and redemption forward on God's behalf, as stewards and as intended. Language and speech, along with their symbols, signifiers, and encoding, become the mechanisms for protecting the integrity of the Word and promulgating an authentic narrative of Creation and its purposes.

Because creation is a one-off event in other myths, the role of language after creation shifts. The language and speech of mythical gods no longer operate with creative properties but instead assume a transactional

10. Smith, *Biblical Monotheism*, 54–66.

11. Ps 89:1.

12. Rom 3:3.

nature. They are meant to inform, threaten, entice, seduce, or mislead, but they do not continue to create. God's purpose for Creation was that all of Creation would worship Him and live in perfect harmony with Him. To the extent that the gods of myth created for a purpose at all, it was far more utilitarian. Language, in that sense, became transactional. It satisfied ministerial purposes, but it had no creative power. The focus of the relationship between man and the gods of myth was participatory, familiarizing and engaging whatever the universe, at any moment in time, had to offer. It was not a process of reclamation or redemption. It was a *quid pro quo*: each party needing one another at a very elemental level for justification, a symbiotic relationship that has been used as a literary device for thousands of years.[13]

What sets Creation, and the language of Creation, apart is the journey from Creation corrupted to Creation completed. The language of Creation remains vital and creative because it is the language of an immediate and intimate journey of perfecting the relationship between God and humanity. As is often the case, it is Paul who captures the essence of this process perfectly:

> For the creation was subjected to futility, not willingly, but because of him who subjected it, in hope that the creation itself will be set free from its bondage to corruption and obtain the freedom of the glory of the children of God. For we know that the whole creation has been groaning together in the pains of childbirth until now. And not only the creation, but we ourselves, who have the firstfruits of the Spirit, groan inwardly as we wait eagerly for adoption as sons, the redemption of our bodies.[14]

It is still a work in progress and, as such, the powers of language and speech must retain their initial creative vitality. And since the Creator is holy, the language and speech of the Creator also retain their holy characteristics. A language that is not sanctified, structured merely for mutual convenience, cannot achieve the objective of a perfected relationship with God.

13. An episode of the television series *Star Trek* (season 2, episode 2, "Who Mourns for Adonais") portrays a godlike figure who exhibits precisely this type of relationship. A quick internet search suggests that the first century Latin poet Statius, in his unfinished epic poem "Achilleid," seems to have been the one who introduced this device. It is credited as an influence in works by Dante (*The Divine Comedy*) and Percy Bysshe Shelley ("Adonais").

14. Rom 8:20–23.

God does not need humanity in any conventional sense. He does not need sacrifices for sustenance or temples for housing. He loves sacrifice and worship because He loves the obedience of His Creation, not for self-aggrandizement but because obedience leads to the perfection of relationships. "For I desire steadfast love and not sacrifice, the knowledge of God rather than burnt offerings."[15]

The nature of obedience to God differs dramatically from the human perspective of obedience. The latter stems from a corrupted human desire to control people and events. Whether the objective is noble or not, it is still driven by a more self-centered human compulsion. Compare that to the binding of Isaac, found in Gen 22. Here, Abram's obedience to God's commands, as horrific as they must have seemed at the moment, led to Abraham's status as patriarch and progenitor of nations. Perfected relationships between God and humans and between human beings lead to salvation, and salvation to everlasting life, the completion of Creation's initial purposes. In his second farewell speech, Moses referred to this process as the circumcision of the heart.[16]

God spoke with creative power when He established the covenants with Abraham, Noah, Moses, and David. He continued to assert His creative will when He spoke through the prophets, to urge His creation to obey His commands so that they may obtain His promises. His creative Word became flesh and was sacrificed, not as reaffirmation of God's power but to inaugurate the kingdom of heaven here on earth in real time and space. And through this sacrifice, humanity was offered the opportunity to assist in building the kingdom.

The power of speech to create includes the power to destroy as well. And lest the power of speech become an impediment to salvation, God demands that mankind respect the creative and sanctified nature of the gift of speech. Admonitions, cautions, directions, and guidance on the use of language and speech populate the entirety of Scripture. If, after Creation, language was merely a device to administer a completed process, there would not be the heavy emphasis on preserving its creative integrity or anointing it as a component of redemption and salvation. Corrupted language could not maintain the vitality of the Creation narrative.

15. Hos 6:6.

16. Deut 10:12–22.

Semiotics, in its simplest terms, is the study of signs and symbols and how they are used in communication. The relationship between the sign or symbol and its meaning can be natural, such as thunder indicating rain, or smoke fire. Some of them become universal by general agreement. In a cognitive sense, think of the color red on a stop sign or a stop light. There is nothing inherent in the color red that means stop, and until the idea of controlling traffic became an issue, it did not mean stop. Others are uniquely tied to a culture. A thumbs up sign in America is generally welcomed, but in Greece, it is more likely to generate ill will if not outright conflict. Still others may be as much technological, as in the case of a ringing phone. Where there are no phones, the ring is meaningless.

As interesting and important as the study of semiotics is, this is not a study in semiotics. But the concept is important, since the meaning and intent of words and how they are signified are deeply encoded in an individual culture. Signs, symbols, and signals are intimately tied up in language, and how one uses language imparts the values reflected in the symbols and signs embedded in that language. This is true in the language of faith as well as that of cultures and societies. Resurrection elicits a very different visceral reaction to a faithful Christian than it does to a script writer or novelist, who molds the concept to fulfill a literary device. So, too, does the symbol of the cross, which seems to hang around the necks of individuals who have absolutely no sense of what the cross means to a follower of Christ. So, while we are talking about language and speech as reflections of the power and majesty of God and their role in guarding and passing on the faith, we are also talking about protecting the values behind the symbols and signs of faith.

Two questions are inevitably raised whenever the matter of scriptural authority is introduced. In the first instance, given the importance of language and speech in protecting and guiding the narrative, it is important to affirm that such power and authority are genuine and intended. Secondly, the matter of inconsistencies within the scriptural narrative is always cited as an objection. It is appropriate to dispense with them now.

The claim that there is a unique power and authority in the gift of language and speech, and that protecting the integrity of the narrative is of paramount concern, can be defended through seven logically consistent premises.

First, God's creative agency was an act of speech. God called the universe into being *ex nihilo* (out of nothing) by His spoken Word. The pattern was set in the third verse of Genesis: "And God said, 'Let there be light,' and there was light." That pattern was followed for every detail of Creation thereafter. C. S. Lewis gives us a wonderful and lyrical version of Creation in *The Magician's Nephew*, where Narnia was sung into existence by Aslan.[17]

Second, as the animating source of Creation, language and speech reflect the powerful properties of the Creator. The nature of the Creator and the nature of His words cannot be at odds with one another. For the narrative to be authentic, the language and speech that convey the narrative must contain the same properties as the words employed at the initial Creation. Any corruption of the narrative is therefore a rejection of God's value proposition

Third, since the nature of the Creator is unchangeable, the subsequent fall from grace did not nullify the sanctity of the gift, the character of the giver, or the responsibilities of stewardship. The powerful qualities of language and speech were not diminished by the act of human disobedience, as Paul asserted in the earlier citation from his letter to the Romans. The task at hand became the redemption and salvation of Creation, which required the same powerful agency for re-creation that was necessary for Creation. Thus, the authentic narrative of Creation is the means by which God moves through history to protect the integrity and purpose of His design for the universe.

Fourth, accepting the obligation to faithfully represent the narrative creates a sanctified relationship between those speaking on God's behalf and those to whom they are speaking, a relationship governed by the terms of God's covenants. One must be both speaker and hearer. "So faith comes from hearing, and hearing through the word of Christ."[18] Failing to abide by the covenants is an act of separation contrary to God's intentions. This fact alone elevates language and speech and reinforces just how critical the Creation narrative is to redemption and salvation.

Fifth, God's words are evidence of His continuing love for His people. They are not simply codified once and forgotten. They are specific and purposeful, alive and active, directed towards the immediate circumstances within which actual people live, operate, and strive to survive. They are not simply abstractions; they are intended to profoundly impact lives in real time. Human language and speech either reflect or reject God's value proposition. The entirety of the scriptural message is

17. Lewis, *Magician's Nephew*, 125–39.

18. Rom 19:17.

to be diligent in guarding against anything that removes mankind from under the umbrella of God's love.

Sixth, the ramifications of language and speech extend beyond the individual. Individual sin, as expressed in personal rebellion, threatens the salvation of the sinner. Sin that causes others to sin is far more serious. Jesus says, "Whoever causes one of these little ones who believe in me to sin, it would be better for him if a millstone were hung around his neck and he were thrown into the sea."[19] By little ones, Jesus was not referring exclusively to children. He was also referring to those new to the faith. As mankind struggles to acquit its stewardship responsibilities, to order society according to God's ethical and moral strictures, it must be constantly aware that chaos and disorder will undermine the reclamation of Creation. Paul warned the Galatians that disorder and strife would ultimately destroy them. The letter of the apostle James carries the same message. Both identified Satan as the author of chaos, and language and speech the vehicle. "For God is not a God of confusion, but of peace."[20]

Finally, God moves through history and controls history. At various points in history, His Word freed the Jews from bondage in Egypt, protected and fed them in the wilderness, helped conquer the promised land, built a nation, and guided the remnants of the nation of Israel through exile and return. Ultimately, His Word was formed in Jesus and, after the resurrection, the Holy Spirit, spoken through the apostles. God's continual communication through the Word represents His unfailing commitment to see humanity through to the end. His words are immediate and vital. Getting His words right arm the faithful for eternity. As one of the psalmists proclaimed, "We will not hide them [God's words] from their children, but tell to the coming generation the glorious deeds of the Lord, and his might, and the wonders he has done."[21] God's words are not tokens of a past era; they speak to humanity at all times and in all places.

The second issue at hand is the matter of conflicting accounts of events within the Bible. A vast amount of time and effort has gone into identifying instances in which one account of an event differs from another account of the same event. As an example, even those only marginally conversant with Scriptures are familiar with the David and Goliath story. One noted archaeologist has identified a number of inconsistencies

19. Mark 9:42.

20. 1 Cor 14:33.

21. Ps 78:4.

in the recounting of the tale.[22] The evidence is clear. What to do with this information is a different matter. This is a problem associated with biblical redaction. It demands explanation.

Some scholars will attribute inconsistencies to errors in translation or imperfect interpretations. Others may acknowledge discrepancies but simply dismiss them as trivial in light of the enormity of the entire narrative and its message. Still others will assign malign motives, suggesting that it is a bald-faced attempt to twist information for the benefit of orthodoxy. For them, the Bible is one huge conspiracy.

From the viewpoint of this study, setting aside conspiracy theories, there may be elements of truth in all these viewpoints. The Bible was compiled over thousands of years, by numerous and disparate contributors. It has been translated and interpreted in many languages, and the product as we know it today was developed over centuries of intense and meaningful debate. But I might add, so has the history of any other extraordinary secular event. As this country approaches its 250th anniversary, the players and the details of the American Revolution are still subjects of heated discussions. More importantly, the intellectual and philosophical undertones of the Revolution, and the impact they continue to have across the entire globe, appear in such diverse guises that one would be excused for questioning whether folks are engaging the same question.

And this is the way it should be for events and movements so seminal, so overarching, so definitive that the entire world shifts. It would be dismissive were this not the case. The theologian N. T. Wright, as an example, refers to Jesus' crucifixion as the day the revolution began.[23] The Scriptures and the Creation narrative deserve this scrutiny and debate. It is evidence of their continuing vitality and their meaning in the lives and circumstances of real, everyday people. In the end, this attention is the most significant evidence of God's commitment to His people.

The Bible demonstrates that, despite human error, the Creation narrative remains consistent and integral to human experience, both in the past and in the present. Barton Swaim, writing in a *Wall Street Journal* editorial, makes the point in a different way. Speaking to current events and the actions of world leaders, he writes, "But the Bible's histories often

22. Cargill, *Cities*, 176–77.

23. Wright, *Revolution*.

reveal patterns of human behavior so recognizable as to seem ripped from yesterday's headlines."[24]

But when it comes to the particular question of whether Creation is a myth as contemporarily defined, these issues are somewhat superfluous. Even in those instances where there may be a difference in dates, individuals, and places, the fact still remains that the premise retains its integrity. God's words have meaning. They have been, and continue to be, impactful. The narrative of redemption and salvation is consistent and unchanged, and the message across the entire width and breadth of the Scriptures consistently insists that this narrative be protected. What we will discover going forward is a continual defense of monotheism, human responsibility as governed by God's covenants, and the demand that the creative intensity of language and speech be carefully guarded and regulated.

Idolatry, false prophets and teachings, or any other word or deed that seeks to put human understanding on a level equal to or greater than God's wisdom assaults the underlying premises of monotheism. Following the conditions of the covenants God made through the ages grants the authority to act on His behalf. Faithfulness assures peace and prosperity, while disobedience results in separation from the protection of God. Cultural syncretism, the accommodation of other patterns of governance and worship, undermines the covenants. The covenants are a living reminder of the commitment of God to His Creation. Finally, God demands that human behavior be governed by His value proposition. Social justice, fairness, and compassion for the needy are all reflections of His moral and ethical standards. They are conveyed through language and speech. Ignoring the sanctified nature of the language of Creation, either through carelessness, wickedness or attempts to accommodate the wants and needs of other cultures, destroys the authenticity of the narrative and the integrity of worship. The words of the prophets confirm this premise. "Being unfaithful to God by apostasy (putting other gods *before* Him) or syncretism (putting other gods *beside* Him) will doom them to subjugation and exile from which the only hope of escape and restoration is to repent of these terrible sins and turn back and walk in His ways."[25]

24. Swaim, Barton. "Like Pharaoh," A13.

25. Podhoretz, *Prophets*, 107.

Hannah's prayer in 1 Samuel very clearly spells out this relationship.[26] The road map is a faithful narrative.

With the incarnation of the Word in the humanity of Jesus, the powerful language and speech of Creation and re-creation became real and immediate. "And the Word became flesh and dwelt among us."[27] Humans were now endowed with the same power as prophets and priests to pass on the sacred narratives in accordance with His will. In Luther's words, "Hence all of us who believe in Christ are priests and kings in Christ as I Pet. 2[:9] says: 'You are a chosen race, God's own people, a royal priesthood, a priestly kingdom, that you may declare the wonderful deeds of him who called you out of darkness into his marvellous light.'"[28]

The responsibility to use the tools of language and speech in ways that reinforce the fullness of the one true God, and to conduct oneself justly in the moral and ethical image of the Creator, falls on the individual. The chosen people were now anyone who followed the Word made flesh, not just the Jews. After Christ's death, resurrection, and ascension, the new kingdom was established on earth. It is real, manifest in time and space. Sanctified language continues to address matters such as idolatry, social justice, and God's value proposition, but now sins can be forgiven and mankind is called to work alongside God, through the Holy Spirit, in redeeming all of Creation. Protecting and guiding the language and symbols of kingdom building became a New Testament imperative as well.

26. 1 Sam 2:1–10.

27. John 1:14.

28. Roper, *Martin Luther*, 144–45.

# Chapter 4

# Creation by Wisdom and the Word

The only living things in the garden over which Adam and Eve had no dominion were two special trees. One was the tree of life and the other was the tree of the knowledge of good and evil—essentially, the powers of eternal omnipotence and omniscience. These authorities were reserved for God alone. While Adam and Eve were not supposed to touch or eat of either tree, they were nonetheless growing in the center of the universe. God does nothing haphazardly. The trees were not a mistake or a lapse in judgment. At the very least, these trees were an attractive nuisance, a risk that was nonetheless appealing. Calling attention to something that is readily accessible but forbidden is difficult to resist. Why would God put such a temptation right under their noses?

The answer lies in an understanding of wisdom and wisdom's relationship with the Word. The Word that was with God and was God at the Creation is the perfect wisdom of God. God created a perfect universe through wisdom and the Word. God wanted man and woman to grow in wisdom, to grow in their knowledge of Him, to mature in their relationship with the Word, and to remain invested in Him as He was, and is, invested in us. To respect the sanctity of the Word through the gift of language and speech was to respect and nurture the narrative. The concepts of Word, wisdom, and an authentic narrative are inextricably entwined.

But true wisdom also includes the recognition of boundaries and limits:

> Then you will understand the fear of the Lord and find the knowledge of God. For the Lord gives wisdom; from his mouth come knowledge and understanding; he stores up sound wisdom for the upright; he is a shield to those who walk in integrity.

> . . . For the upright will inhabit the land, and those with integrity will remain in it, but the wicked will be cut off from the land, and the treacherous will be rooted out of it.[1]

Only those who possess true wisdom will understand what it means to fear the Lord and know Him ("find the knowledge of God"). This knowledge and understanding are directly associated with the Word ("from his mouth come knowledge and understanding"), the agency of Creation. To those willing to follow the Word, He will continue to provide wisdom and store it up for the generations to follow. All of this is summed up in the term integrity, a concept found throughout wisdom and poetic literature. It is meant to convey the sense of uprightness, perfection, and fullness, the very qualities found in the image of God in which man was formed.[2] Paul reflects this same understanding when, in his instructions to Titus, he tells him, "Show yourself in all respects to be a model of good works, and in your teaching show integrity, dignity, and sound speech that cannot be condemned."[3] And only those with integrity can produce "speech that cannot be condemned," that is, doctrine so sound that it cannot be challenged. Protecting the authentic narrative requires sound wisdom.

Through His wisdom and the Word, made manifest in Creation, God made an agreement, a covenant, with Adam. Adam was to have dominion over all living things, governing in accordance with God's value proposition.[4] Adam was to raise generations of faithful people who would come to know God, and whom God would know, by wisdom imparted through a perfected testimony to the power of the Word.

But this perfected relationship could only be maintained by accepting the boundaries established by God's commands, reflected in the reality and immediacy of these two trees. This was not some divine trap. The power of God, physically represented by the trees, was to be feared and respected. They were not to be corrupted by human contact. The trees represented the standards for proper behavior and obedience. Their existence required Adam and Eve to acknowledge that whatever power and authority the grant of dominion brought with it, it did not rise to a level comparable to God. This was precisely how the serpent tempted Eve.[5]

1. Prov 2:5–7, 21–22.

2. Job 2:3, 2:9, 27:5, 31:6; Ps 7:8, 25:21, 26:1, 26:11, 41:12, 78:72; Prov 2:5–7, 21–22, 11:3, 19:1, 20:7.

3. Titus 2:7.

4. Gen 2:15.

5. Gen 3:4–5.

The trees symbolized the depth of human obedience; the contractual requirements Adam and Eve were expected to fulfill. These trees were the exclusive purview of the Creator and represented something far more awesome and terrible. The power over life and death and the full omniscience of the Creator are two concepts humanity could never understand or control. Further, possessing these qualities would extinguish any distinctions between the Creator and the created.

When God said, "Let us make man in our image, after our likeness," He was not intending to signal whatever, if any, physical manifestations of the Creator might be reflected in human form. Instead, God intended that humanity be imbued with the characteristics of reason, morality, language, creativity, beauty, and the capacity to develop relationships built on the unconditional love and commitment that His image projected. "It is more probable . . . that some less material resemblance is intended: that human beings, in distinction from the animals, possess the unique capacity to communicate meaningfully with God."[6] Adam's mission to populate the earth, governing with integrity and wisdom, required the capacity to not only hear God but accurately communicate His wishes and desires. The gifts of language and speech were the vehicles designed for those specific purposes. Society could not be properly ordered without the quality of integrity referenced in Prov 2 and Paul's instructions to Titus.

Fully embracing God's image provides insights into Creation and how it is to be ordered and governed. Paul acknowledges these characteristics and their relationship to the image of God in his letter to the Colossians: "But now you must put them all away: anger, wrath, malice, slander and obscene talk from your mouth. Do not lie to one another, seeing that you have put off the old self with its practices and have put on the new self, which is being renewed in knowledge after the image of its creator."[7]

God's image is nothing less than His value proposition for all of Creation. Wisdom is a quality of the omnipotent and omniscient Word that humanity is permitted to share. It is a place where God permits greater insight into Himself. It is the foundation of His gift of language and speech. It is the source of Christian semiotics, its symbols and signs.

The relationship between the Word, wisdom, and the image of God is restated in the opening to the Gospel of John:

6. Barton and Muddiman, *Oxford Bible Commentary*, 43.

7. Col 3:8–11.

> In the beginning was the Word, and the Word was with God, and the Word was God. He was in the beginning with God. All things were made through him, and without him was not any thing made that was made. In him was life, and the life was the light of men. The light shines in the darkness, and the darkness has not overcome it.[8]

The choice of words here is important. Since Greek was the language of the New Testament writings, John could have used either *mythos* or *logos* for the opening lines of his Gospel. The authenticity of *mythos* is derived from its general acceptance as opposed to empirical verification. *Mythos* carries with it a sense of story or fiction. Obviously, *mythos* gave us the term and concept of myth. *Mythos* is exclusively negative in the New Testament, meaning "an invented story, a rumor or a fable."[9] *Logos*, however, refers to a certain validity that can be tested, argued, independently validated, and demonstrated in some empirical way. It reflects the Old Testament sense of wisdom, which was, as we shall see momentarily, tantamount to divine presence. John used the word *logos*.

Of course, the Word also refers to Jesus who, along with God, existed through history, had a divine relationship with God, and was God. Since Jesus was God, was present at the creation, but took on the nature of a man, we now have another reference point against which we can begin to understand the purpose, the absolute reality, of Creation. The image of God, not merely the physical but the moral, relational, rational, and beautiful, appears as His Son—the perfect exemplar of absolute, unchanging, and unchangeable core values. Jesus is the physical manifestation of wisdom, present in real time and space.

John, writing as he did after the events of Jesus' life, death, and resurrection (70–100 CE), speaks not only to physical realities but the spiritual realities of wisdom manifested as the Holy Spirit. "Through the Word, who is both light and life, the invisible and unheard God is revealed."[10] And again in chapter 14, "Jesus said to him, 'I am the way, and the truth, and the life. No one comes to the Father except through me. If you had known me, you would have known my Father also. From now on you do know him and have seen him.'"[11] We can continue to know Him and see Him through wisdom conveyed by the Holy Spirit. In His high priestly

8. John 1:1–4.

9. Metzger and Coogan, *Oxford Companion*, 539.

10. Barton and Muddiman, *Oxford Bible Commentary*, 962.

11. John 14:6–7.

prayer, offered just before His arrest and crucifixion, Jesus restates this reality: "I made known to them your name, and I will continue to make it known [through the Holy Spirit], that the love with which you have loved me may be in them, and I in them."[12]

Given the significance of wisdom as revealed in Creation, it is not surprising that there is a robust legacy of wisdom literature that informs both the Old and the New Testaments. The book of Wisdom, which was written sometime in the first or second century before Christ, situates the Word within wisdom and, through wisdom, offers a window into Creation: "With thee is wisdom, who knows thy works and was present when thou didst make the world, and who understands what is pleasing in thy sight and what is right according to thy commandments."[13] God wants us to be wise—in other words, to know Him. The wiser we become, the better we know Him. "Send her forth from the holy heavens, and from the throne of thy glory send her, that she may be with me and toil, and that I may learn what is pleasing to thee."[14] "For God created man for incorruption, and made him in the image of his own eternity."[15] This is the spiritual reality of Creation to which John refers and is freely offered to mankind. Spirituality and salvation are not simply a matter of interpolating the mysteries of myth; they are imbedded in God's Word at Creation. They become accessible through obedience that reflects the true image of God, and through the presence of the living Word in Christ. We are called to grow in wisdom, to know Him better, and share that wisdom through the faithful recounting of His Word. As Paul puts it, "Formerly, when you did not know God, you were enslaved to those that by nature are not gods. But now that you have come to know God, or rather to be known by God, how can you turn back to the weak and worthless elementary principles of the world."[16]

Poetic and wisdom literature were not limited to Jewish traditions. Throughout the ancient Middle East every culture had wisdom traditions. Some grew out of tribal histories; some reflected official worship patterns; and still others had roots so distant that they can only be referenced in the abstract. Whatever the source, poetic and wisdom literature were widely distributed and universally recognized. Wisdom could take

12. John 17:26.
13. RSV, Wis 9:9.
14. RSV, Wis 9:9–10.
15. RSV, Wis 2:23.
16. Gal 4:8–9.

on the complexion of simple, commonsense instructions on how to live. It could also appear as sage advice on matters of a deeply contemplative and profoundly theological nature, or as rich, beautiful, and lyrical reflections on the natural world.

Poetic and wisdom literature are equally applicable to both individuals and communities. The slow unraveling of the nation of Israel after the death of Solomon marked a shift in emphasis from God's building and sustaining a discrete nation to the prophetic appeals to individuals to turn away from evil and embrace the eternal truths of God's wisdom. It was also a time when God's call extended beyond the confines of Israel and the Jewish people. He invited, if you will, anyone into a covenanted relationship without regard to nationality. God did not turn away from His chosen people, but His call no longer remained exclusive. The fact that poetic and wisdom literature were generally familiar to the people of neighboring nations and tribes, to distant empires and their faith traditions, brought a certain familiarity to the messages of the prophets. Speaking, as they did, to the remnants of Israel now dispersed among other nations and peoples meant that many of those hearing the prophets may not have understood specific references to the Jewish experience, but they would certainly have recognized the language of wisdom.

The beauty of wisdom is that it transcends history, and the Scriptures include a broad tradition of poetry and wisdom literature.[17] Here we can see wisdom and the Word in a timeless context, one that allows the faithful to rise above their historical context and feel the fullness of Creation in its entirety. It is not tied to a unique point in time; its meaning is not dependent on specific places or people; and its value transcends chronological constraints. "Poetic and wisdom literature tends to resist a straight-forward chronological setting. Rightly understanding the Bible's histories and prophetic literature depends to an extent on taking their historical context into account; such is not normally the case for Israel's hymns and wisdom."[18] They are a medium for instruction and guidance: "Because of the individualistic emphasis, wisdom placed no stress on historical events as the arena of divine disclosure."[19]

Examples of poetry and wisdom literature extend far back in time. While the author of Job may have been a contemporary of Ezekiel in

17. The books of Job, Psalms, Proverbs, Ecclesiastes, and the Song of Solomon are classified as poetic and wisdom literature in the modern Bible.

18. ESV, 867.

19. Metzger and Coogan, *Oxford Companion*, 802.

the sixth century BCE, individual psalms can be dated back as far as the thirteenth century BCE, and most were composed in the tenth. Proverbs is generally agreed to have been written during the era of Solomon in the tenth century BCE, as were Ecclesiastes and the Song of Solomon. During the period of exile, the prophets relied heavily on poetic and wisdom traditions, as did Jesus during His ministry. Roughly 200 BCE, in the midst of the exile, a Jewish scribe and teacher of ethics began writing down many of the oral wisdom traditions that would have been familiar to generations of Jews. While the collection of Jesus the son of Sirach did not make it into the canon, the apocryphal book of Ecclesiasticus is considered a profoundly important piece of inspired wisdom literature and is frequently incorporated in the liturgies of both Roman and Protestant denominations. References to these traditions are abundant in the New Testament and the writings of the patristic fathers as well.

Focusing on the three defining characteristics of Creation (monotheism, covenantal promises, and language and speech), there are four particular themes woven through wisdom literature that reinforce the conclusion that the distinguishing characteristics that place Creation beyond the constraints of conventional mythology are identified, reinforced, and imbedded within the historical wisdom tradition. They sufficiently demonstrate that the distinctions between Creation and myth have been informing the Creation journey since the beginning of time and are not merely interesting intellectual ponderings.

Because these traditions are not bound by history, the characteristics of Creation assume a more timeless and universal profile. In the traditions of wisdom literature, they can be read, heard, and experienced through four thematic strains: 1) the reconciliation of good and evil; 2) the ordering of the righteous (wise) and the wicked (fools) within the universe; 3) the necessity of obedience and faithfulness as prerequisites to experiencing the fullness of God; and 4) the inadequacy of relying exclusively on human wisdom. Collectively, they offer individuals insights into the inadequacy of idols, false teachers, and human understanding. They speak to the outcomes of an obedient life, Creation's demands for a just and ordered society, and the dangers of falling prey to outside influences. Consistent with their didactic emphasis, wisdom and poetic literature reflect these tensions through the lens of language and speech and the responsibility to fully and accurately maintain the narrative tradition.

For our purposes, the best place to begin is with Job. Unlike the rest of wisdom and poetic literature, Job offers a dynamic conversation between Job, his antagonists, and God. As Job contends with the presumption of his erstwhile friends, he also engages directly with God. Throughout the course of this dialogue, the interplay of the four thematic strains, the wisdom of God, and ultimate redemption are on full display.

In replying to Zophar's argument that the wicked suffer, Job reacts by asserting the contrary, that the wicked do not seem to suffer at all. "Why do the wicked live, reach old age, and grow mighty in power," further on adding, "How often is it that the lamp of the wicked is put out? That their calamity comes upon them? That God distributes pains in his anger?"[20] Here, Job is wrestling with the age-old challenge of reconciling the existence of both good and evil in a loving God.

The reader is given greater insight to this question at the opening of the chapter. Job is acknowledged to be "blameless and upright, one who feared God and turned away from evil."[21] Satan immediately challenged God's characterization of Job, suggesting that the only reason Job is blameless and upright is because God has been protecting him. God then granted Satan permission to deal with Job as he wished, with one exception. He is not permitted to take Job's life. Apart from Jesus' crucifixion, there is no clearer example in Scripture of God as the ultimate authority over both good and evil. Satan could only act if God granted him the authority to do so. He could not act on his own authority.

Job acknowledges God's wisdom in ordering of the universe, recognizes his own weaknesses, and repents.[22] God rebukes Job's friends, pointing out the folly in relying on their own understanding. God not only redeems Job but makes the redemption of Eliphaz, Bildad, and Zophar contingent upon Job's prayers.[23]

Job is not the only place within the collection of poetic and wisdom literature where the aforementioned themes are addressed. With respect to the apparent imbalance of pain and suffering between wicked and the wise, in Ps 94, the writer cries out, "O Lord, how long shall the wicked, how long shall the wicked exult? They pour out their arrogant words; all the evildoers boast."[24] In Ps 31, the psalmist is seeking refuge from those who pursue and destroy the faithful. "Let the lying lips be mute, which speak insolently against the righteous in pride and contempt."[25] The fear

20. Job 21:7, 17.

21. Job 1:1.

22. Job 24, 28, 42:1–6.

23. Job 42:7–9.

24. Ps 94:3–4.

25. Ps 31:18.

of opening one's mouth and saying something that will only enable the wicked testifies to the power of speech to distort the will of God. One psalmist, suffering from grief and confusion, acknowledges the risks of not carefully choosing his words in the face of his pain but understands that, eventually, he must speak.

> I said, "I will guard my ways,
> that I may not sin with my tongue;
> I will guard my mouth with a muzzle,
> so long as the wicked are in my presence."
>
> I was mute and silent;
> I held my peace to no avail,
> and my distress grew worse.
>
> My heart became hot within me.
> As I mused, the fire burned;
> then I spoke with my tongue.[26]

Psalm 39, from which this passage is taken, reminds the readers that it is more important to sustain the narrative than it is to risk misrepresenting it. The risk of speaking in the company of the wicked is offset by the knowledge that words spoken through worship, which is the focus of the remainder of the psalm, is the correct way to express one's concerns and fears to the Lord.[27] Psalm 105 reminds the reader to "tell of all his wondrous works."[28] That constitutes true wisdom, the understanding that pain and suffering are transitory but that God is in control. Pain and suffering do not define the relationship between God and humanity during any individual's lifetime, because the distinctions between good and evil are shattered in the end. It is how humans respond under these tensions that matters, not the tensions themselves. It is the duty of the faithful to continually share this message and speak to the order of Creation, where "God is light, and in him is no darkness at all."[29]

To the second point, language and speech are frequently cited for their role in defining the correct relationship to God, which wisdom defines as the righteous and the wicked, the wise and the fool. Nearly a quarter of the one hundred fifty psalms draw a distinction between the wicked person and the wise by referring to the utterances of their mouths, what proceeds from their lips, and the products of their tongues. While wisdom literature, and indeed all of Scripture, offer other litmus tests for

26. Ps 39:1–3.

27. Ps 39:1–3.

28. Ps 105:2.

29. 1 John 1:5.

righteousness, there is a very clear and undeniable linkage between faithfully passing on the narrative and a right relationship to God.

In the fifth psalm, David sets the tone. "You destroy those who speak lies; the Lord abhors the bloodthirsty and deceitful man," later adding, "For there is no truth in their mouth; their inmost self is destruction; their throat is an open grave; they flatter with their tongue. Make them bear their guilt, O God; let them fall by their own counsels . . . they have rebelled against you."[30]

Two psalms later, David restates the defining characteristics of the wicked: "Behold, the wicked man conceives evil and is pregnant with mischief and gives birth to lies."[31] The psalmist, in Ps 10, cries out to God to reveal Himself as the poor continue to suffer at the hands of the rich and powerful. Again, the characteristics of the wicked are obvious. "For the wicked boasts of the desires of his soul, and the one greedy for gain curses and renounces the Lord." "His mouth is full of cursing and deceit and oppression; under his tongue are mischief and iniquity."[32] In describing one who opposes the faithful, "The words of his mouth are trouble and deceit; he has ceased to act wisely and do good."[33] Righteousness and destructive speech are mutually exclusive, as Ps 52 pointedly reminds the reader: "Why do you boast of evil, O mighty man? The steadfast love of God endures all day. Your tongue plots destruction, like a sharp razor, you worker of deceit. You love evil more than good, and lying more than speaking what is right. You love all words that devour, O deceitful tongue." The consequences: "But God will break you down forever; he will snatch and tear you from your tent; he will uproot you from the land of the living."[34]

The third point is that, in addition to drawing bright lines between the righteous and the wicked, the wisdom of the psalms identifies the qualities of language and speech that reflect proper obedience and faithfulness. "Who shall ascend the hill of the Lord?" Among those who will "stand in his holy place" are he "who does not lift up his soul to what is false and does not swear deceitfully."[35] Those fervently praying for redemption must honestly claim, "I do not sit with men of falsehood, nor

30. Ps 5:6, 9–10.

31. Ps 7:14.

32. Ps 10:3, 7.

33. Ps 36:3.

34. Ps 52:1–5.

35. Ps 24:3–4.

do I consort with hypocrites."[36] A wisdom section of Ps 34 warns those who would be wise to "keep your tongues from evil and your lips from speaking deceit."[37] In the psalm "He Will Not Forsake His Saints," the reader is advised that "the mouth of the righteous utters wisdom, and his tongue speaks justice. The law of his God is in his heart; his steps do not slip."[38] God is the ultimate judge, as Ps 50 reminds us, and there is only one way in which the faithful live:

> But to the wicked God says: "What right have you to recite my statutes or take my covenant on your lips? For you hate discipline, and cast my words behind you. . . . You give your mouth free rein for evil, and your tongue frames deceit. You sit and speak against your brother; you slander your own mother's son.'"[39]

God will harshly judge those who do not discipline their tongues. Their sinful speech has not gone unnoticed and will be repaid. "These things you have done [referring to lies, deceit, and slander], and I have been silent; you thought that I was one like yourself. But now I rebuke you and lay the charge before you."[40] Similar condemnation awaits those of wicked speech, in Ps 64, "who whet their tongues like swords, who aim bitter words like arrows. .. But God shoots his arrows at them; they are wounded suddenly. They are brought to ruin, with their own tongues turned against them."[41] Cries to defend against lying, deceitful, and violent men will be answered.[42] The judgment in Ps 58 is harsh: "The wicked are estranged from the womb; they go astray from birth, speaking lies."[43]

The prayer in "Deliver Me from My Enemies" reveals the anguish that inevitably accompanies distorted and perverse speech: "For the cursing and lies that they utter, consume them in wrath; consume them till they are no more, that they may know that God rules over Jacob to the ends of the earth."[44] God is not silent in His response: "No one who prac-

36. Ps 26:4.
37. Ps 34:13.
38. Ps 37:30–31.
39. Ps 50:16–20.
40. Ps 50:21.
41. Ps 64:2–5, 7–8.
42. Ps 140, 144.
43. Ps 58:3–5.
44. Ps 59:12–13.

tices deceit shall dwell in my house; no one who utters lies shall continue before my eyes."[45] There can be no question of God's intentions toward the profane in that passage. And it was not simply judgment on the individual. Psalm 120 is a corporate lament, attributing God's punishment to the "lying lips" and "deceitful tongue" of the entire community.[46]

It is easy to assume that the mouth, tongue, and lips can only be authors of evil and judgment, but the Psalms also remind us that salvation can be found in language and speech, specifically worship and prayer. How are we to respond to God's mercy and grace, His answers to our petitions and lamentations? "Then my tongue shall tell of your righteousness and of your praise all the day long."[47] After promising rebuke for lies and slander, God tells the reader that there is one way to amend the wrongs of deceitful language. "The one who offers thanksgiving as his sacrifice glorifies me."[48] Psalm 119 is one of covenant instruction and praise. In one stanza the psalmist celebrates God's steadfast love and prays that He keeps the words of the psalmist perpetually in his mouth. In rejecting the language of evil, "I will also speak of your testimonies before kings and shall not be put to shame."[49] Not only are worship and praise the antidotes to lies and deceit, they can be trusted to guide and protect the one who prays and worships, delighting in His commandments.

The psalms are not the only place in the wisdom tradition that addresses the distinctions between the righteous and the wicked in terms of language and speech. The Proverbs, which tend to be more practical in nature, also identify rash or ill-advised speech as potential threats to redemption and salvation. "Put away from you crooked speech, and put devious talk from you."[50] An adulterous relationship begins with lips that "drip honey" and are "smoother than oil."[51] Proverbs attributed to Solomon are just as pointed. "Blessings are on the head of the righteous, but the mouth of the wicked conceals violence."[52] "The wise of heart will receive commandments, but a babbling fool will come to ruin."[53] "The

45. Ps 101:7.
46. Ps 120, note.
47. Ps 35:28.
48. Ps 50:23.
49. Ps 119:46.
50. Prov 4:24.
51. Prov 5:2–5.
52. Prov 10:6.
53. Prov 10:8.

mouth of the righteous is a fountain of life, but the mouth of the wicked conceals violence."[54] "The wise lay up knowledge, but the mouth of a fool brings ruin near."[55]

The theme continues throughout Proverbs. "The mouth of the righteous brings forth wisdom, but the perverse tongue will be cut off. The lips of the righteous know what is acceptable, but the mouth of the wicked, what is perverse."[56] While most of Proverbs can be attributed to Solomon, the counsel of one Agur, who resided far from Solomon's court, is evidence of the extensive reach of wisdom traditions. "Every word of God proves true. . . . Do not add to his words, lest he rebuke you and you be found a liar."[57] "Remove far from me falsehood and lying."[58] Ecclesiastes continues in the same vein. "The words of a wise man's mouth win him favor, but the lips of a fool consume him. The beginning of the words of his mouth is foolishness, and the end of his talk is evil madness."[59]

Far from just distinguishing the wise from the fool, the heart of point three is that positioning oneself in that right relationship is an absolute prerequisite for experiencing the fullness of God. Here, wisdom is expressed in a radically different way. It is described as the fear of the Lord. But fear, in this usage, is not the cowering fear one feels if fearing for one's life or anticipating doom and destruction. Fear, in this case, is the awe-inspiring recognition of the Creator, the *numinous* as described by Rudolf Otto.[60] It is the recognition that all else in Creation pales in comparison to the power and authority of the Creator. It is the understanding that God not only demands but deserves our love, reverence, worship, adoration, and honor. Furthermore, we cannot survive without offering all this to Him. It is true wisdom.

Anything spoken can reflect or reject this totally consuming reverence for the Lord. It is, therefore, not surprising that wisdom literature would broach the subject of fearing the Lord as a function of language and speech. As noted earlier in Ps 39, the psalmist is afraid to express his dismay at the suffering of the faithful until he realizes that if one speaks

54. Prov 10:11.

55. Prov 10:13–14.

56. Prov 10:31–32. Chapters 11–19, 21, 24, and 29 all contain similar passages, stressing the point that language and speech must be carefully guarded.

57. Prov 30:5.

58. Prov 30:8.

59. Eccl 10:12–13.

60. Otto, *Idea*, 20–24.

within the boundaries of honor and reverence, one's words will neither condemn the speaker nor discourage the hearer. This topic is expanded in the oft quoted verses in Proverbs: "The fear of the Lord is the beginning of wisdom, and the knowledge of the Holy One is insight. For by me your days will be multiplied, and years will be added to your life."[61] The writer goes on to state that Folly is loud and demanding, calling out to any who would listen. Those who pay heed to the words of Folly, the wicked, do not know that its guests are "in the depths of Sheol."[62] Wisdom, by contrast, delivers "you from the way of evil, from men of perverse speech," and "from the adulteress [those who would turn the obedient from the true path] with her smooth words."[63] Ecclesiastes concludes with the command to fear God and keep His commandments. "The Preacher sought to find words of delight, and uprightly he wrote words of truth. The words of the wise are like goads, and like nails firmly fixed are the collected sayings; they are given by one Shepherd. My son, beware of anything beyond these."[64] Goads are sharp sticks used to herd animals. The obvious reference is to the authentic narrative of Scripture. As noted earlier in Proverbs, the truth of God is sufficient. Do not add to it or take anything away. If you stay within the fullness of God's Word, and faithfully represent the journey, you will be called righteous.

The fourth and final area addresses the limitation of human wisdom, particularly when compared to the incomprehensible wisdom of God. "Whatever has come to be has already been named, and it is known what man is, and he is not able to dispute with one stronger than he. The more words, the more vanity, and what is the advantage to man?"[65] The risk here is that even the pious can become presumptuous with their words. Job's three friends had become so captivated by their own intelligence that their piety had lapsed into self-absorbed arrogance. They would have been better served to remain humble, understanding that no amount of human wisdom or understanding can approach the wisdom of God.

Humility is reflective of true piety, accepting the limitations of human understanding. Psalm 66 speaks to the obligation to live in a condition of always honoring God, praising Him for His goodness and mercy. The note accompanying this psalm draws a distinction between trying

61. Prov 9:10–11.

62. Prov 9:18.

63. Prov 2:12, 16.

64. Eccl 12:10–12.

65. Eccl 6:10–11.

to manipulate God through vows and promises and responding to God with our words and our prayers. It contrasts the inadequacy of human wisdom, which presents itself as arrogance, with the humility of submitting to the magnificence of God's wisdom. At the end of the psalm, the psalmist commits to a life of continual worship and prayer, not as a *quid pro quo* with God but as his joyous duty. True piety is described much later in Ps 145: "The Lord is near to all who call on him, to all who call on him in truth."[66] A characteristic of the pious is language and speech which is truthful and honors the core of God's value proposition.

As noted earlier, wisdom literature is not limited to just the current biblical canon. The wisdom collected and catalogued in the apocryphal book of Ecclesiasticus fully and accurately reflects the themes of canonical wisdom writings. In addition, it speaks to matters such as justice and fairness, vigilance in speech, wickedness and virtue, and obedience. During the formative centuries of Christian doctrine, there were a number of apocryphal gospels circulating. While none of them were ultimately adopted, a few actually imparted useful information. Unfortunately, as Jerome is quoted as saying, "One might find *aurum in luto*, 'gold in amongst the muck.'"[67] This is not to suggest that the apocryphal gospels should be recognized as inspired wisdom but that the traditions were robust even into the common era.

These examples, and many others too numerous to recount, are bright lines. There is no equivocation in the Scriptures when it comes to the power of language to uplift or destroy, not only at the individual level but the corporate as well. The worship of a monotheistic God and the success of the covenants are dependent upon the judicious use of His gifts of language and speech in justly ordering Creation. The process of re-creation is wholly dependent upon an accurate and authentic narrative. Wisdom is required, and wisdom is the reward.

Since the idea of wisdom is not linked to historical events and circumstances, poetic and wisdom literature offer a unique perspective on the purpose of Creation. God created so that He could be worshiped and obeyed. In return, He promises salvation, a life of joy and peace in a perfected relationship with Him for all of eternity. Because of original sin, the ability of humans to properly apply the authority inherent in the power of language was distorted and corrupted. The new reality after the fall was

66. Ps 145:18.

67. Gathercole, *Apocryphal Gospels*, xix.

twisted into the idea that somehow humanity was the central point of Creation. However, Creation was never about the individual. Unless, and until, we can understand that the salvation of the whole of Creation is the greater purpose, not the salvation of an individual, true wisdom can never be achieved. In many respects, the individual is inconsequential in Creation. One has the right to ignore God completely, even if he does so at his own peril. God is loving and merciful and clearly wants to see all of humanity redeemed and saved. This is His promise freely offered. But the greater goal of reclaiming the whole of Creation cannot be put at risk by the actions of any one individual. He cares deeply about all of us. He knows us and wants to be known by us. He wants us to be saved and to share a perfected life in Him at the end of time. But reclaiming the entirety of Creation at the end of time is His primary objective. If that does not succeed, the individual has no basis for hope anyway. It was not until the Word became incarnate, and forgiveness became an option, that the Good Shepherd could seek after the one lost without endangering the entire enterprise. But even Jesus acknowledged that if one wishes to sin and alienate himself from the Father, he is free to do so.

If looking at poetic and wisdom literature from the vantage point of the individual as the center of creation, the true depth of these writings will be missed. Sometimes this section of Scripture is treated more as *Poor Richard's Almanack* or an eighteenth-century sampler, tatted and hanging over the fireplace, dispensing homespun platitudes. The profundity of wisdom in the scriptural context is easily overlooked, even while its sayings are uplifting in any number of circumstances, Christian or otherwise. Wisdom, a true, deep understanding of God and Creation, is the essential ingredient for the salvation of both the individual and Creation. This was not lost on the prophets. Jeremiah reached back into Psalms, Proverbs, and Job as sources for one of his exhortations on the magnificence of God. He attributes the Creation to wisdom and reminds his listeners of this fact. "It is he who made the earth by his power, who established the world by his wisdom, and by his understanding stretched out the heavens."[68] Wisdom keeps us on the right track by informing the language and speech of the faithful.

68. Jer 10:12, 51:15.

# Chapter 5

# Creation Under the Law

When discussing the Old Testament, sanctification is frequently spoken of as "under the law." The idea of something "under the law" is a New Testament term, used in comparison to someone subject to the Holy Spirit or under the new covenant. It is highly unlikely that anyone living in the period of the Old Testament would have used the term in that context. Paul spends a great deal of time comparing the two, particularly in his letter to the Romans. The Law was covenantal law, particularly the covenant with Moses as expressed in the Ten Commandments. It was not originally intended to extend beyond Israel. The Law was meant to structure the relationship between God and His chosen people. The covenants were foundational statements for a nation that was to be set apart. As such, they were uniquely focused on the arc of Jewish history, but they would succeed only to the extent that they were accurately delivered, obediently followed, and rigorously enforced.

Under these circumstances, there were only two options. One obeyed and avoided judgment or disobeyed and was condemned. There was no forgiveness for sin, as a Christian would understand it, whether the sin be purposeful or accidental. The Law was strict and specific. When Aaron's sons, Abihu and Nadab, lit the incense in front of the altar, they were immediately consumed by fire.[1] As the Philistines were returning the ark to Israel, they stopped in Beth-shemesh. As the people of Beth-shemesh were celebrating its return with burnt offerings, the Lord struck down seventy men for staring too intently at the ark.[2] During that same journey, when Uzzah tried to steady the cart carrying the ark, he

1. Lev 10:1–2.
2. 1 Sam 6:19.

was killed instantly.[3] Aaron was mortified and somewhat embittered by the seemingly cavalier manner in which his sons were struck down. The enormity of the incident with Uzzah was not lost on even David, who was so stunned by Uzzah's demise that he chose not to deal with the ark for months. On the surface, it does not appear to be any suggestion that disrespect, idolatry, or apostasy were involved in any of these incidents. But at this stage in the Creation narrative, strict compliance was an absolute necessity. There was no latitude for error, no matter how trivial it might seem. Whatever the motives of Abihu, Nadab, the men of Beth-shemesh, or Uzzah, they had violated the strict letter of the Law. The terms of the covenants with Adam, Noah, and Abraham had been established as guidelines for human behavior. The Mosaic covenant would soon follow, codifying the earlier agreements.

There is no such thing as a small sin. In the Old Testament, the closest thing to forgiveness under the Law is found in the rituals designed to seek mercy or avoid condemnation. These rituals were very specifically detailed within the Law. In other words, to seek redress under the Law was to follow the Law itself. It was not until the appearance of Jesus that forgiveness of sins was an option. If the Israeli community was to succeed, Yahweh must be acknowledged above all other gods, the covenants were to be strictly obeyed, and there could be no equivocation on what God said or how the message was transmitted.

After the fall, it is clear that the essential nature of humanity was at odds with the essential nature of the Creator. Human nature was no longer ordered or governed according to Creation's purposes. That being the case, does it necessarily follow that if the stewards of the universe were flawed, then the universe itself must be flawed? God did not create a flawed universe. Its flaws grew out of the imperfect nature of its stewards. Absent the perfected relationship between humans and God, the guidelines for properly governing and ordering Creation now needed to be codified. Hence, the need for the Law. If the Law was not obeyed, that could only mean that the universe was being governed contrary to God's wishes. The stewards would then be replacing the authority of God with something of human provenance, either its own wisdom or that of other gods. This denial of the essence of the Creator is something the Law was designed to confront and correct. The idea of eternal life was a concept that only slowly evolved in the Old Testament. There are certainly no

3. 2 Sam 6:3–8, 1 Chr 13:7–11.

references to eternal life in the first five books of the Bible (the Pentateuch). Thus, the Jewish concept of salvation was grounded in knowing and following the Law.

This also established God as the sole authority to judge. Consistent with the patterns of monotheism, it was He alone who determined right or wrong, and He alone who meted out punishment. Individuals could make appeals for mercy, and rituals were established for that purpose. In the last analysis, however, judgment and punishment were purely godly prerogatives. Not until the appearance of Jesus could anyone stand in the place of the sinner and appeal for forgiveness. That is why failing to strictly adhere to the word of God had such immediate and severe consequences. The Law was not subtle. In a very literal sense, God was speaking Judaism and the Israeli community back into existence. He was reordering Creation to accommodate the sinfulness and frailty of humanity.

This created a very strict theocracy, one that departed so dramatically from the governing principles of neighboring tribes that it caused the Israeli community to stand out even more. This not only isolated them socially and culturally but created an even greater level of distrust and fear among surrounding communities. They were not only seen as interlopers but as threats to the stability of the status quo, which only got worse the stronger the Israelis grew. Nonetheless, it was impossible to survive without some interaction with those around them. We know, for example, that trade and economic interactions between Jews and other groups were common.[4] By necessity, there developed some level of communication that permitted these divergent cultures to coexist. The more familiar and comfortable these interactions became, however, the greater the risk of diluting Jewish standards. The process is one of cultural acclimation or syncretism. The Law had to be firm and unmovable if this community, with its strange practices, was to survive. God's covenantal agreement was to eventually build a strong nation led by a faithful king. For that to happen, Jewish standards had to remain uncontaminated.

The matter of cultural acclimation is more than simply the erosion or loss of habits and idioms. For a small minority that stood apart for its strange beliefs and behaviors, and whose social and political governance was inextricably tied to its religious foundations, acclimation meant relinquishing the rights to its own language. In a purely theocratic

4. Gordon and Rendsburg, *Bible and Ancient Near East.*

environment, there were no distinctions between the language of worship and faith and that of commercial or social transactions. Any accommodation threatened the wholesale replacement of God's language by those of other cultures. What first might seem to have been harmless agreements on questions of political, economic, or social interaction resulted in seriously undermining the language of faith in an increasingly and uniquely monotheistic Jewish community.

> Because activities in most areas of society—business, education, law—were now being conducted in Greek, and Jewish children were learning Greek so that they could survive in the hellenized economy, there came a point where Aramaic-speaking Jews began to learn and know Greek better than the Hebrew they learned as children.[5]

Intermarriage was the most extreme example of this interaction, and it posed an even greater threat. Until there was a more universal appeal to those outside of the immediate circle, such as began to occur during the exile, cultural syncretism had to be avoided at all costs.

The Pentateuch opens with the Creation story in Genesis and the garden of Eden. Interestingly, given the significance of the garden as the site of Creation itself, Eden does not appear anywhere else in Scriptures except for brief references in Ezekiel and Isaiah,[6] and there only for the purposes of identifying the absolute perfection of God. It does not run through Scriptures as a thematic literary or theological device. This should come as no surprise, since the importance of the garden in Genesis lies not in recapturing or reclaiming a physical experience but in the perfected nature of the garden relationship. By overemphasizing the physical characteristics of the garden experience, the intended purposes of the divine-human relationship are lost. It is that relationship God seeks to reclaim, not specific physical circumstances.

The Pentateuch and the Law set the tone for the remainder of the Creation narrative, and all of the linguistic and semiotic themes of the salvation journey are introduced here, although not necessarily fully developed. The tenets governing the garden experience are those that are reinforced within the Law. They are to protect and secure the narrative as it is passed down from generation to generation, and these are the tenets that will eventually be replicated in the new kingdom. They are precisely

5. Cargill, *Cities*, 141.

6. Ezek 28:13; 31:9, 16, 18; 36:35; Isa 51:3.

those that give hope and promise to the Jewish people throughout the Old Testament. The message of the Law is that a reconstructed, perfected relationship with the Creator is achievable but only through complete obedience. Order will eventually replace the disorder of a fallen people, but it could only be obtained through obeying one true God, within the context of the covenants, faithfully reflecting the Creator's ethical and moral constitution. Of course, the idea that perfect obedience could be achieved was absurd, even amongst the early Israelis, hence the idea of salvation took the form of a human Messiah. He would be one who would rule with an absolute authority granted by Yahweh and who alone could create the conditions that would permit perfection to be achieved.

God continued to interact directly with Adam and Eve's descendants, albeit with mounting frustration. By the time Noah had arrived, God's patience had worn sufficiently thin that He flooded the earth and destroyed the Jewish community. But He did not give up on Creation, nor did He simply walk away and leave history to its own devices. God instructed Noah on the most minute details of building the ark. He specified who and what should be loaded on the ship and when it was to be boarded. Throughout the flood, God guided every step. God's words continued to be creative, carrying the same power of the words that brought the universe into form at the beginning and to the same end: the reconstruction of human society and its relationship with God. After the flood had receded, God made another covenantal agreement with Noah, and so the Old Testament pattern of divine-human relationship continued.

The point here is not to view the original relationship as a negotiation with God, who is finally driven by exasperation to become petulant and wrathful. It is to highlight the intimacy of God's relationship with mankind and His continuing commitment to humanity's success. But it is strictly on His terms, modeled upon His value proposition. Obviously, language and speech are meant to project and protect this model. There is no better example of how critical this gift is to God's overall plans than the story of the tower of Babel.

The incident at Babel is an intricate and complex story, despite being limited to one paragraph, rich in what is left unsaid. It opens with this: "Now the whole earth had one language, and the same words."[7] The residents of this burgeoning community expressed a desire to "make a

7. Gen 11:1.

name for ourselves, lest we be dispersed over the face of the earth."[8] Unfortunately for the citizens of Babel, being dispersed over the face of the earth is exactly what God had in mind for His Creation when He told Adam and Eve to be fruitful and multiply. The mechanism for achieving Babel's objective was to be a tower that reached to the heavens. Both the dismissal of God's intentions and the arrogance of assuming that they could simply create a connection with the heavens demonstrated a "human independence and self-sufficiency apart from God"[9] that is totally at odds with His designs for Creation. Humanity does not govern the divine-human relationship nor can it perfect that relationship by virtue of its own efforts. By preempting God's authority and order, those in Babel were diminishing the singularity of God and denying the imperatives laid out in the covenant with Adam.

God's response: "Come, let us go down and there confuse their language, so that they may not understand one another's speech. So the Lord dispersed them from there over the face of all the earth."[10] His reaction to Babel's behavior is telling for two reasons. First, it continues to demonstrate His ongoing purpose for Creation. His initial directive to Adam and Eve was to go forth and populate the earth and, by extending humanity's domain, to fulfill the Creation expectation that His authority over the rest of Creation would be properly ordered. Whether the population of Babel intended to or not, they were sent forth to populate the earth.

Secondly, there were any number of ways He could have dealt with the situation. He could have rained destruction and devastation on the city. He could have dispersed the people through the military intervention of hostile neighbors or caused natural disasters to wreak havoc on their enterprise. Instead, He simply confused their language. Confusion, the opposite of order, was the price humanity paid for disobedience. Under these circumstances, the integrity of the gifts of language and speech could only be protected by making them less accessible. Language and speech remained chaotic until the Pentecost, when Christ reclaimed their holy properties. At that point, the original creative intentions of the Word were reinserted into history.

It is important to look at this process more carefully. The simplest and most generally accepted reading of the tower story is that God

8. Gen 11:4.

9. Gen 11:2–4, note.

10. Gen 11:7–8.

responded by creating a series of languages that made it impossible to coordinate the building of something that reached the heavens. But that would present an internal inconsistency: the whole pattern of Genesis up to this point and beyond is that the power of God would have made such a task impossible. More contemporary interpretations suggest that the tower story was an invention inserted after the description of the flood by much later apologists to explain the appearance of different languages, when that fact had not been pertinent up to that point in the narrative.

But the Pentecost offers an alternative to either of these approaches. The answer may be better understood as one of understanding and sharing divine intentions within the structure of existing languages, not necessarily one of inventing new languages. In this sense, the tower story and the Pentecost are bookends to a subtheme in Creation. Disobedience creates confusion. Wisdom and the Word had been rejected completely. The sinful state that gave rise to the flood and the pursuit of the tower could very well have created a situation where understanding godly intent now required hearing a different "language"—not a spoken language but one that drew from the vestiges of the original Creation relationship between God and humanity. The incident at Babel erased any remaining innate understanding of God's purposes. It is not that new languages were created but that existing languages no longer had access to the "holy language" of Creation by virtue of humanity's sinful nature.

This is not that extreme an explanation. A very popular book published in 1992 entitled *Men Are from Mars, Women Are from Venus* addresses a set of circumstances where profound misunderstanding occurs even when people speak the same language. It is quite possible that after the flood, the steady erosion of obedience to the Word so diminished the gift of language and speech that any deep-seated understanding of divine stewardship and humanity's responsibility to properly order the universe was rendered impossible. Prior to that point, various speakers of different languages had the innate capacity to acknowledge and understand godly purposes that, after the tower, was taken from them. That understanding was returned at the Pentecost. Where sin created chaos, the ascension of Christ and the inauguration of the new kingdom eliminated chaos for those seeking to redeem and reestablish the Creation relationship now completed in Jesus. At the Pentecost, accessibility to the sanctified gift of language and speech was restored. People were able to hear and understand, in their own diverse languages, the good news. It is important to note that there was no effort to suggest that Pentecost eliminated all languages, just as there is no need to rationalize the existence of different languages after Babel.

Returning to the matter at hand, the outlines of the Law as eventually revealed through Moses became increasingly evident as God directed the affairs of the patriarchs Abraham, Isaac, and Jacob—not only the expectations but the consequences for non-compliance. Additional covenants were made with Abram and Moses, and the purposes of these covenants remained unchanged. The descendants of Abraham were destined to be chosen for the task of continuing the Creation narrative and redeeming its original intent. Their success was directly related to faithfully accepting the primacy of Yahweh and accurately passing on the authentic narrative of Creation.

The Ten Commandments are only a segment, although an important segment, of the Mosaic covenant. The totality of the covenant includes very specific rules and regulations designed to reinforce the intent of the Commandments and more thoroughly define the obligations of the people.[11] The presentation of the Commandments and their accompanying protocols were the first time the Law began to be written down. It was also the first time that a specific class of people were charged with superintending the liturgy of the Law. Jewish worship was being formalized.

The message reflected on the tablets established the four fundamental principles to ordering a godly society: the primacy of God (no other gods are to be acknowledged), the worthiness of God (setting aside time specifically to honor the Creation), the social model of God's perfected creation (rebellion, murder, lust, and envy assault the balance of Creation), and the language of God (speech is not to be used to dishonor His name or pervert justice).[12] These tenets of faith define the salvation journey going forward and encapsulate the linguistic and semiotic themes of the Old Testament. They also highlight the importance of monotheism, covenantal relationships, and the obligation to order society through language and speech. This structure, which thousands of years later would become instrumental in distinguishing Creation from myth, was set out very early in the narrative.

The first set of instructions contained in the expanded covenant were, not surprisingly, specific direction regarding idols and altars. Altars were of concern because that was the primary mechanism for displaying

11. Exod 20:1—23:33.

12. Exod 20:7, 16.

and worshiping other gods. There are constant references to Asherim or Asherah throughout the Old Testament. These were poles or posts erected alongside Canaanite altars to honor the goddess Asherah. Depending on which tradition one followed, Asherah was the wife of El, the chief Canaanite god, and either the mother or adoptive mother of Baal. Thus, a Jewish altar had to have characteristics that clearly distinguished it from anything that might reflect the worship of idols. Prior to the period of the temple, and excepting the tabernacle that moved with the Israelis in the desert, they were to be simple altars of earth, not elaborate constructions that might celebrate human accomplishments.

Just as importantly, a perfect community must reflect the values of the Creator. The characteristics necessary to order society in a way that conforms to the Creation include such traits as justice, harmony, respect for authority, and obedience. In the Mosaic covenant, these behaviors were specifically identified. Take the following for examples:

> You shall not spread a false report. You shall not join hands with a wicked man to be a malicious witness. You shall not fall in with the many to do evil, nor shall you bear witness in a lawsuit, siding with the many, so as to pervert justice. . . . You shall not pervert the justice due to your poor in his lawsuit. Keep far from a false charge, and do not kill the innocent or righteous, for I will not acquit the wicked. And you shall take no bribe, for a bribe blinds the clear-sighted and subverts the cause of those who are in the right.[13]

Justice and fairness, hallmarks of a properly ordered society, are guaranteed only by respecting and carefully guarding God's value proposition. Language that suborns this value proposition is evil. Although introduced in Exodus, this is the theme that will become increasingly important during the latter stages of Old Testament history. The Pentateuch, very early on, established the significance of idolatry and a properly ordered society as themes for the redemption and reclamation of Creation.

Finally, the period under the Law revealed to us the nature of God, what the theologian Rudolf Otto understood as a *numinous* experience. In the early twentieth century, Otto developed the concept of a *numinous*, a non-rational sense of the divine or transcendent that is universal to all of humanity. The *numinous* is experienced in two distinctive ways: the *mysterium tremendum* and the *mysterium fascinans*. The first is the sense

13. Exod 23:1–3, 6–8.

of something terrifying and awesome, beyond all human understanding. In its presence, an individual feels almost helpless, diminished and humbled. As its polar opposite, the *mysterium fascinans,* imparts a sense of something fascinating and comforting. It is the source of spiritual joy and the fullness of the Creation experience.[14]

The *mysterium tremendum* is first seen when Moses ascended the mountain. The enormity of God's spoken Word was not lost on the people: "Now when the people saw the thunder and the flashes of lightening and the sound of the trumpet and the mountain smoking, the people were afraid and trembled, and they stood far off and said to Moses, 'You speak to us, and we will listen; but do not let God speak to us, lest we die.'"[15]

The Law had been set by the time of Moses' death. The very specific guidance of the Law are the themes that work through both the Old and New Testaments. The existential dangers of idolatry, the very specific guidance within the Law on properly ordering society, and the awe-inspiring nature of God are first introduced in Genesis and the development of the Law. The Ten Commandments affirmed the agency and power of the Word, and the four truths expressed in the commandments, as noted earlier, placed language and speech in the prominent position of protecting the integrity of wisdom.

It is important to remember that the Law did not pass away with the advent of Jesus or His death and resurrection. "Do not think that I have come to abolish the Law or the Prophets; I have not come to abolish them but to fulfill them."[16] He reaffirmed the authority of the Law and said that those who accurately teach the tenets of the Law "will be called great in the kingdom of heaven."[17] The Word was purposeful, authoritative, and trustworthy. It was to be guarded, passed on, and obeyed. By referencing the kingdom of heaven, Jesus makes clear that the Word is everlasting. Paul argued in Romans, "For Christ is the end of the law for righteousness to everyone who believes."[18] As the commentary in the English Standard Version puts it, Jesus is both the goal of the Law and, by His resurrection, the completion of the Law in the new kingdom.

14. Otto, *Idea.*
15. Ex 20: 18–19.
16. Matt 5:17.
17. Matt 5:19.
18. Rom 10:4, and note.

# Chapter 6

# The Pentateuch: The Foundation of Faith

As we follow the Creation process from Genesis to the Revelation, it becomes increasingly apparent that Creation has never been a myth, in the contemporary sense, and that the characteristics of the Creation narrative differed dramatically from those of other myths from the very beginning. It is also apparent that the need to protect the integrity of the Creation narrative became an imperative almost immediately after the end of the garden experience, and each of the distinct characteristics upon which the narrative is based were intended to move through history as God redeems Creation. One characteristic does not become more or less important than another, and the interconnectedness of the three remains, but the beauty of Creation is its structural ability to respond to different circumstances as the needs arise. This stands in stark contrast to the examples of myths noted earlier that could not adapt to change and required the renegotiation of their values and semiotics to rationalize their beginnings and their culture.

The Pentateuch reaffirms this argument. Myths and explanations of the mysteries of the cosmos appeared as soon as humans began to comprehend the world around them, but even at their earliest stages, these myths differed substantially from the framework of Creation. They did not elevate or worship one unique God as the source of all power and authority, and there was no sense of commitment by the Creator to deliver humanity to a perfected state at the end of time. The agencies of creation in other myths were everything but a dynamic Word, and nothing like a Creative Word was bequeathed to humanity as a responsibility to act as guardians of the narrative or set in place guidelines for ordering the universe.

The first five books of the Bible are the source of both the Creation narrative and the Law. The Law created the baseline for what would emerge as a truly monotheistic theology, defending the unique status and provenance of Yahweh. It created the boundaries for properly ordering Creation. The history of the patriarchs is contained in the Pentateuch, and covenants with Adam, Noah, Abraham, and Moses were established during this period. The Law, the covenants, and the strictures outlined within these first five books of the Bible formed the faith of Jesus, the apostles, and the first generation of Jewish Christians. Over time, the Law became corrupted by the constant interaction between the Jews and their neighbors. Indeed, the mission of Jesus was to free the Law from the constraints of a corrupt political alliance. The Pharisaic defenders of the Law had negotiated an unholy alliance with the Romans, and Jesus' defense of the Law precipitated the political and social tensions that led to the crucifixion and ascension. In a very substantive way, the Pentateuch provides the context for Jesus' ministry.

These five books do not, in and of themselves, constitute a comprehensive set of rules for human behavior, nor can it be said that they create a fully blown theological system. But they do, in a sense, establish a theological foundation for history in that they record and interpret the relationship between God and mankind as it was meant to be at the beginning of time. They document the period after the original separation of humanity from God, when He could have chosen any of the paths the gods from other myths had taken. The events documented in the Pentateuch make clear God's unwavering commitment to the purposes of Creation. They are instructional books, aimed at an audience corrupted by sin, and to the extent that they reveal the values of the Creator, they are ethical books. The Pentateuch not only recounts the beginning of history, but it presents a pattern for God's continuing involvement in history to sustain and support His original purposes.

Aside from God, the central character in all five books is Moses. Some have suggested that Moses may have recorded all the events detailed therein, or even written them himself, but forcing the issue of authorship has the tendency to obscure the most important aspect of these books. They were divinely inspired and serve to firmly ground all that follows.

The question of timing is also hotly debated, but most scholarship points to the fifth century BCE as the most likely time frame within which these thousand-year-old oral traditions coalesced into a widely accepted written format.[1] The Pentateuch can be studied as both a unit or through its individual components. There is a historical linearity, from Creation to the promised land, which presages later conversations about the new kingdom and the end of time. Issues such as idolatry, false teaching, ordering Creation, cultural syncretism, and protecting the narrative, all of which have threatened to derail the process of re-creation from the fall to today, are identified as such as well. Since the life of Moses was a relatively compact period of time, roughly one hundred and twenty years, these issues are not introduced in any discernible historical pattern. For example, stressing the uniqueness of Yahweh, which should be of paramount concern, is not a huge part of Genesis. That marker is not unequivocally laid until nineteen chapters into Exodus.

It is also important to remember that this all took place in a cauldron of competing geographic and dynastic tensions. Until Judaism had time to truly emerge as a fully structured system of faith, worship, and behavior, and until Israel could obtain the promises of land for a nation, the uncertainty of their circumstances created serious challenges to both theological and national identity. There is a sense that Moses dealt with whatever constituted the crisis of the moment.

One might try to argue that such behaviors as idolatry, false teachings and prophecies, concerns for justice and righteousness, or the risks of cultural syncretism are present at all places and in all times. Therefore, there is nothing that truly distinguishes Creation from other myths. They would, of course, be wrong. Those protecting or promulgating other creation myths would simply not have recognized any of these circumstances as either unique or threatening. There could be no idols, since there were no false gods. What an early follower of Yahweh would recognize as an idol was to his or her neighbors merely a representation of another, equally relevant, god. Teachings and prophecies were all true for somebody, since they messaged matters of significance to various worshipers. The idea of justice was tied to power structures that were fluid, not to universal or transcendent value systems. Syncretism, or cultural acclimation, was a concept with no meaning when the status of a god depended simply on its utility to the user. Found to be useful, that particular god was adopted into the community with little or no concern for a language

1. ESV, 35–37, as well as the introductions to each individual volume, offer a much more thorough discussion on authorship, timing, and the role of the Pentateuch in the development of Jewish and Christian theology.

that protected the narrative or its symbols. Identifying such threats, and setting the patterns for dealing with them, is one of the most significant accomplishments of the Pentateuch. The patterns for behavior going forward are all God and Creation centered.

By the end of the Pentateuch, each of the three qualities of Creation that are central to differentiating Creation from myth have been introduced, identified as an authentic characteristic of Creation, and become the subject of rules for their protection. There is only one God, His covenants describe the arc of history, and speech was gifted to humanity for the sole purpose of protecting and governing the processes of re-creation, redemption, and salvation.

All five books are replete with references to a singular God, an invested God, a fair God. The rules and regulations for maintaining the integrity of these qualities are carefully and specifically detailed, as are matters of language and speech that are intended to sustain the narrative for future generations. A quick tour through each book will serve to reinforce the point.

In Genesis, with the exception of "In the beginning, God created the heavens and the earth,"[2] there is no ongoing defense of monotheism or the uniqueness of Yahweh. But the first two chapters do serve to firmly establish the ethical structure of Creation. Humans were created in the image of God, reflecting not so much His physical characteristics but His moral and ethical nature. Humanity was charged with being stewards of Creation, populating the earth, and governing it according to His standards. The covenant with Abram (Abraham) was established, marking the first of the post-fall agreements that God would remain invested in the welfare and success of His Creation.

Interestingly, the matter of speech and its role in the process of redeeming Creation appears early in Genesis. The incident in Babel has already been introduced, but it is more nuanced in this context. As noted in the previous chapter, it was said at that time, "Now the whole earth had one language and the same words."[3] Again, as discussed in the previous chapter, this may actually have been the case from the standpoint of the divine-human relationship before the original sin. More than building a tower, the people were harnessing the power of a shared, sanctified language to create a new universe, one where humanity and God were

2. Gen 1:1.

3. Gen 11:1.

on a much closer footing. There was a real danger to a unified humanity demanding a larger share of godly authority. "And the Lord said, 'Behold, they are one people, and they have all one language, and this is only the beginning of what they will do. And nothing that they propose to do will now be impossible for them.'"[4] But the concern has nothing to do with actually displacing God. An omnipotent and omniscient God can never be meaningfully challenged by humans. The real issue presented in the story of the tower has to do with God's design for re-creating and redeeming Creation and the threat that "one people" leveraging sanctified language poses to the process.

God was doing two things here. In the first instance, He was acknowledging the creative powers of language and speech and their ordained role as a holy gift. The risk with the tower was that humanity's responsibilities as stewards of Creation would be corrupted. It was necessary to disperse the people throughout the earth. There is nothing new in this development since it was a directive given to Adam and Eve at Creation. But a more important matter was to constrain, for the moment, the power to restate godly intentions and risk contaminating the purity of an authentic narrative. As we saw in the last chapter, when the Word became incarnate, that authority was now concentrated in the form of Jesus and protected by the Holy Spirit. The focus in the Pentateuch needed to remain on His representatives obediently fulfilling their side of the bargain with Adam, not exercising the incredible power of language to disrupt it.

Secondly, to carve out a separate nation for Israel, distinct nations with localized customs and languages had to exist in order to demonstrate and glorify the power of God inherent in the Abrahamic covenant. Time and time again, from Moses through the Prophets, the ability of God to overcome rulers and kingdoms far mightier than Israel was evidence of His unique power and authority, His covenantal investment in seeing humanity through to a perfected relationship with Him at the end of time, and the ethical standards to which God expects Creation to be ordered.

In Exodus, the initial steps in fulfilling the Abrahamic covenant were taken. Moses was selected as the instrument through which God reveals the terms of the covenant, and through whom the discipline of performing covenant obligations was enforced. Moses assumed the stewardship responsibilities initially assigned to Adam and Eve. When Moses

4. Gen 11:6.

responded to God's call from the burning bush, God told Moses that He has seen the afflictions of the people and knows of their oppression under the Pharaohs. God's command: "Come, I will send you to Pharaoh that you may bring out my people, the children of Israel, out of Egypt."[5] It is Moses alone to whom God speaks, and who sees God face to face.[6] "And he said, 'Behold, I am making a covenant. Before all your people, I will do marvels, such as have not been created in all the earth or in any nation. And all the people among whom you are shall see the work of the LORD, for it is an awesome thing that I will do with you."[7]

Included with the Ten Commandments are guidelines for structuring and properly ordering Creation. Specific instructions for the tabernacle and its furnishings are delivered, as well as those for patterns of worship. Very specific rules regarding idols are included.[8] The very first Commandment specifically addresses the primacy of Yahweh. While the people of Israel may not have immediately become monotheistic in their theology, as evidenced by the ease with which the golden calf was built and worshiped during Moses' absence, it clearly sets the tone going forward. With the first commandment, God made clear that there was no other source of absolute authority or power and that He was unique in that regard.

The Pentateuch is the life story of Moses, and cementing the singularity of Yahweh was his legacy. This is at the core of the contest between Moses and Pharaoh, which appears in Exodus and frames the narrative of these five books. Pharaoh had the earthly power to release the Israelis, but it was the Lord's words that made the event real. "Moses said, 'Be it as you say, so that you may know that there is no one like the Lord our God.'"[9] This is an interesting exchange. It takes on the appearance of a negotiation between equals. Pharaoh, we should recall, was a god to the Egyptians and all within their orbit. This is an enormous test, a struggle for hegemony between Pharaoh and Yahweh playing out on a world stage. Not even the servants of Pharaoh were exempt. There were no disinterested actors. When warned that a great plague of hail threatened livestock and slaves, those of Pharaoh's subjects who followed the

5. Exod 3:7–12.
6. Exod 34:29–35,
7. Exod 34:10.
8. Exod 20–31.
9. Exod 8:10.

advice of Yahweh were protected from its devastation.[10] At the institution of the Feast of Unleavened Bread, Moses reminded the people precisely which god prevailed: "And it shall be to you as a sign on your hand and as a memorial between your eyes, that the law of the Lord may be in your mouth. For with a strong hand the Lord has brought you out of Egypt."[11]

Speech alone had the ability to turn people towards God or, as was too often the case, compel the people to turn from Him to idols and pagan practices. "Pay attention to all that I have said to you, and make no mention of the names of other gods, nor let it be heard on your lips."[12] The generations of access to alternatives other than Yahweh had conditioned the Israelis to turn to other gods during periods of distress. In the desert, the concept that there was only one God that could be relied upon for deliverance was made manifest. He was Lord.

By the end of Exodus, God had delivered the message that Israel was to be His chosen people and, by virtue of the covenants with Abraham and Moses, that He intended to remain among them. He expected society to be ordered in accordance with His moral and ethical standards, and He would remain invested in humanity's success. Since the people of Israel demonstrated a propensity to revert to sinfulness and disobedience, how was the perfected nature of God reconciled with such a recalcitrant group of people? That is the focus of Leviticus, Numbers, and Deuteronomy. Here the model for a truly moral and ethical social structure is more fully developed.

Exodus and Leviticus tend to stress the relationship between God and His people, whereas Numbers and Deuteronomy emphasize the preparations for entering the promised land. But all four speak to the covenantal nature of God's relationship with humanity. They encourage strict adherence in all matters that could upend the covenantal promises. Exodus and Leviticus identify those behaviors that damage the prospects of the faithful as individuals, while Numbers and Deuteronomy turn more towards corporate behavior that could put at risk the promise of a national identity.

Leviticus is an almost encyclopedic collection of instructions on offerings, ritual cleanliness, feasts, personal preparation, blessings and curses, and vows and dedications. It reaffirms God's intentions to reside among the people, and what that should look like under the tensions of

10. Exod 9:20–21.

11. Exod 13:9.

12. Exod 23:13.

daily community life. Leviticus outlines how the community should be ordered so that sin and impurity do not obstruct the spiritual relationship. The uncompromising nature of the Law, and the precarious standing of the Jews during this period, required every thought and behavior to be strictly defined. The covenants are not merely agreements that God would stay involved but a commitment to so carefully detail every facet of life that redemption and salvation under the Law would be possible. God was defining the stewardship responsibility originally entrusted to Adam and Eve.

In chapters 4 and 5, as an example, great care is given to repairing broken relationships, both with the Lord and with one another. Continuing idolatry led to a broken relationship with God. Idolatry was not only an act of fashioning and worshiping idols, it celebrated the arrogance of assuming human wisdom to be superior to Yahweh's grand designs. Arrogance generated dissatisfaction and distrust, which in turn gave way to incidents such as God chastising Miriam and Aaron, and Moses striking the rock at Meribah.

Although idols and idolatry profaned God, broken relationships within the community made it impossible to meaningfully order Creation. If humans are to order society as God's stewards, what is spoken is consequential for both personal and community salvation. "If anyone sins in that he hears a public adjuration to testify, and though he is a witness, whether he has seen or come to know the matter yet does not speak, he shall bear his iniquity." Justice is the strict purview of God and distorting the administration of justice is a sinful affront to order. Later in that same chapter—"If anyone utters with his lips a rash oath to do evil or to do good, any sort of rash oath that people swear"[13]—he is required to make a sin offering.

Note that it is less important that the oath be for evil or good than that an oath was invoked at all. It is quite common in a polytheistic environment to make oaths with many gods for specific requests. Swearing by a god, followed by some commitment to sacrifice, was not proscriptive. One could swear as many oaths and offer as many independent sacrifices depending on his or her immediate needs. This rather cavalier approach to swearing oaths had to be curtailed if Yahweh was to be worshiped as omniscient and omnipotent. The warnings Moses offered in God's name were to remind people there was but one God and you were not to trifle

13. Lev 5:4.

with His name or diminish its significance by swearing oaths for every triviality. Oaths were made in the name of the Lord, and any utterance that does not magnify the name of the Lord is anathema. Furthermore, breaking that oath, evil or good, tarnishes the divine nature of God.

The theme of a just and ordered society, just as that condemning the worship of idols, is a recurring theme in Leviticus. Moses says to the people, "You shall not steal; you shall not deal falsely; you shall not lie to one another. You shall not swear by my name falsely, and so profane the name of your God: I am the Lord."[14] Dishonesty in human relationships destroys the purposes of Creation. God ordered society at the Creation and He continued to reorder society after the fall. Each word of warning and instruction had meaning; no utterances of God were casual suggestions. God turned to Aaron to deliver the ultimate message: "You are to teach the people of Israel all the statutes that the Lord has spoken to them by Moses."[15]

Numbers chronicles Israel's final preparations for entry into the promised land as partial fulfillment of the covenant with Abraham. God's constant presence among the tribes of Israel is a palpable reminder of His covenant promises. God's appearances are persistent and dramatic. Sin and disobedience were harshly punished. A man found gathering sticks on the Sabbath was stoned to death.[16] Hundreds of followers of Korah were swallowed up or burned for opposing Moses,[17] and thousands died of the plague for following the idolatrous traditions of Moab and intermarrying with the women of other nations.[18] Not only were the promises of the covenantal relationship being challenged but idolatry and accommodating the practices of other nations were being allowed to undermine the purity of worship. This was a critical time in Israel's history. There was no time to waste and God's patience was growing thin.

At this crucial time in Israel's history, the power and authority of Yahweh, when compared to other gods, were put to the test. God led the people to the boundaries of the land of Canaan and directed Moses to send twelve spies to report on the circumstances in this new land. Presumably out of fear for the unknown and a lack of trust in the Lord, this commission of spies returned with a negative report. With the exception

14. Lev 19:11–12.
15. Lev 10:11.
16. Num 15:32–36.
17. Num 16:31–35.
18. Num 25:1–9.

of Joshua and Caleb, the other ten insisted that the Israelis would be quickly overwhelmed by the current inhabitants. The people responded by cursing their fate and seeking new leaders that would take them back to Egypt.[19]

The unspoken fear was that the wealth and power of Canaanite cities was a reflection of the power of their gods and a corresponding concern that the God of Israel was not up to the task. It is telling that the spies referred to the presence of descendants of the Nephilim, people of unknown origins who were thought to be the offspring of rebellious angels. At this crucial time, second-guessing the singular power of God put the entire program at risk. If this was the mindset of the Israelis, it was clearly in their best interests that God delay the project.

The entire incident was enough to even rattle the confidence of Miriam and Aaron, two of God's most consistent and faithful followers. They were questioning the qualifications and leadership of Moses, God's chosen. God pointedly responded with finality: "And he said, 'Hear my words: if there is a prophet among you, I the Lord make myself known to him in a vision; I speak with him in a dream. Not so with my servant Moses. He is faithful in all my house. With him I speak mouth to mouth, clearly, and not in riddles, and he beholds the form of the Lord.'"[20] There were to be no arguments. Moses was God's immediate representative on earth. Test him and you tested God. When we talk about the Pentateuch, we are talking about a cosmic reality that was unequaled until the presence of Jesus.

In Deuteronomy, we find Moses' last three sermons and two prophetic poems that both recount the history of God's involvement to that point, and reflect upon the future. This is the only book in the Pentateuch that speaks to the full scope of our inquiry: the uniqueness of God (monotheism), His covenantal investment in Israel, the ethical structure and order of society, and the importance of protecting the authenticity and integrity of the Creation narrative.

The covenantal faithfulness of God is referenced in the historical prologue, which made up Moses' first speech,[21] and throughout the second speech.[22] The requirement to order society according to God's moral

19. Num 13:1–29, 14:1–4.

20. Num. 12:6–8.

21. Deut 1—4:43.

22. Deut 1:8, 19–46; 7:1–26; 8:1–20; 9:1—10:11.

and ethical standards is recalled in his second speech,[23] as were warnings about cultural acclimation and idolatry.[24] Throughout, there are continual warnings about speaking in such a way that the magnitude of the message is diminished or the narrative is corrupted.

Most importantly, in a long passage, Moses makes the case for one God who stands apart from all other gods. Moses makes a persuasive case that Creation is not a myth by pointing out His uniqueness:

> For ask now of the days that are past, which were before you, since the day that God created man on the earth, and ask from one end of heaven to the other whether such a great thing as this has ever happened or *was ever heard of*. Did any people ever hear the voice of a god speaking out of the midst of the fire, as you have heard, and still live? Or has any god ever attempted to go and take a nation for himself from the midst of another nation, by trials, by signs, by wonders, and by war, by a mighty hand and an outstretched arm, and by great deeds of terror, all of which the LORD your God did for you in Egypt before your eyes? To you it was shown, that you might know that the LORD is God; there is no other besides him.[25]

The passage goes on for a number of additional verses, all challenging the Jewish people to test for themselves the stories and experiences of other nations and their gods. While scholars point to the prophet Isaiah as the first to express a fully formed monotheistic theology, Moses speaks to the singularity of Yahweh with passion and conviction.

This was a clear message that the values of the Creator, powerfully represented in the Word and through His words, were sufficient. To live was not just to survive but to experience the fullness of God. They were spoken as the people of Israel were on the verge of entering the promised land. They experienced a hope and expectation that was not equaled until the resurrection and ascension of Christ.

As Moses concludes his second speech, he offers a wonderful benediction that speaks to the nature of God and sets the proper tone for the specific teachings and instructions that follow throughout Scripture:

> Know therefore today that he who goes over before you as a consuming fire is the Lord your God. He will destroy them and subdue them before you. So you shall drive them out and make

23. Deut 12:1–32; 19:1—25:16.

24. Deut 5:1–21; 9:1—10:11; 13:1–18; 24:5–22.

25. Deut 4:32–35.

> them perish quickly, as the Lord has promised you. . . . Do not say in your heart, after the Lord your God has thrust them out before you, 'It is because of my righteousness that the Lord has brought me in to possess the land,' whereas it is because of the wickedness of these nations that the Lord is driving them out before you. Not because of your righteousness or the uprightness of your heart are you going in to possess their land, but because of the wickedness of these nations the Lord your God is driving them out from before you, and that he may confirm the word that the Lord swore to your fathers, to Abraham, to Isaac, and to Jacob.[26]

We do not earn our salvation. It is gifted to us. It is a theme that Peter reiterates in his first epistolary letter. "Blessed be the God and Father of our Lord Jesus Christ! According to his great mercy, he has caused us to be born again to a living hope through the resurrection of Jesus Christ from the dead."[27] It is through God's mercy, freely given, that we are saved. This truth was not the result of New Testament thinking. Moses pointed it out very early on.

26. Deut 9:3–5.

27. 1 Pet 1:3.

# Chapter 7

# From Tribe to Kingdom

In the Pentateuch God began the process of developing a cohesive faith system based on the Law. In addition, He was guiding a somewhat amorphous tribal community into a new land where He could shape a nation that reflected His ethical and moral standards. The challenge was twofold. First, to foster and protect a group of people in an inhospitable environment, set apart from their neighbors by beliefs that were so glaringly different from those around them that they were impossible to ignore. Secondly, while so doing, continue to define the relationship between God and humanity through the very covenants and Law that isolated the Jews in the first place. The process was not one of accommodation and compromise but of doubling down, so to speak, on the uniqueness of Creation.

God now assumed the role of a warrior God. Just as He carefully and particularly designed the physical and liturgical practices of worship and community during the exodus, He just as specifically ordered the movements of people and armies during the early national period. Moses, Aaron, and Joshua were selected to lead a collection of tribes that had been wandering in the desert without any attachment to territory or political authority. A different leadership structure was necessary to reflect the needs of national development, theological orthodoxy, unity, and conquest. Idolatry obviously remained a problem. But now, as a nation with land to protect and a community to develop, the issue of a just and faithful society ordered according to God's value proposition became equally important. While not a new dimension, its significance increased dramatically. And as always, carefully managing the language that would define the characteristics of this new order and push the Creation narrative forward continued to be of paramount concern.

The success of twelve relatively loosely connected tribes wandering in the desert, eking out a living, was not as severely threatened by disobedience as was a developing, unified state with political, economic, and social relationships to maintain. Disobedience now jeopardized not just a collection of tribes and individuals, but the salvation of a nation chosen to stand apart as an example to neighboring communities. God's sovereignty over all the universe now had to be dramatically reasserted. He stopped the river Jordan, made the sun and moon stand still, and extended His blessings to outsiders if they acknowledged His absolute sovereignty. All this was critical for the next step in ordering Creation, the establishment of a theocracy, governed by strict adherence to His will in all matters large and small.

When we arrive at the period of Joshua and the Judges, roughly the thirteenth through the eleventh centuries BCE, Israel had emerged as a discrete and recognizable nation, although not yet particularly powerful or commanding. The Law had been established as its founding principles. In a very real sense, God's Word, now spoken through Joshua, continued the patterns of the initial Creation. God spoke and the next step in reclaiming Creation, the nation of Israel, took shape.

The historical books of Joshua and the Judges mark the period between the covenants with Abraham and Moses and the fulfillment of the promises to Abraham of a cohesive, united kingdom. In the Pentateuch, Creation values were established and codified by a specifically designated group of priests and scribes. Moses was commanded to write a song and "teach it to the people of Israel." The song of Moses was written in a book that was to be placed by the ark of the covenant as a witness against the nation for their rebellious behavior.[1] More systematically developed statements of faith, now joined to earlier oral traditions, were emerging as a structured theological canon proclaiming the absolute and inviolable sovereignty of God. His words, spoken, recorded, and passed on to the people, were foundational moral and ethical value statements. Accordingly, the language and speech that powered His creative acts were to be treated with awe and respect and, in so doing, not only replaced chaos with order but reinforced the singularity of Yahweh.

1. Deut 31:19–29.

> Assemble the people, men, women, and little ones, and the sojourner within your towns, that they may hear and learn to fear the LORD your God, and be careful to do all the words of this law, and that their children, who have not known it, may hear and learn to fear the LORD your God, as long as you live in the land that you are going over the Jordan to possess.[2]

God set the ground rules right after Moses' death, when He commissioned Joshua. "This book of the Law shall not depart from your mouth."[3] The Lord's commission to Joshua was also a warning to the people of Israel. They are to meditate on the Law day and night, "so that you may be careful to do according to all that is written in it. For then you will make your way prosperous, and then you will have good success."[4] The litmus test for success was a just and ordered society, not merely the survival of twelve tribes wandering in an inhospitable environment. It also took on a new dimension. This was more than a commission to Joshua, it was now a commission to all of Israel, which Joshua demanded the officers of the people affirm. Their response: "Whoever rebels against your commandment and disobeys your words, whatever you command him, shall be put to death."[5] Through Joshua, God was continuing His efforts to reclaim and redeem Creation. The extraordinary power of these words over the laws of the universe was evident when, after speaking with the Lord, Joshua was able to command the sun and moon to stand still. "There has been no day like it before or since, when the Lord heeded the voice of a man, for the Lord fought for Israel."[6]

Joshua marks a significant development in both Creation and salvation history. In fulfillment of the covenant promises to Abraham, it was essential that the promised land assume the characteristics of a nation of faithful people, not merely a collection of like-minded folks. The collective, identifiable qualities of the community were now as important, if not more so, than those of tribes and individuals. This new nation was to be large and powerful, totally obedient to God, and totally dependent upon God for critical decisions and essential direction. The Lord's presence was central to decision making. He was to be consulted on all matters, large or small, and failure to do so led to bad outcomes, both personal

2. Deut 31:12–13.
3. Josh 1:8.
4. Josh 1:8.
5. Josh 1:18.
6. Josh 10:12–14.

and collective. While at times, the punishment might seem excessive, the rewards for obedience were extraordinary. The militant Lord secured successes on the battlefield that defied logic and, once completed, the Lord provided a peace and rest that seemed to pass all understanding. The nation state of Israel was to be defined by the centrality of God in all things, the unity of all people under God's divine leadership, and the fulfillment of His covenantal promises. The continued efforts to drive out other gods and order society around God's value proposition also worked to cement the monotheism that would increasingly define Judaism by the time of Saul, the first King of a united Israel.

As Joshua closes, all Israel's enemies have been defeated, the land has been divided between the twelve tribes, and for "a long time afterward," peace and rest settled in on the nation.[7] Towards the end of his life, Joshua gathered the leaders of Israel to remind them of all that God had done and admonish them to "be strong to keep and to do all that is written in the Book of the Law of Moses, turning aside from it neither to the right hand nor to the left."[8] He warned of the dangers of mixing "with these nations remaining among you or make mention of the names of the gods, or swear by them or serve them or bow down to them, but you shall cling to the Lord your God just as you have done to this day."[9] The reminder to remain vigilant not only points back to early commandments dealing with language and speech but also specifically points to the inherent dangers of simply the "mention of the names of the gods, or swear[ing] by them." As small a matter as this might seem, particularly in light of the recent period of bloodshed, warfare, and conquest, the language of idolatry was not only blasphemous, it threatened to undermined the faith of the entire community. It put at risk all the efforts to conquer the land, stabilize relationships with neighbors, and govern a commonwealth of twelve tribes. This was particularly true since this was to be a government entirely built around theological principles, not political or economic expediency. God had designed a nation set apart.

The power of the Lord is beyond measure, and the people of Israel had been given a unique gift in time and space, to see mighty works of God that surpassed human comprehension. Great armies that far exceeded the capacity of the Israelites had fallen before them in combat. The people were living in material comfort without care or concern for

7. Josh 23:1.

8. Josh 23:6.

9. Josh 23:7–8.

their well-being. "I gave you a land on which you had not labored and cities that you had not built, and you dwell in them. You eat the fruit of vineyards and olive orchards that you did not plant."[10] They had committed themselves completely to God, and He delivered on all His promises.

Moses had already issued a strict commandment not to intermarry.[11] Joshua reiterated Moses' message in a warning that would become a prophetic challenge for all generations that followed. In language that also anticipated New Testament warnings found in John, 1 Corinthians, Romans, James, and elsewhere, Joshua describes the seductive risks associated with the world around them:[12]

> For if you turn back and cling to the remnant of these nations remaining among you and make marriages with them, so that you associate with them and they with you, know for certain that the Lord your God will no longer drive out these nations before you, but they shall be a snare and a trap for you, a whip on your sides and thorns in your eyes, until you perish from off this good ground that the Lord your God has given you.[13]

Accommodating outside cultural patterns gave strength and legitimacy to those cultures, particularly when the authority of Israel's culture was based on a vastly different premise. By tolerating cultural and religious differences, individuals accept and speak the language of another authority. It is reflected in how civil governance is conducted and worship is practiced. All these were authorities that God had retained for His exclusive purview and expressly laid out in the Book of the Law and His covenantal promises.

This was not merely idolatry. Speaking the language of a competing culture did not reflect the values of the Creator. While taking physical action against another is obvious and immediate, the language of other cultures is subtle and far more destructive. It is easy to punish the obvious and thereby maintain some semblance of order. Not so with the seemingly harmless language of governance and authority, which can pervert the intent of Creation and bring others down with it. Subtle and creeping accommodation with the faithless, adopting and incorporating their language and symbols in order to marry, raise families, govern

10. Josh 24:13.
11. Deut 7:3–5.
12. John 2:15, 15:19, 17:14–16; 1 Cor 5:9–10; Rom 12:2; Jas 1:27.
13. Josh 23:12–13.

and function as a community was a significant threat, which the Lord identified and Joshua warned against. Such accommodations might be sustainable on the occasional individual basis, when small family groups were wandering the desert. But the choices were different when managing across a larger social or cultural spectrum. If blending Jewish and non-Jewish practices was the path to effective governance, the outcomes may be practical but they were not godly. Incorporating the language and speech of the faithless into the very fabric of Jewish culture would simply eat away at its substance until it ceased to exist. The only real option, the one God designed and Joshua commanded, was to avoid any level of cultural contamination. Accommodation with other cultures may be practical for the management of mundane matters, but it insidiously eats away at value systems. Hundreds of years later, Ezra, Nehemiah, and Malachi would confront the same threat as they sought to rebuild the temple.

At this point in the story, Joshua has the people of Israel collectively renew the covenant in Shechem. In stark contrast to the comforts and pleasures the Israelites were experiencing under God's regime, Joshua describes the costs of disobedience. "If you forsake the Lord and serve foreign gods, then he will turn and do you harm and consume you, after having done you good."[14] Recalling the gravity of oaths and pledges, Joshua cements this covenant agreement: "Then Joshua said to the people, 'You are witnesses against yourselves that you have chosen the Lord, to serve him.' And they said, 'We are witnesses.'"[15] The people of Israel had now invoked the name of the Lord through the solemnity of a community oath. Joshua did not underestimate the enormity of this oath and the use of God's name, although it appears those swearing the oath did. An oath was underscored by the word and authority of God, and failing to follow through was tantamount to rejecting His word. It diminished the stature of God and His reign in Creation. Joshua acknowledges this in his powerful declaration of faith: "And if it is evil in your eyes to serve the Lord, choose this day whom you will serve, whether the gods your fathers served in the region beyond the River, or the gods of the Amorites in whose land you dwell. But for me and my house, we will serve the Lord."[16]

What Joshua said quite pointedly is, if you want to choose, then choose, but do not hide behind false oaths or spoken pledges you have no intention of honoring. Do not dishonor the life-giving covenants of

14. Josh 24:20.

15. Josh 24:22.

16. Josh 24:15.

the Creation narrative with hollow commitments, pious recitations, or cynical behaviors clothed in a false language of faith.

Of course, this did not last long and may have started unraveling shortly after the covenant was renewed at Shechem. The book of Judges opens with the continued conquest of Canaan but, before the end of the first chapter, the leaders of Israel were already equivocating on the terms by which the Lord would deliver the other cities and nations into their hands. One would have thought that with Joshua's passionate insistence on obeying the Law, the enthusiastic renewal of the covenant, and Joshua's emotional appeal to faithfulness, Israel would have remained obedient for a somewhat longer period of time. The fear of just such a rapid descent into chaos was at the core of the Lord's warnings about the risks of assimilating local practices. For a better understanding of why these warnings were so often repeated, and why these concerns were so well placed, we need to inject a historical context.

The land that the Lord had promised to Abraham generations earlier happened to be in an area called Canaan. While the area had been settled for more than eight thousand years before Christ, beginning in the twelfth century BCE, a robust Phoenician civilization had grown up. During its heyday, the Phoenicians successfully established colonies across the Mediterranean, through North Africa and as far as Spain, and were "one of the most economically prosperous cultures of the late second to early first millennium BCE."[17] Eventually, the colony of Carthage became its *de facto* capital, and Carthaginian Phoenicians came to be known as Punics. That status was eventually settled by a series of wars with Rome.[18]

The work of archaeologists, such as Robert Cargill, Mark Smith, and many others, have in recent years provided a far more complete picture of what Canaan looked like when the Jews arrived. This body of work fills in gaps in the biblical picture. What the Israelis confronted was a very powerful and wealthy number of city-states, the magnitude of which is absent in Old Testament accounts of the conquest of Canaan. Although a few cities were recognized in the Scriptures, such as Tyre and Sidon, the enormity of their impact on the ancient world is not immediately evident in biblical references. It was an area that exhibited sophisticated traditions of art, architecture, trade, and literature. This had to be particularly

17. Cargill, *Cities*, 16. Gordon and Rendsburg, *Bible and Ancient Near East.*

18. Hanson, *End of Everything*, 69.

unsettling for a loose community of semi-nomads, who had been wandering in the desert for forty years, living in tents, gathering produce, and herding their animals. The report that was delivered by the spies sent out by Moses not only describes the beauty and fertility of the land but captures the sense of awe and inadequacy that the spies felt upon seeing the land and its inhabitants.[19]

Not only was this land agriculturally fertile, it was theologically fertile as well. El was the principal god of the region, but other gods appear frequently: Baal, Resheph, Asherah, and Astarte, to name a few that are identified in the Scriptures as posing an ongoing threat to the stability of the Jewish community. There was a strong undercurrent of sexuality and sensuality in the prostitute cults of Canaanite worship, which was devastatingly tempting to the people of Israel. The rejection of idolatry and sins of the flesh that characterized Jewish behavior were in such stark contrast to the behaviors of those around them that their singularity was difficult to either disguise or accommodate. The Jews themselves were not that far removed from a time when family gods and local cults were part of their traditions, and they had repeatedly shown a predilection to resort to these traditions while wandering in the desert. This was a tempting environment indeed.[20]

It should come as no surprise that the leaders of the Jewish community, particularly Joshua, should so heavily stress the importance of not allowing relationships with other cultures to enervate or erode their faith, and that punishment would be meted out for failing to completely excise the influence of local populations during the conquest of Canaan. This was the serpent in their garden of Eden. It was under these circumstances that the judges appeared, and their assigned task was to reinforce the moral character of the Israeli communities, rejecting chaos and committing themselves to properly ordering society.

Even before Joshua died, the people of Israel had begun to accommodate existing cultures, adopting local practices, and marrying members of other tribes and nations. Eventually, as Joshua had warned, they began to rely on and worship other gods. This included the judges themselves. The most famous example may be that of Sampson. His wife was an outsider, and he later consorted with harlots, most notoriously, Delilah. During the period of the judges, Israel sank deeper and deeper

19. Num 13.

20. Arnold and Beyer, *Readings from Ancient Near East*; Smith, *Origins*.

into apostasy and the record documents both the national and spiritual decline of the state of Israel that resulted. Judges ends with the following verse: "Everyone did what was right in his own eyes."[21]

The history of Israel had moved from an isolated group of tribes that God guided out of Egypt, through the conquest of Canaan and the establishment of the nation of Israel, to the eventual kingship of David and the realization of the covenantal promises to Abraham. The most remarkable characteristic of the period of the judges, which immediately precedes the kings, is the constancy of God, not the competency of the judges. Despite flagrant and cavalier rejections of the words of the Lord and His prophets, God did not turn His back on His Creation. He set up judges as His representatives to rule over the people, particularly in a military capacity and, when they were obedient, God delivered them. When they were not, they felt His wrath. The judges were selected to not only serve as God's representatives, but they were the mechanism through which God tested the people. "I will no longer drive out before them any of the nations that Joshua left when he died, in order to test Israel by them, whether they will take care to walk in the way of the Lord as their fathers did, or not."[22]

Between the scriptural records of the judges and the advent of Samuel and the kings sits the beautiful story of Ruth. It is a pause in the historical flow from the spiritual estrangement of the judges to the rise of a powerful kingdom. It begins with Elimelech, his wife Naomi, and their two sons leaving Bethlehem because of severe and prolonged famine. Of all places, they settled in Moab, a hotbed of idolatry and sexual excess, a country particularly anathema to Moses and Joshua. The sons, contrary to all that was holy, took Moabite women for wives. Eventually, Elimelech and his sons die, leaving Naomi and her two daughters-in-law in Moab without family connections or any means of support. Naomi decided to return to Bethlehem and encouraged Ruth and Orpah to stay in Moab where they might find some measure of assistance from their families. Orpah remains, but Ruth takes an oath to follow Naomi, return with her to Bethlehem, and adopt Naomi's Jewish patterns of belief and worship. Her faith, which exceeded that of many of her new neighbors, bore fruit and, in the end, she was redeemed. She ultimately gave birth to Obed,

21. Judg 21:25.

22. Judg 2:21–22.

who became the grandfather of David. This places Ruth the Moabite in the direct lineage of the Messiah.

The story would be poignant under any circumstances, but its placement between the judges and the rise of the kingdom of Israel makes it so much more. Once Ruth was redeemed by Boaz, Naomi's and her situations improved dramatically. The book of Ruth reminds readers that redemption is possible for even those most separated from God and that David's kingship is an eternal example of God's salvation made available to all through the agency of Jesus Christ. In the end, whether acknowledged as such or not, Ruth is a covenant book, a record of God's never-ending commitment to that which He created.

The experiment with the judges was spotty at best. After roughly four hundred years, the Lord called Samuel. The period of the kings began, and with it, the eventual rule of David and the establishment of his line. Here the lineage and promise of the Messiah is firmly cemented into Jewish theology.

# Chapter 8

# The United Kingdom

God had intended from the beginning that when the Jewish nation was formed, it would be governed by a king. "No longer shall your name be called Abram, but your name shall be Abraham, for I have made you the father of a multitude of nations. I will make you exceedingly fruitful, and I will make you into nations, and kings shall come from you."[1] When speaking of Sarah, God again says to Abraham, "She shall become nations; kings of peoples shall come from her."[2] The theme is repeated elsewhere throughout Genesis. But this was to be a different kind of king. Rather than "the king as warrior, Israel's king was to focus on keeping the Mosaic law (Deut 17:18–20)."[3] The Hebrew word used for ruler in Deut 17:14–20, which establishes the guidelines for this eventual kingship, makes clear that the king, no matter his power or authority, was ultimately beholden to God alone.[4] The king was not to "acquire many horses for himself," or "acquire many wives for himself, lest his heart turn away, nor shall he acquire for himself excessive silver and gold."[5] Well before Joshua and the judges, the authors of Deuteronomy understood that elevating oneself above others for personal gain was contrary to the moral and ethical structure of Creation. It was the antithesis of service and humility. Personal aggrandizement undermined the created order. This passage also anticipated the dangers of the acclimation of other cultural

1. Gen 17:6.
2. Gen 17:16.
3. ESV, 434.
4. The Hebrew word is *mashal*. Strong, *Concordance*, 175.
5. Deut 17:16–16.

standards. Solomon's reign was distinguished by this type of destructive excess, and its outcome was the eventual dissolution of the kingdom.

This distinction is critical. One would think that physically securing the boundaries of the nation would be the primary task for a king, especially a nation in the midst of unfriendly neighbors. Instead, the role of king in this context was first and foremost to abide by the Law and enforce a strict adherence to the substance and form of worship. Absolute faithfulness was sufficient. All else would follow as God intended. The whole point of Creation, and the re-creation reflected in the new Jewish nation, is that all else will work for good if the people turn first to God and rely upon Him exclusively. When strictly followed, it was a formula that had worked during the exodus through the arrival at the promised land and had been constantly reinforced by the words of the Lord spoken through both Moses and Joshua. There was no room for human arrogance or self-aggrandizement under these circumstances.

Samuel serves a transformational role in the history of the Jewish people and the journey to salvation. The calling of Samuel as a prophet marks the end of the era of the judges. Israel had evolved from the traditional authority of a priestly class to that of the judges. The Jewish people would evolve yet another step, from the loose confederation of tribes and communities under the spiritual leadership of the judges to a strong, wealthy nation under some influential and successful kings. Samuel is the one whom God chose as His instrument to eliminate the position of judges and inaugurate the era of the kings. It was as a prophet that Samuel, through God's authority, called Saul to be the first king. Saul would, in turn, be succeeded by David. This shift from judges to kings sets the stage for the kingship of David and the Davidic line that would come to fruition with the kingship of Christ.

The period of the judges, roughly four hundred years, was largely one of apostasy, chaos, and disobedience. Tucked away in a sea of Canaanite degradation, Israel turned away from the Lord. At the time of Samuel's call, "The word of the Lord was rare in those days; there was no frequent vision."[6] The absence of His Word was as powerful as its presence, as the chroniclers of 1 and 2 Samuel felt compelled to note in the rendering of the narrative. He created by the Word, and He tested by His Word. And when it came time to set the history of Creation and salvation back on course, it was His revealed Word that did so.

6. 1 Sam 3:1.

"And the Lord appeared again at Shiloh, for the Lord revealed himself to Samuel at Shiloh by the word of the Lord."[7] After the degeneration of the Jewish community occasioned by the judges' frequent accommodation of foreign beliefs and practices, the Lord reinserted Himself more actively into history, delivering the king He had foretold in His covenant with Abraham. "As they were going down to the outskirts of the city, Samuel said to Saul, 'Tell the servant to pass on before us, and when he has passed on, stop here yourself for a while, that I may make known to you the word of God.'"[8]

Unlike the judges, the ideal king was to be formed in the image of God. As noted previously, the expectations for a king in this context were different. Not only was the king formed in God's image, fully imbued with His moral and ethical nature, but he ruled exclusively at the pleasure and authority of God alone. This was to be a providential monarchy where all things worked together for good under the aegis of a loving, all-powerful Lord, an earthly mirror of the perfected social order of Creation. A king was called according to God's purpose and His sovereign will, which was to be honored and respected in every aspect of the lives of the king and his subjects. Sufficiency for these purposes lay in the fullness of God, not in human preparation, training, or upbringing. The intersection of God's sovereignty and the king's success was obedience, without which His purposes in the lives of the individuals under the king's authority could not be achieved. Under a godly kingship, the king was a servant, enforcing God's will for the salvation of all. The eternal hopes of both the king and his subjects were inextricably intertwined.

This is a critical distinction that separates the divine kingship of Israel from kingship derived from human understanding. The king was meant to be God's immediate representative. Without a faithful king, individual blessings were impossible. The body politic was corrupted if the king was corrupted. This was a spiritual corruption, not merely political or economic. This codependence between Jewish leadership and individual salvation continued through history until God's Word, manifest in another King, the Christ, altered the pattern. With the arrival of the Messiah in the form of Jesus, the salvation of mankind was no longer dependent upon the wisdom and faithfulness of an ordained, albeit worldly, leadership. The real King was present, in space, time, and

7. 1 Sam 3:21.

8. 1 Sam 9:27.

for a short period, matter, and it was loyalty to that King that assured salvation, not obedience to earthly rulers.

Although the line of kings begins with Saul, his kingship was successful only to the extent that the tribes were united and the possibility of a cohesive nation was proved. But his kingdom began to unravel almost as soon as it started. Saul was given authority and direction by God to destroy the Amalekites. The orders were clearly stated: everything, without exception, was to be destroyed. The military campaign was successful, but Saul decided to hold back some of the best of the herds and flocks and unilaterally decided to show mercy to the leader of the Amalekites.

On the surface, this would seem to be a wise and politically expedient conclusion to a successful military campaign. There were a few problems however. Specifically, Saul was ordered to "devote to destruction" all that the Amalekites had, with no exception. The phrase "devote to destruction" carries with it some theological connotations. "This practice, known also as 'imposing the ban,' denotes setting aside something as the Lord's share."[9] Saul unilaterally chose to diminish the Lord's share by holding back livestock and sparing the life of the Amalekite leader. This was a direct violation of God's word and Saul's oath to rule as an obedient and godly king. It fell to Samuel to complete the sacrifice when he later called for the king of the Amalekites and "hacked Agag to pieces before the Lord in Gilgal."[10] When Samuel found it necessary to strictly enforce the Word of God, which Saul had ignored, that was it. "And the Lord regretted that he had made Saul king over Israel."[11]

Saul tried to explain the matter of the livestock as part of a sacrifice to the Lord, blaming it on the people. Samuel would have nothing to do with lying, deceit, and avoiding personal responsibility:

> Has the Lord as great delight in burnt offerings and sacrifices, as in obeying the voice of the Lord? Behold, to obey is better than sacrifice, and to listen than the fat of rams. For rebellion is as the sin of divination, and presumption is as iniquity and idolatry. Because you have rejected the word of the Lord, he has also rejected you from being king.[12]

9. ESV, 515.
10. 1 Sam 15:33.
11. 1 Sam 15:35.
12. 1 Sam 15:22–23.

This was not simply a private matter between the Lord and Saul. When he was first anointed, Saul gathered the people and "told the people the rights and duties of the kingship, and he wrote them in a book and laid it up before the Lord."[13] This was now an oath, a binding agreement between the Lord and the people of Israel, with Saul as His regent. Saul now had the power to enable or undermine the stability and salvation of a just and faithful society. Saul's commands, his words, to the people had now become tantamount to "iniquity and idolatry," and the bond between Saul and the Lord—and by extension, the Lord and His people—had been broken. If you are the king, there is no such thing as casual speech. Every spoken word had an enormous impact on the salvation of his subjects. Israel moved from the blessed comfort of a nation under authority to the chaos and danger of a nation in disarray because of the cavalier notion that Saul could take the Lord's words lightly. As David would later sing, "The word of the Lord proves true; he is a shield for all who take refuge in him."[14]

The story of the ascension and rule of King David can be found in 1 Chronicles, 2 Samuel, and the first two chapters of 1 Kings. But the language of an ordered society worshiping a monotheistic God comes through most clearly in David's own words. Although part of the tradition of wisdom literature, it is through specific psalms that we can see clearly how David viewed the language and symbolism of a perfected social order and how its holy nature drove his behavior and guided his theology.

The number of psalms actually authored by David, or whether he personally wrote and sang any psalms at all, is subject to some conjecture. However, a case can be made, beginning with Samuel's testimony, that David wrote a number of the psalms. First, he was an accomplished musician. When Saul was suffering from a "harmful spirit from the Lord" because he had lost favor in the Lord's sight, he sought out "a man who is skillful in playing the lyre."[15] David was described by one of Saul's servants as one "skillful in playing," and after Saul had brought David into his closest circle, it was said that "whenever the harmful spirit from God was upon Saul, David took the lyre and played it with his hand."[16] David was chosen by God, so it is not surprising that David's songs were

13. 1 Sam 10:25.

14. Ps 18:30.

15. 1 Sam 16:14–16.

16. 1 Sam 16:18, 23.

sanctified and thereby were sufficient to quiet the harmful spirit that troubled Saul. After all, only God had the authority to calm His own spirit. In 2 Samuel, it was confirmed that David was equally skilled as a songwriter, "the sweet psalmist of Israel."[17] So, whatever the number, there is no doubt that many of the psalms can be directly attributed to David, and they accurately reflect his thoughts and beliefs.

The discussion is worth joining since David's wisdom is most prominently displayed through his language. The questions of monotheism, God's commitment to His people, and a fair and just society are all addressed through David's songs. Here, the perfection of language and speech, as intended in God's initial gift to mankind, are on full display. David can be viewed as a prophet as much as a king.

In Ps 4, David acknowledged that God listens to the prayers of the faithful, has been gracious to David, and has heard his prayers in the past. In the second verse, David asks, "O men, . . . How long will you love vain words and seek after lies?" and immediately warns that slanderous and deceitful words differentiate the godly from the ungodly: "But know that the Lord has set apart the godly for himself."[18] In Ps 5, also attributed to David, he continues the theme: "You destroy those who speak lies; the Lord abhors the bloodthirsty and deceitful man."[19] Later in that same psalm, David describes what defines those who have rebelled against God:

> For there is no truth in their mouth; their inmost self is destruction; their throat is an open grave; they flatter with their tongue. Make them bear their guilt, O God; let them fall by their own counsels; because of the abundance of their transgressions cast them out, for they rebelled against you.[20]

The reader of Ps 5 will note that there are no references to any other type of sin. The whole context of this psalm is the gravity of deceitful, slanderous speech. The gift of language, given at the Creation, was for the purposes of adoring and worshiping God and properly ordering Creation. After the fall, language and speech were to reflect the values of the Creator and further the completion of Creation, salvation, and eternal

17. 2 Sam 23:1.

18. Ps 4:2–3.

19. Ps 5:6.

20. Ps 5:9–10.

life. To disabuse these gifts was to profane God Himself. It was a corruption of the Creation order that could derail the salvation promise.

The pattern of sin is straightforward, and the consequences are severe. "Behold, the wicked man conceives evil, and is pregnant with mischief and gives birth to lies. He makes a pit, digging it out, and falls into the hole he has made."[21] A lament written by David describes the impact that lies and deceit have on communities of faith, and the manner in which such behavior upends social order and justice. It juxtaposes the flattering lips of humans with God's pure words.

> Save, O LORD, for the godly one is gone;
> for the faithful have vanished from among the children of man.
> Everyone utters lies to his neighbor;
> with flattering lips and a double heart they speak.
>
> May the LORD cut off all flattering lips,
> the tongue that makes great boasts,
> those who say, "With our tongue we will prevail,
> our lips are with us; who is master over us?"
>
> "Because the poor are plundered, because the needy groan,
> I will now arise," says the LORD;
> "I will place him in the safety for which he longs."
> The words of the Lord are pure words,
> like silver refined in a furnace on the ground,
> purified seven times.
>
> You, O LORD, will keep them;
> you will guard us from this generation forever.
> On every side the wicked prowl,
> as vileness is exalted among the children of man.[22]

The message here is clear. When God's "pure words" are distorted by "flattering lips," Creation is turned upside down. The poor are plundered and the deceitful prevail; the just ordering of society is denied. The power to corrupt the intent of Creation by the injudicious use of language and speech is real and immediate. To make sure that the power of speech is not lost on the readers and hearers of the psalms, David reinforces the point when he offers a description of the Lord's voice: "Smoke went up from his nostrils, and devouring fire from his mouth; glowing coals

21. Ps 7:14–15.

22. Ps 12.

flamed forth from him; . . . The Lord also thundered in the heavens, and the Most High uttered his voice, hailstones and coals of fire."[23]

In another psalm, David answers the question, "O Lord, who shall sojourn in your tent? Who shall dwell on your holy hill?" The answer, "He who walks blamelessly and does what is right and speaks truth in his heart; who does not slander with his tongue and does no evil to his neighbor, nor takes up a reproach against his friend."[24] Note here that David makes a clear connection between what is in the heart and what leaves the mouth. The two cannot be separated. Sins of language and speech stem from a broken relationship with God.

Of the one hundred fifty psalms, as many as half may be attributed to David, either as author or subject. The themes of rejecting idols, fulfilling the covenantal obligations of justice and righteousness, and protecting the authentic narrative by carefully guarding language and speech are constant refrains. David knew the destructive power of language and speech, and he constantly stressed the need to be vigilant in profaning God's word or distorting it to either the benefit of the ungodly or the destruction of the godly.

At the same time, it should be noted that David was not without sin. He took Bathsheba, the wife of one of his generals, fathered a child, and had her husband killed. He was punished with the loss of that child, unrest among his followers, and the rebellion of Absalom. He called for a census, which insulted the Word of God by questioning the strength of the army God had ordained to succeed. But the Lord did not entirely withdraw His favor, and David had an heir, Solomon, whose kingship outshone David's in many respects. The Davidic lineage was secured and led directly to the Messiah. What, it may be asked, was different about the magnitude of David's sin that differentiated his disobedience from that of Saul, who completely lost the Lord's favor and his kingdom?

The clue lies in the nature of each sin and the threat each posed to the process of salvation. "So Saul died for his breach of faith. He broke faith with the Lord in that he did not keep the command of the Lord, and consulted a medium, seeking guidance. He did not seek guidance from the Lord. Therefore the Lord put him to death and turned the kingdom over to David the son of Jesse."[25]

23. Ps 18:8, 13.

24. Ps 15:1–3.

25. 1 Chr 10:13–14.

Saul defied the direct Word of God and profaned it by his disobedience. He violated his oath to God, which had been professed in front of the people, and tried to shift the blame for his behavior to his subjects. These were corporate sins that threatened to undermine the majesty of God by blaspheming His words and minimizing the sovereignty of God. Saul's sins put at risk the entire narrative of the Abrahamic covenant, the Davidic line, the Messiah, and ultimately, the new Creation and salvation itself. David's sins were just as abhorrent to the Lord, and David was punished. But the actions David took were not corporate sins that could put the nation's salvation at risk.

It would not do well to belabor the point. God does not condone sin or create a hierarchy of misbehavior. All sin is anathema to God. But it is important to understand that God's purpose is the salvation of all mankind, and jeopardizing that goal, threatening the theological survival of the entire community by upending the just ordering of society, required a punishment of the same magnitude as the sin. Saul was creating a reality that God did not intend and that was a public assault on His plan for the new Creation and salvation. It required public punishment. David's sin was individual, and his punishment was personal, but the community was not put to a theological test by his behavior.

From a purely secular point of view, Solomon's reign was the zenith of the Davidic line. Its popularity in books and movies tends to obscure the fact that Solomon's successes in the early part of his reign were based on his faithfulness and obedience. With the ascension of David to the throne, there was a new dynamic in play. Saul was chosen to become king but was undone by his disobedience. In David's case, the Lord made a covenant with him that assured the continuation, although not necessarily the political or economic success, of the Davidic line. In this covenant, God promised He "will raise up your offspring after you, who shall come from your body, and I will establish his kingdom. . . . When he commits iniquity, I will discipline him with the rod of men, with the stripes of the sons of men, but my steadfast love will not depart from him, as I took it from Saul, whom I put away from before you. And your house and your kingdom shall be made sure forever before me. Your throne shall be established forever."[26] Solomon was ordained by the Davidic covenant to succeed.

26. 2 Sam 7:12–16.

And yet there were qualifications. The Davidic line was secure, but implicit in the covenant is the understanding that the life of the nation, and the degree of success of each succeeding King, was dependent upon absolute obedience. Smooth sailing was not guaranteed. It required strict conformance to the Word of God. David reaffirmed as much when he gave Solomon his final instructions:

> Be strong, and show yourself a man, and keep the charge of the Lord your God, walking in his ways, and keeping his statutes, his commandments, his rules, and his testimonies as it is written in the Law of Moses, that you may prosper in all that you do and wherever you turn, that the Lord may establish his word that he spoke concerning me, saying "If your sons pay close attention to their way, to walk before me in faithfulness with all their heart and with all their soul, you shall not lack a man on the throne of Israel."[27]

While this might seem to be a qualification of the covenant promise to David, it is not. The covenant is clear, and God's oath and commitment cannot be qualified. They are paramount, and David clearly understood that. The point he was making was that only through faithfulness would uninterrupted success be guaranteed. The journey would not be linear, but it had a promised conclusion, a Messiah.

So it followed that Solomon ascended to the throne as David's successor. Although it is said that "Solomon loved the Lord, walking in the statutes of David his father," like his father, Solomon's life was not without sin, and he fell in and out of favor with the Lord. When Solomon was obedient, his territories expanded, his enemies were defeated, and his wealth increased.[28] When he gave way to disobedience and idolatry, Solomon fell out of favor. Solomon's successes did not follow him after his death, and the united kingdom of Israel broke apart and eventually disintegrated.[29] The patterns established with the behavior of Saul and David are replicated in Solomon, and the wording is clear. When Solomon was "walking in [David's] ways and keeping his statutes," all was well—remembering, of course, that David was not without personal sin. But David did not commit the corporate sin that would corrupt the

27. 1 Kgs 2:2–4.
28. 1 Kgs 3—11; 2 Chr 1—9.
29. 1 Kgs 11—12; 2 Chr 9—10.

salvation narrative and put the kingdom at risk in the way in which Saul had. Unfortunately, Solomon made the same mistake as Saul.

Solomon had seven hundred wives who were part of the royal retinue, a formal position within the national structure, and very visible throughout the kingdom. He is also credited with keeping over three hundred concubines, who, as consorts to the head of state, occupied a public role as well. By no means were all one thousand of these faithful and obedient Jews. In fact, Solomon allowed his foreign wives to build shrines to their pagan gods outside of the city walls. It was referred to as the Mount of Corruption.

It was politically advantageous to develop personal relationships and bonds with other leading figures in the territories now controlled by Israel. While politically expedient, it nonetheless ran afoul of the warnings dating back to Joshua to avoid making accommodations with those outside the faith. The very public behavior of the head of state blending, and thereby diluting, the cultural and religious practices of the faithful and the non-faithful was ultimately destructive to the entire body politic. The public versus the personal nature of Solomon's sin and David's is borne out in the observations in 1 Kings: "His wives turned away his heart after other gods, and his heart was not wholly true to the Lord his God, as was the heart of David his father. . . . So Solomon did what was evil in the sight of the Lord and did not wholly follow the Lord, as David his father had done."[30]

The point was not the relative sinfulness of David and Solomon. No one, including the authors of Kings, felt that David was free of sin. The fact is that idolatry and other acts of cultural assimilation produce a language of disobedience that, when encouraged by the head of state, resulted in the corruption of God's Creation and salvation narrative. Personal sin damages the relationship between God and the individual. Corporate sin damages the relationship between God and His people. The kingdom of Israel was rent by schism and divided into the competing kingdoms of Israel and Judah. The Davidic lineage was preserved through the kings of Judah, but the Jewish state suffered military conquest, economic deprivation, cultural disintegration, and exile as a result of Solomon's apostasy.

30. 1 Kgs 11:4–6.

# Chapter 9

# The Rise of the Prophets

If one were merely perusing the Bible, looking at book titles, one might assume that at a certain point in time, a group of prophets suddenly appeared on the scene. The books of the Prophets follow the historical books of Kings and the Chronicles of their reigns. After the last Prophet, Malachi, the Old Testament ends and the New begins. It would be easy to conclude that this was a linear pattern, both historically and theologically. The kings failed, the prophets tried, and finally, Jesus arrived. The Abrahamic and Davidic covenants did not produce a Messiah who vanquished all earthly enemies, so that historic phase was over. Theologically, the Mosaic covenant of the Law was insufficient and needed to be replaced, so the theological phase ended as well. In many circles, this has become a presumptive narrative. It would do well to look more closely.

Those prophets after whom books of the Bible were named lived in an era often referred to as that of the Classical Prophets. It began with Amos (c. 760 BCE) and concluded with Malachi, whose activities ended around 430 BCE—a span of roughly three hundred years. This period coincided with the dissolution of the kingdom of Israel, moved through the Assyrian conquest of the northern kingdom and the Babylonian exile of Judah, and ended with the rebuilding of the temple under Ezra and Nehemiah. After Malachi, the scriptural narrative is quiet for three to four hundred years, until the New Testament picks up with the birth and ministry of Jesus.

Rather than being just one of a number of discrete segments of the Creation narrative, the Classical Prophets are best seen as part of a much broader history of prophets and prophecies. There were rich oral traditions of prophecy, some of which are accessible only by reference in other accounts. There were also literary traditions that were preserved in other forms and passed on through the centuries, such as those captured and compiled by Sirach in the apocryphal book of Ecclesiasticus. Simply limiting the tradition of prophesying to the Classical Prophets in the Old Testament would diminish the importance of prophets to the Israeli people. Abraham, Moses, Samuel, Elijah, Elisha, Deborah, Huldah, Nathan, Gad, Shemaiah, and Ahijah, to name a few, all met the criteria as God's messengers or prophets and should be considered an important part of a rich prophetic legacy.

In fact, in older Jewish versions of the Torah, Joshua, Judges, 1 and 2 Samuel, and 1 and 2 Kings are considered books of the Former Prophets. In 1 Samuel, there are references to groups or schools of prophets.[1] The prophet Obadiah took one hundred prophets to the caves outside of Sidon to escape Jezebel's wrath.[2] Elisha is described as being surrounded by so many sons of prophets that they were having trouble accommodating all of them.[3] Although the teachings and prophecies of earlier prophets have not been collected and codified as systematically as were the words of the Classical Prophets, they were clearly witnessing to God's will amongst the Jews of their time.

Historically, prophets specifically identified as Former Prophets were primarily active during the roughly four hundred years of the judges. The Classical Prophets appeared during the dissolution of the kingdom of Israel, which followed the period of the judges. Samuel can be seen as either the last prophet of the Former Prophets or the first of the Classical Prophets. When 1 Samuel opens, God had not spoken or given a vision for three or four generations, dating back to the last prophet Deborah, who happened to also be a judge.[4]

It is important to recognize that prophets were not unique to the Hebrews.[5] Throughout the ancient Middle East, references to prophets appear in Hittite literature, Sumerian texts, and the records of Mesopotamia, Assyria, and ancient Iran. In the Old Testament, prophets in the countries around the Jewish settlements, such as Moab, Edom, Ammon, Tyre, Sidon, Philistia, and Phoenicia, are mentioned frequently. In addi-

1. 1 Sam 10:5; 19:20.

2. 1 Kgs 18:4.

3. 2 Kgs 6:1.

4. 1 Sam 3:1.

5. Metzger and Coogan, *Oxford Companion*, 620–23; Arnold and Beyer, *Readings from Ancient Near East*; Gordon and Rendsburg, *Bible and Ancient Near East.*

tion to theological matters, many of the issues prophets dealt with were of social, political, or ethical interest. Prophets were often allied with a dominant ruling order, some were drawn from guilds or trade associations, or were formal representatives of political territories and conquered regions. They were alternately referred to as diviners, necromancers, magicians, and seers as well as prophets. The pharaohs of Moses' time had their house prophets; the ancient Romans had cults of prophets; and the kings of Babylon surrounded themselves with royal seers, diviners, Chaldeans, and prophets. Every political entity in Canaan had prophets who were called upon to speak on behalf of their gods and advise leadership on matters of public policy.

Being a prophet during this era, particularly one representing a dynastic or economic interest, was not an inconsequential thing. Honor and status were accorded to many of the prophets who spoke for rulers or represented established dynastic religions. Daniel's account of his exile in Babylon references prophets, magicians, seers, and wise men, all of whom were highly placed within Nebuchadnezzar's royal retinue. It is easy, in this modern era, to portray prophets as somewhat marginalized, standing out for their bizarre behavior, strange dress, and dire exhortations. Some, indeed, fit that description. But by and large, they were generally respected in Middle Eastern society of the time. There are even examples in the Bible of rulers and authorities outside of Jewish circles granting a certain level of respect to Jewish prophets prior to the diaspora. God's decision to work through prophets was a familiar and effective way to reach an audience.

In nearly all these iterations, the prophet was there to support the ruling order, not to make waves. Such was not the case with Jewish prophets. "However, unlike their counterparts in the surrounding cultures, who mainly encourage their royal patron, and who, on those rare occasions when they issue admonitions, do so very mildly. Gad and Nathan, like Samuel, dare to defy, contradict, and chastise the king."[6]

This gets to the crux of what constituted a true prophet within the Israeli experience. But it should be noted that just because an Israeli king referred to someone as a prophet did not mean that they were genuine prophets. Part of the reason Obadiah and his one hundred prophets had to flee was that he did not tell King Ahab, who had married Jezebel, what the king wanted to hear in preparation for Ahab's military engagement

6. Podhoretz, *Prophets*, 77

with the Syrians. It is said that Ahab gathered four hundred prophets to consult after he could not get the answer he wanted from Obadiah.[7]

What, then, defined a true prophet? True prophets provided both hope and encouragement as well as condemnation and judgment. When reading the accounts of various prophets, it is clear that prophesying on the Lord's behalf during the Classical period brought with it some wrenching personal pain and discomfort. They were decrying the very circumstances in which they were born and raised. Idolatry, the great threat to salvation, was practiced in the homes and communities in which they lived and, very likely, by those closest to them. Through the prophets, God made it clear that He would judge all peoples, eradicate sin, and, if necessary, make Israel an example and warning to other nations. This was not a simple matter of delivering unfortunate news and hoping someone listened. Prophetic messages were serious matters of life and death. They reflected both God's love and anger and spelled out the consequences of misbehavior. Prophets not only delivered prophecies but were able to understand and describe the consequences of people's choices. As one noted historian of religion described it, the messianic nature of the Old Testament prophets was unique. They looked forward to a future theological state, not merely the historical future.[8]

This could not have been an easy task, physically, emotionally, or psychologically. Jonah was apparently content with his current station, or he would not have chosen to run off to Tarshish when God called. He was disappointed that God did not punish Nineveh after Jonah had left the comfort of his surroundings to rail at the Ninevites. Isaiah might very well have been related to Amaziah, the king of Judah, and in any event was a married man and a father living in Jerusalem, conversant with royal counselors and the royal family.[9] Jeremiah was a descendant of Abiathar, a high priest under King David, whom Solomon exiled for supporting Adonijah for the throne instead of Solomon. Jeremiah was a priest, living and working in a small community near Jerusalem. He was in close proximity to the lifestyle and behaviors of a class from which he had descended.[10] In a world where lineage and kinship were extremely important, breaking away and criticizing familial and community

7. 2 Chr 18:5.

8. Young, *Old Testament Prophecy.*

9. Isa 7:3; 8:2–3, 18.

10. 1 Kgs 1:13–27. See also, discussion in ESV, 1363–64.

relationships, which all true prophets did, had to be fraught with a great deal of emotional and psychological tension.

There are several characteristics common to all true prophets. Clearly, they were all called by God in a way that could not be impeached. They were called through a vision, a dream, the mediation of another prophet or holy man, or a visitation from one of God's emissaries. Prophets were always aware that they were prophets, although in certain instances, such as in a trance or an ecstatic condition, they may not have clearly appreciated what they prophesied.

It is also clear that prophets had the ability to intercede on behalf of others, but that was not their primary mission. Given the nature of the threat, their greatest asset was the ability to understand and, most importantly, make others understand that there was only one true God and that He had chosen Israel as His instrument to reveal the Law to surrounding populations.[11] The poetry of Isaiah, as an example, not only calls out the bad behavior of Israel but also provides a vision for the future. A vision that boldly declares that there would be a time when all people of every walk of life would live in a perfected state with God.

Another interesting characteristic of the prophets is illustrated in 2 Chronicles, when Ahab, king of Israel, is seeking an alliance with Jehoshaphat, king of Judah, in his battle with the Syrians. Jehoshaphat asked Ahab whether he had sought the word of the Lord. This is the point noted earlier at which Ahab gathered four hundred prophets, who essentially endorsed Ahab's plan to proceed. Jehoshaphat resisted and asked if there was one more prophet who could be trusted to speak God's truth. Ahab concedes that there is another, Miciah, but in Ahab's words, "I hate him, for he never prophesies good concerning me, but always evil."[12] Nonetheless, Miciah was called. He initially concurred with the advice of the four hundred, but Ahab makes Miciah swear that he is speaking the Lord's truth. Miciah recants and denounces the four hundred, saying that the Lord has put lies in their mouths to "declare disaster concerning you."[13] With that, Ahab orders Miciah to be jailed, to which Miciah replies, "If you return in peace, the Lord has not spoken by me."[14] Ahab is defeated and dies. The point here is that Miciah, like all other genuine prophets, was incapable of speaking anything other than God's truths even when

11. Podhoretz, *Prophets*, 22.

12. 2 Chr 18:7.

13. 2 Chr 18:22.

14. 2 Chr 18:27.

he tried. They knew only what God wanted them to know and spoke only what God wanted them to speak.

A true prophet would not encourage the worship of any god other than Yahweh. They would speak only God's words, not those of spirits or oracles. A genuine prophet would speak truth about the future, no matter how painful. The outcomes of their prophecies could be verified and subjected to testing, as Miciah had sworn to Ahab. Finally, the true prophet's words would conform to, and reinforce, the tenets of the covenantal arrangements between God and His people.[15] Interestingly, since they are singularly focused on speaking God's truth, true prophets tended not to perform miracles, unlike so many accounts of false prophets. There are many instances of miracles being performed by such prophets, beginning with the miracles the pharaoh's prophets performed in response to Moses' miracles. But as a rule, Elisha's raising a dead child notwithstanding,[16] the Classical Prophets did not perform miracles. The act of performing miracles, again, with a very few exceptions, presents an alternative to worshiping the one true God. It ran the risk of exalting the prowess of the one performing the miracle and increasing the status of the ruler. This was a form of idolatry, and a true prophet did not teach idolatry. They were incapable of saying or doing anything that in any way represented a path other than through the one sovereign God. As with Miciah, when they spoke, they lived out the prophecy by example.

While most false prophets probably lived relatively comfortable lives under someone's patronage, true prophets in the Classical period frequently ended up living lives of destitution and privation. But not as a punishment or sign of disfavor. Again, using Daniel as an example, Old Testament prophets often chose to adopt such a lifestyle to prepare themselves for divine revelation, as when Daniel chose to voluntarily fast and mourn prior to receiving his fourth vision.[17] Fasting, rejection within their own communities, condemnation, and punishment by the authorities were largely the result of voluntary behaviors. We do not see Classical Prophets being martyred for their beliefs or opinions until John the Baptist was beheaded.

The rise of the Classical Prophets was, in part, driven by the political situation within the kingdom of Israel. As Solomon's reign drew to a close, the Davidic line was secured and the lineage of Jesus firmly established. It

15. Deut 13, 18; Jer 14, 28.

16. 2 Kgs 4:32.

17. Dan 10:2–3.

was not, however, a smooth path. In the later stages of his reign, Solomon imposed unfair and repressive tax policies to support his many construction projects. A new layer of bureaucracy arose, one made up of royally appointed superintendents from each tribe charged with overseeing the execution and completion of the king's projects. There was no historical or cultural affinity between this new class and those on the bottom layer of society. The natural empathies and responsibilities that are part of a less rigid tribal class structure tend to disappear under formal bureaucracies. This added a new source of tension within the kingdom.

One of the superintendents appointed by Solomon was Jeroboam, from the tribe of Ephraim. Jeroboam saw firsthand the discontent of the people and conspired to replace Solomon. The plot was discovered, and Jeroboam sought sanctuary in Egypt, where he remained until Solomon's death.[18] Rehoboam, Solomon's son and heir, assumed the throne. The conditions in Israel at this time were vaguely reminiscent of the circumstances under the pharaohs prior to the exodus. Rehoboam traveled to Shechem, where the nation gathered to pledge their loyalty to the new king. Jeroboam heard of this, left Egypt, and led a delegation to Shechem to plead their case for social justice. "Your father made our yoke heavy. Now therefore lighten the hard service of your father and his heavy yoke on us, and we will serve you."[19] Rehoboam chose to reject the advice of his father's seasoned counselors and threatened to increase the burden. In a scene echoing that of Moses beating to death one of the pharaoh's overseers, Rehoboam "sent Adoram, who was taskmaster over the forced labor, and all Israel stoned him to death with stones."[20] This led to rebellion among the ten northern tribes of Israel, who called Jeroboam to be king of Israel. Rehoboam gathered an army from the house of Judah and prepared to attack Jerusalem. But the Word of God, delivered by the Prophet Shemaiah, warned Rehoboam not to wage war against "your relatives the people of Israel."[21] This time, he listened and disbanded his army. Specifically, God's command was "every man return to his home, for this thing is from me." Despite the intense despair the people of Israel must have felt, God made it very clear that this was His call, and He would continue to control history.

18. 1 Kgs 11:26–40.
19. 1 Kgs 12:4.
20. 1 Kgs 12:18.
21. 1 Kgs 12:24.

It was an ignominious end to the glory of David and Solomon. Jeroboam became the first king of the new Israel, consisting of the ten northern tribes of the old kingdom, and Rehoboam was the king of Judah, essentially the tribes of Judah and Benjamin.[22] The northern kingdom would lose its identity in roughly sixty years. It was absorbed into the Assyrian Empire, and its capital was situated in the city of Samaria. Judah survived for another two hundred years until its capital Jerusalem fell, and its people were sent to Babylon in exile. But this remnant contained the bloodlines of David, so the promise of a Messiah was unbroken.

The period of the kings and, to a lesser extent, the judges created a whole new dynamic in which the challenges of language, speech, and semiotics play out. While idolatry remained a serious issue, the question of ordering social justice according to God's moral and ethical values took on a new dimension, and the idea of a more broadly based faith gained greater acceptance.

Jeroboam became concerned that the people of the northern kingdom would continue to journey to Jerusalem to worship at the temple. The intensity of the worship experience might very well have led to a healing of the nation, which would not have been in Jeroboam's personal plans. So he set up two sites within the territory he controlled, Dan on the northern border and Bethel on the southern border with Judah, that were to become new centers of worship. In both places, Jeroboam installed golden calves as substitutes to the Israeli God and commanded, "Behold your gods, O Israel, who brought you up out of the land of Egypt."[23] He went even further, creating a whole new system of faith, including festival days, building new temples, and replacing the Levites with a new priestly class.[24]

Monotheism was, by this time, the accepted practice in the Davidic line of Jewish theology. The Jerusalem temple remained the place of worship in Judah, and God was acknowledged as singular, omnipotent, and omniscient. With Jeroboam's actions, the northern kingdom was no longer a Jewish state, and the rift between what would become Jews (Judah) and Samaritans (Israel) was firmly entrenched by the time of Jesus. By

22. In order to avoid confusing the old united kingdom of Israel with the new kingdom of Israel going forward, the ten northern tribes (the new kingdom of Israel) will be referred to simply as the northern kingdom. The southern kingdom, the tribes of Judah and Benjamin, will be referred to as either the southern kingdom or Judah.

23. 1 Kgs 12:28.

24. 1 Kgs 12:25–33.

eliminating the language and symbols of Jewish worship, Jeroboam created the conditions that led to the complete eradication of any sense of being Jewish. The political, social, and economic identity of the northern kingdom was quickly subsumed by the Assyrians and, absent a Jewish faith system that was built around the Law, their Jewish identity was destroyed as well.

This was more than an act of personal idolatry on Jeroboam's part. It was now official behavior. The challenge the prophets faced was no longer one of confronting individual failure. It was now institutional failure. In earlier times, prior to the establishment of a meaningful political and economic entity with unquestioned authority to enforce laws of its own making, questions of idolatry and social justice were enforced by moral suasion and tribal pressure. While individual acts of sin still threatened the cohesion of the community, when these patterns became accepted patterns of official behavior, the problem was quite different. Who governs the governors now became the issue at hand.

But notwithstanding the diminishing stature of Israel and the capacity of the kings and the ruling class to influence others through political or economic leverage, God still expected the Jewish people to speak and act in ways that reinforced His value propositions. Now, prophetic warnings on idolatry and social justice were aimed more towards reinforcing obedience within faithful subsets of the nation, embracing the sovereignty of God, and submitting to His kingship.

With Israel an increasingly less powerful and influential political player in the region, individual communities of Jews struggled to reclaim their inheritance, jealously guard their unique identity, protect the tenets of their faith, and persevere in the face of powerful empires inimical to their interests. The importance of what was said and how it was said was critical for the survival of their faith. Speech, the language of the heart, was what one needed to get right with God and was by and large the only tool available to do so within a politically and economically enervated community.

This was the void the Classical Prophets filled. They became the voice of God's value proposition. The circumstances had radically shifted. The patriarchs and judges were clearly not operating on their own authority. The kings, however, were acknowledged to have authority and dominion over the people greater than that of the patriarchs or judges. They were, in fact, God's earthly emissaries. When they crossed the line, there was no appeal to a greater earthly authority. With the demise of functional government, the Assyrian domination in the north, and the recurring geopolitical challenges in the south, the prophetic message continued to include corporate warnings but increasingly extended to individuals.

Here, the joy and beauty of poetic and wisdom literature became an important feature for the Classical Prophets. Poetic and wisdom literature was timeless. It did not derive its meaning from a particular point in time or series of events. Writings that fell within this category were commonplace, familiar to both the Jews in exile and the prophets of that period. This literature can fairly be described as oriented towards individual instruction, although it carried portentous meaning for the larger community. Given the shift in emphasis in the prophetic era from divine guidance aimed at nation building to more personal appeals for a return to obedience and faithfulness, it is not surprising to find many of the same themes of poetic and wisdom literature appearing in the words of the prophets. God's message to individuals remained unchanged, in language and speech, informed wisdom literature and prophetic warnings alike. The thematic tones echoed in poetic and wisdom literature with respect to language and speech remained particularly instructive.

The prophets continued to appeal to the faithfulness of the kings, and a number of them in Judah were receptive. But notwithstanding the exceptions, individual salvation became as important as institutional salvation because it would be the individuals who returned to rebuild and reenergize Israeli identity. Prophets continued to stress the rejection of idolatry and the importance of social justice as a reflection of God's image, but the appeal went beyond Jews. Since the prophets were speaking to diverse and eclectic communities, non-Jews heard the message and were welcomed in a way that they had not been before. The Creator's appeal was now truly universal. And it was this expanded call that ultimately played out in Paul's missions to the gentiles.

The subject of social injustice increased in emphasis during the Classical period. But that should not be viewed as a departure from prior prophetic activity—more of a shift in intensity. Both Moses and Joshua spoke about matters of fairness and justice. No message on behalf of the Creator could ignore social concerns, since it has always been the Creator's intent that people live with their neighbors in a way that fully embraces the value system of Creation. You simply cannot divorce good social behavior from good theological behavior in God's world.

In part, the increased focus on social justice was due to the change in circumstances after the death of Solomon. During the brief period of national stability under Saul, David, and Solomon, the theological encompassed the social because the liturgy of worship was also the language of social and cultural behavior. It should be noted that there is a school of thought that the Classical Prophets were exclusively focused on reforming Judaism and rehabilitating Yahweh from its corruption in Canaan. There is no question that the matter of Canaanite influences reached back to the warnings of Joshua when the Jews were about to enter the promised land, and it remained a central focus. As another scholar put it, "They represent the true prophet as the agent and defender of Yahweh in opposition both to religious apostasy and syncretism and to the authority of kings when these failed to uphold the cause of Yahweh or flouted his moral demands."[25]

The case that speaking against idolatry was the sole purpose of the Classical Prophets, however, is a bit overstated. While the principal task of the prophets recorded in Scriptures was to order the right relationship with God as designed in covenantal agreements, that right relationship was all-encompassing. It did not preclude fairness, justice, or even redemption for those outside of traditional Jewish circles, and that case is borne out in all the books of the prophets.

The kingdom of Israel had proven unable to remain faithful to God as a political entity, but individual communities and family groups remained obedient and struggled to retain their Jewish identity. God did not renege on His covenant promises, but He suspended His support for the Jewish people in their political and economic capacities. God no longer actively directed the affairs of the Jewish nation in the same manner as He had during the exodus and the national period. He nonetheless continued to influence history through the agency of foreign kings and local prophets as He worked His will on a rebellious people. No longer is a warrior God directly guiding His people in the building of a nation, but a jealous God is demanding obedience and a return to the relationship He had always intended from the outset. The "eighth and seventh-century prophets addressed themselves not only to kings and other individuals and particular groups, but also to the whole people."[26] At this time, the greatest risk to the Jewish people was not in their national capacity, since it had been, for all intents and purposes, erased, but to the souls of His remaining followers. Idolatry, absorption into other cultures, and false

25. Metzger and Coogan, *Oxford Companion*, 621.

26. Metzger and Coogan, *Oxford Companion*, 621.

prophets who sought to seduce the hearts and minds of the remaining faithful were the primary concerns after the dissolution of the kingdom. It is not at all helpful to view this as simply a matter of idolatry. Any mythical god can demand absolute obedience and still not care whether an obedient people are a just people. The God of Creation demands obedience for the purposes of a perfected relationship between the Creator and the created, built around His moral and ethical standards.

Under the circumstances of exile, with the dispersion of families throughout the Babylonian Empire, small clusters of Jews were particularly susceptible to the importuning of false prophets and false teachers. This was not new to the exiled diaspora. False prophets and false teachers had been a problem from the beginning of time and remained an issue even at the end of times, as described in the Revelation.[27] Because Israelis survived only in isolated pockets, the presence of competing faith systems increased the vulnerability of these small groups of Jews to false teachings. Often, false prophets preyed on their isolation by suggesting that hope was right around the corner.[28] Distinguishing false prophets became far more problematic during the Classical period. Early efforts "to establish criteria for identifying the genuine prophet"[29] were attempted long before the matter rose to the level that it did during the Classical period. But absent the social, cultural, and theological discipline of a cohesive community structure, the challenge became far greater.

For our purposes, this falls right in line with the ongoing process of reclaiming the authentic Creation narrative and the importance of preserving the power of the Word. The integrity of language, speech, and the semiotics of Creation relied upon the eradication of idolatry and the rejection of syncretic accommodation. False prophets and false teachers were authors of idolatry and syncretism. The themes of idolatry and social justice are embedded in classical prophecy, with the additional quality of a broader, more universal appeal. The purposes of Creation were the obedient unity of the faithful under the guidance of a loving God and the ultimate salvation of mankind in the new kingdom. By their words, the prophets clearly communicated God's vision. The distinguishing characteristics of prophetic language were its godly attributes and the reflection of a perfected moral condition, which the listener ignored at

27. Rev 13:11–18; 19:11–21.

28. Jer 28; 29:24–32. These chapters and verses tell of Hananiah and Shemaiah, false prophets who minimized the duration and, by extension, the severity of Judah's exile.

29. Metzger and Coogan, *Oxford Companion*, 622.

his own peril. It was the powerful speech of God, delivered through human agency, guiding His people toward salvation.

For idolatry to take hold and succeed, the language and speech of idolatry must become the dominant currency for all transactions, secular as well as divine. The integrity of the authentic narratives of faith can only be preserved if both the worship of anything other than God and acculturation with the secular environment are repudiated. While it may seem that an effective firewall can be built between sacred and secular language, that is simply not the case. If secular language alone is allowed to adjudicate matters of fairness and justice, for example, then the sacred language must give way. That can fundamentally alter the godly intentions behind fairness and justice. What one says honestly reflects one's heart, but an individual's heart can be profoundly impacted by how he or she is pressured to speak. This is particularly true if secular language becomes the dominant linguistic currency, and the sacred is consigned to the perimeter of social behavior. While that may seem counterintuitive, people will respond to popular patterns of speech and eventually inculcate the message. How people react, what they accept or reject, and their position in society are conditioned by how speech conforms to accepted patterns. Once the decision is made to conform to the language patterns of the surrounding culture, behavior will change. It is very difficult, once accepted into certain circles, to put that status at risk by challenging conventional thought. Under those circumstances, God's purpose becomes increasingly at odds with popular notions. When Antiochus IV sought to viciously Hellenize Canaan after failing to conquer Egypt, a number of Jews succumbed in order to conform and succeed under Seleucid rule. The subsequent Hasmonaean revolt was as much a civil war to rid the land of apostate Jews as it was a revolt against Antiochus's rule. This is the reality and the burden of sanctified speech.

There is an interesting passage in Isaiah that speaks to the easy conflation of the mundane with the divine and the importance of remaining diligent. In Isa 44:9–20, entitled "The Folly of Idolatry," Isaiah speaks to the process by which a humble carpenter carefully culls trees from the forest, replanting their eventual replacements. Some of the wood he burns for warmth, and some he uses to bake bread and cook meat. All these behaviors are consistent with the original, harmonious purposes of creation. But then, in a jarring departure, "the rest of it he makes into a god, his idol, and falls down to it and worships it. He prays to it and says,

'Deliver me, for you are my god!'"[30] The irony of man's behavior, and the intentional blindness God has visited upon the disobedient, is not lost on Isaiah. "He feeds on ashes; a deluded heart has led him astray, and he cannot deliver himself."[31] Creation has been corrupted. Idolatry, leveraged by the language of prayer into a denial of the kingship and authority of God, has destroyed the relationship between mankind and his Creator. Speech and reality have become so distorted that the carpenter cannot even deny the falsehood of his own heart.[32]

The ease with which mankind can move seamlessly from the sublime relationships of Creation to worshiping idols is a stunning example of the dangers of cultural acclimation. That is why an overarching and continuing concern of the prophets was calling out the dangers of idolatry, false teachings, and cultural accommodation. The book of Lamentations, with its confessional prayers, reminded the faithful of the promises of hope and renewal but stressed the point that these promises are wholly dependent upon strict obedience to God. Lamentations, most clearly of the Old Testament writings, speaks very specifically to the real experiences of pain, suffering, and sorrow that inure to willful disobedience. There is an abiding sense of sorrow in these prayers, since they acknowledge that none of this was necessary. God had not intended this path but for the rebellious and sinful nature of mankind. Lamentations says, in ways other writings do not, that the unified kingdom collapsed specifically because of turning away from God, both at the individual and corporate levels. The rejection of God took the form of personal and social sin, the sins of apostasy, idolatry, cultural accommodation, and an inequitable society. The language of God was preempted by the language of sin. One could choose to embrace the language and speech of God or to reject it. The first led to joy and redemption, the second pain and sorrow.

This point is reinforced by the Prophet Joel. As he is bemoaning the sinfulness of the people, he proclaims, "Alas for the day! For the day of the Lord is near, and as destruction from the Almighty it comes."[33] Joel repeatedly returns to the themes of judgment and punishment, but juxtaposed to the threat of divine punishment are calls to return to the Lord. "Return to the Lord your God, for he is gracious and merciful, slow

30. Isa 44:17.

31. Isa 44:20.

32. Isa 44:9–20.

33. Joel 1:15.

to anger, and abounding in steadfast love; and he relents over disaster."[34] There are reasons for hope in the midst of God's anger. The judgments and punishments of the present will lead to the renewal of the future. Unwillingness to acknowledge God's sovereignty will result in pain and sorrow, but sincere confession and prayer, the language of reconciliation, can restore the relationship.

The words of all the prophets during this period in history contain that same hope. There is a specific promise and expectation of a Messiah that will deliver mankind from sin and death and a new covenant that will be extended to all believers. The earth will finally be cleansed of sin and the new Creation inaugurated. Both implicitly and explicitly, the prophets proclaim God's clear intention to purge the world of disobedience and sin, and they herald the era of a triumphant Messiah. But a fallen people will endure much in the interim.

The prophets speak to Israel's rejection of the language of wisdom in favor of accommodating the cultural language of the larger, non-Jewish communities within which they resided. It should be noted that social justice in the Old Testament context does not carry the same flavor as social justice does today. In the postmodern era and beyond, social justice is driven by compliance with generally accepted cultural norms. This is not to say that many issues that are identified in that environment are unworthy of attention and deserve to be corrected. However, it is fair to say that grounding in culturally derived norms can be fluid and transitory, as it is not based on any transcendent, unchanging set of values. One only need compare political correctness and the "woke" culture with the consistent values of language and speech embodied in scriptural truths to see the difference. It was to God's value system and sense of social justice that the prophets spoke. They could do no other since their language was informed directly by God. What the prophets shared with the people of Judah and Israel were the never-changing truths and values that were the foundation of history from the beginning, which is why it is not at all surprising that words in the wisdom tradition and prophetic utterances remain fresh and relevant today.

34. Joel 2:13.

# Chapter 10

# Prophetic Voices: Idolatry, False Prophets and Teachers

*"You shall have no other gods before me."*

Before the conversation shifts to the individual prophets, three observations are in order. The prophets whose books appear in the Bible have been classified as either major or minor. The distinction is somewhat unfortunate, although the poetic lyricism of Isaiah, the magnificence of Jeremiah, and the imagery of Daniel and Ezekiel certainly stand out. The size of the book seems to have been a consideration, but Hosea and Zechariah are roughly the same size as Daniel. Whatever the thought processes, it has created an assumption that the minor prophets were in some way less important or impactful. This is simply not the case, and when it comes to the matter at hand, prophets like Amos and Hosea were powerful witnesses to the power and authority of God and the sufficiency of His moral and ethical standards.

Secondly, redaction analyses, which gained popularity during the first half of the twentieth century, have exhausted an untold number of hours debating who may have written a particular biblical passage, who might have edited it, or even how many authors and editors may have been involved. In the case of Isaiah, for example, some have chosen to refer to first, second, and third Isaiah, each segment theoretically composed by a different author. There are even suggestions that there may have been upwards of forty contributors to what is known as Isaiah. While there may be some value in such an exercise, the redaction analysis itself tends to garner more attention and diminishes the majesty of the whole. The approach here is to credit the prophet for what he said and what has been recorded. The message of each prophet is cohesive, powerful, and stands on its own merits.

Finally, one must necessarily select examples of prophecies that address one of the principal themes. To try to capture all the references would essentially entail reciting the entirety of the prophets. However, it would be misleading to draw the conclusion that the prophets specialized in one particular topic or theme. With a few exceptions, each of the prophets expressed concern about all issues the Jews were facing. Despite relying on a sample of work, what follows is a fair and accurate representation of a very large body of work.

The point was made earlier that distinctions between the prophets of the Classical period and those that preceded them might in some way suggest a hierarchy of influence, with the Classical Prophets at the top. Certainly, the transfiguration of Jesus, where Elijah represents the prophetic tradition and Moses represents the Law, belies any such suggestion. Nonetheless, the fact that the Classical Prophets all have their own books lends credence to the idea that they are more significant.

Although it can be overemphasized, the distinction is not without some value. The Classical Prophets represent a new style of prophecy that was an essential ingredient in spreading the message of the Law as well as laying the necessary groundwork for later missions to the gentiles. Prophets prior to the Classical period generally spoke to the leaders of the community and, with the exception of Moses, they did not address the people directly. Their message was as godly and powerful as that of the later prophets, but it was the responsibility of leadership within the Jewish community to establish the structure for following the Law, protecting the processes of worship, and representing, through their behavior, the integrity of the Law. But as Israel's political influence, authority, and national identity began to wane, prophets were increasingly left to face the people directly.

This is the real distinction between the early prophets and those of the Classical period. Now, everyone within earshot, Jew or non-Jew, was exposed to the message. There were no intermediaries. Much the same way Jesus upended the delicate political balance of Jewish communities under Roman authority, the Classical Prophets created a great deal of tension within the disintegrating structure of Jewish political authority.

Because this period of prophecy played out in a very public manner, the interplay between the distinctive characteristics of the Creation narrative and the targets of prophetic criticism is very clear. It proves the logical and cohesive nature of Creation, and God's plan of redemption, re-creation, and salvation for all humanity—a logic and cohesion not in evidence in any other origin story.

Confronting the challenges of idolatry, syncretism, false prophets, and false teaching is to assert the unique and singular authority of God, which is, of course, the principal characteristic of monotheism. Similarly, the insistence on a just and fair society is a reflection of God's continued desire to reclaim and redeem His Creation. This is also a criterion of a covenanted relationship. Monotheism alone does not guarantee fairness and justice. One true god could just as well be a tyrant or tolerate chaos, but a God with a loving commitment to the success of His Creation cannot. The same holds true with respect to the gifts of language and speech. Their integrity must be protected because they not only serve to order Creation according to God's moral and ethical image, but they are also the most powerful vehicle for accurately sustaining and passing on the authentic narrative. Language and speech are the tools that permitted God's message to grow beyond the boundaries of Judaism and become more universal in scope.

## *IDOLATRY*

Idolatry was, and remains, a prominent threat to God's plan for the redemption and salvation of mankind. Presenting alternatives to the preeminence of God diminishes the message. As a result, the question of idolatry is not simply the worship of idols but includes false prophets and false teachers who spoke to an alternative authority. All seek to replace a sovereign God with an authority derived from human convention.

Among many biblical scholars, the question of monotheism as a tenet of Jewish theology was not definitively settled until sometime around the kingship of David.[1] This conclusion is based on archeological records that indicate there was a robust cult of idol worship among Israelis from Abraham through David. That clearly was the case, given the accounts within the Scriptures themselves. But too much can be made of the question. It is equally clear that there was a strong belief in the primacy of

1. For example, see Smith, *Origins*, 163.

Yahweh, even in the face of family gods and idolatrous patterns of worship, prior to David. The Ten Commandments open with the statements, "You shall have no other gods before me. You shall not make for yourself a carved image. . . . You shall not bow down to them or serve them."[2] The blessings for obedience found in Leviticus begin, "You shall not make idols for yourselves or erect an image or pillar, and you shall not set up a figured stone in your land to bow down to it, for I am the LORD your God."[3] Joshua's spirited call to follow the Lord was not unique. The psalms attributed to David make clear his belief that Yahweh was far superior to any other god and was deserving of obedience and worship. Solomon's wisdom consistently reflected David's rejection of gods other than Yahweh.

But it was not until some two hundred years after the death of Solomon that the first real, powerful defense of God's supremacy and the complete inadequacy of idols appears in the Scriptures. Beginning in the fortieth chapter through the sixtieth, Isaiah hammers home the point that orthodoxy in Judaism meant one God and one God only. In some circles, this has been accepted as evidence that the question of monotheism and the singularity of God was not settled until the time of Isaiah. However, if the definition of polytheism rests solely on the existence of other gods, then the argument could easily be made that Jews and Christians today remain polytheistic, since idols of one sort or another continue to be worshiped. Only the form has changed.

Once again, it is not useful to expend a great deal of time debating the matter of when or how monotheism became entrenched in the scriptural narrative. It is just as likely that the Classical Prophets sounded more monotheistic than their predecessors because the authoritative, orthodox, uncorrupted structure of religion began to unravel along with the kingdoms of Israel and Judah. Ultimately, it may be more a matter of the broader nature of the Classical Prophets' audience that elevated the conversation.

It did not take long for the divided kingdom to devolve into rampant apostasy. Jeroboam I, the first King of Israel after the division, built altars worshiping golden calves shortly after assuming the throne. The language Jeroboam used is precisely that which was used to justify the golden calf during the exodus.[4] The reaction should not have been unexpected:

2. Exod 20:3–5.
3. Lev 26:1.
4. Exod 32:4.

> Moreover, the Lord will raise up for himself a king over Israel who shall cut off the house of Jeroboam today. And henceforth, the Lord will strike Israel as a reed is shaken in the water, and root up Israel out of this good land that he gave to their fathers and scatter them beyond the Euphrates, because they have made their Asherim [a totem symbolizing the worship of Asherah], provoking the Lord to anger. And he will give Israel up because of the sins of Jeroboam, which he sinned and made Israel to sin.[5]

Jeroboam's successor, his son Nadab, was no better: "He did what was evil in the sight of the Lord and walked in the way of his father, and in his sin, which he made Israel to sin."[6] This list goes on with discouraging continuity, one king after another doing "what was evil in the sight of the Lord."[7] Only Jehu managed to please the Lord by destroying the house of Ahab: "But Jehu was not careful to walk in the law of the Lord, the God of Israel, with all his heart. He did not turn from the sins of Jeroboam, which he made Israel to sin."[8]

Hosea, a prophet to the northern kingdom who preceded Isaiah by roughly a generation, delivered a powerful message directed at Jeroboam I for encouraging idolatrous beliefs. He saw in Israel's conduct a surrender of the language of faith and adoption of prayers and oaths acknowledging other gods. Hosea declared that idolatry denied the active involvement of God in both the natural world and the immediate lives of the individual. It was blasphemous and profane. It violated the first, second, third, and ninth commandments as well as the covenants offered by God to humanity. In referring to the transgressions of Israel, Hosea prophesied, "And I will punish her for the feast days of the Baals when she burned offerings to them."[9] The terms of repentance: "For I shall remove the names of the Baals from her mouth, and they shall be remembered by name no more."[10]

Hosea was active during the last thirty years of the kingdom of Israel. This was an unstable period, during which six different kings reigned and four were assassinated. The last independent king, Hoshea, conspired against the dominant Assyrian empire, which led to the destruction of

5. 1 Kgs 14:14–16.

6. 1 Kgs 15:26.

7. A chart on page 623 in the ESV contains all the references to the reigns of the kings of Israel.

8. 2 Kgs 10:31.

9. Hos 2:12.

10. Hos 2:17.

the kingdom of Israel. Hosea places the fall of Israel directly at the feet of idolatry. "Israel is a luxurious vine that yields its fruit. The more his fruit increased, the more altars he built; as his country improved, he improved his pillars. Their heart is false; now they must bear their guilt. The Lord will break down their altars and destroy their pillars."[11]

The rejection of a monotheistic God was sufficient to incur the wrath of God, but worshiping Baal entailed all other sorts of abominations and sexual deviations that corrupted the holy image that the chosen people were called to uphold. These were not the reflections of a covenanted people who were called to be a shining example to other nations. In the end, a loving God was committed to their redemption, but isolation and exile were the means by which redemption and restoration were to be accomplished.

Isaiah similarly warned of the cost of idolatry and rejecting God's Word:

> He who makes a memorial offering of frankincense, like one who blesses an idol. These have chosen their own ways, and their souls delight in their abominations; I also will choose harsh treatment for them and bring their fears upon them, because when I called, no one answered, when I spoke, they did not listen; but they did what was evil in my eyes and chose that in which I did not delight. Hear the word of the Lord, you who tremble at his word.[12]

Jeremiah used the Mosaic law of adultery to condemn both Israel and Judah for their idolatry: "You have played the whore with many lovers; and would you return to me? declares the LORD. . . . By the waysides you have sat awaiting lovers like an Arab in the wilderness."[13]

> The LORD said to me in the days of King Josiah: "Have you seen what she did, the faithless one, Israel, how she went up on every high hill and under every green tree, and there played the whore? And I thought, After she has done all this she will return to me, but she did not return, and her treacherous sister Judah saw it. She saw that for all the adulteries of that faithless one, Israel, I had sent her away with a decree of divorce. Yet her treacherous sister Judah did not fear, but she too went and

11. Hos 10:1–2.
12. Isa 66:3–5.
13. Jer 3:1–2.

> played the whore. Because she took her whoredom lightly, she polluted the land, committing adultery with stone and tree."[14]

This allusion to whoredom was nothing new in either prophetic or wisdom literature. Long before Jeremiah prophesied, Ps 106 employed the same theme. "Thus they became unclean by their acts, and played the whore in their deeds."[15] The idea of whoredom as an appropriate analogy for the enormity of Israel's deviation from the Word of God is prominent in Hosea. In fact, God Himself set the circumstances. "When the Lord first spoke through Hosea, the Lord said to Hosea, 'Go, take to yourself a wife of whoredom and have children of whoredom, for the land commits great whoredom by forsaking the Lord.'"[16] This became a living, active metaphor for Israel's unfaithfulness to God.

While Nineveh's repentance disappointed Jonah,[17] it was a much different city by the time Nahum was sent there. The Assyrian Empire had grown, and Nineveh had become the capital of the empire. Nahum's sole mission was to condemn the city and its inhabitants, warning them of eternal damnation. Nineveh fell not because it had gained extraordinary status or power; Nineveh was judged and punished because of the enormity of its sin. "Woe to the bloody city, all full of lies and plunder—no end to the prey."[18] The city was the center of Assyrian cults of idolatry and exported that idolatry to other nations. Its sin was compounded by its role in corrupting all around it. "And all for the countless whorings of the prostitute, graceful and of deadly charms, who betrays nations with her whorings, and peoples with her charms."[19] Nineveh was the antithesis of the moral structure of Creation.

Those resident in Judah were no less practiced in the art of idol worship than their relations in the northern kingdom. In prophesying to Judah, Habakkuk complained, "What profit is an idol when its maker has shaped it, a metal image, a teacher of lies? For its maker thrusts in his own creation when he makes a speechless idol! Woe to him who says to a wooden thing, Awake; to a silent stone, Arise! Can this teach?"[20]

14. Jer 3:6–9.
15. Ps 106:39.
16. Hos 1:2.
17. Jonah 4.
18. Nah 3:1.
19. Nah 3:4.
20. Hab 2:18–19.

Zephaniah, who was a contemporary of Habakkuk's in Judah, also chastised them for their idolatrous ways. "Woe to her who is rebellious and defiled, the oppressing city."[21] "Her prophets are fickle, treacherous men; her priests profane what is holy; they do violence to the law."[22]

Zechariah, in one of his visions, speaks to a fountain in the house of David, which will serve to purify and cleanse the people. Zechariah places idolatry at the center of their sinful state. "This is the sin that 'pierced' the Lord in Zech. 12:10, metaphorically in its original context and physically in the person of Jesus."[23] Once the people have been purified and cleansed, the Lord "will cut off the names of the idols from the land, so that they shall be remembered no more."[24]

## *FALSE PROPHETS AND TEACHERS*

False prophets and teachers were another frequent topic of Isaiah's prophesies. Inasmuch as the Law was the only path to salvation for Jews, the Law must be accurately repeated and disseminated. Both those speaking and those hearing the word must be scrupulous and diligent in their responsibilities. The speaker for the initial accuracy, and the hearer, so that it can be repeated to the generations that follow.

Isaiah placed the blame for Judah's circumstances squarely at the feet of a willful and disobedient leadership who permitted, by their laxity, the appropriation of sanctified speech. This had, in turn, led to the demise of the nation: "The prophet who teaches lies, . . . those who guide this people have been leading them astray, and those who are guided by them are swallowed up . . . everyone is godless and an evildoer, and every mouth speaks folly."[25] In speaking directly to the leadership and the people of Judah, Isaiah reconfirmed the power of speech in very plain terms. "And he shall strike the earth with the rod of his mouth, and with the breath of his lips he shall kill the wicked."[26] "The rod of his lips" is the truth of His holy word. Isaiah's narrative to his contemporaries constantly warns of resorting to cavalier and distorted speech, whether it be through the profanity of appropriating the language of unbelievers for worship

21. Zeph 3:1.
22. Zeph 3:4.
23. Zech 12:10, note.
24. Zech 13:2.
25. Isa 9:13–17.
26. Isa 11:4.

or twisting the truth through false prophets and false witnesses. Isaiah's Jewish audience is described as rebellious people and lying children, unwilling to hear the instructions of the Lord. They are not interested in the hard truths of God's Word, preferring instead that their religious leaders dilute the message of obedience and "speak to us of smooth things, prophesy illusions." The residents of Judah consciously chose to embrace the norms and behaviors of their secular surroundings, wishing to "leave the way, turn aside from the path, let us hear no more about the Holy One of Israel."[27]

The language of the Lord had been usurped by human intentions and self-serving purposes, and the consequences would be dire. "And the Lord said, 'Because this people draw near with their mouth and honor me with their lips, while their hearts are far from me, and their fear of me is a commandment taught by men."[28] This is a passage that Jesus quotes in Matt 15:8–9. The Lord will not permit the narrative of creation and salvation to be turned on its head. All the tools of speech and language will be employed to crush the rebellious: "Behold, the name of the Lord comes from afar, burning with his anger, and in thick rising smoke; his lips are full of fury, and his tongue is like a devouring fire; his breath is like an overflowing stream that reaches up to the neck; to sift the nations with the sieve of destruction, and to place on the jaws of the people a bridle that leads astray."[29]

A hundred and twenty years after Isaiah, little had changed in this regard, and Jeremiah returned to the same theme. Before Jeremiah relayed the judgment of God to the nations, he emphasized the point that none of this would have occurred if not for the distortion and perversion of the message by false teachers and false prophets. They denied God's essential truths.

> Thus says the Lord of hosts: "Do not listen to the words of the prophets who prophesy to you, filling you with vain hopes. They speak visions of their own minds, not from the mouth of the Lord. They say continually to those who despise the word of the Lord, 'It shall be well with you;' and to everyone who stubbornly follows his own hearing, they say, 'No disaster shall come upon you.'"[30]

27. Isa 30:8–14.
28. Isa 29:13.
29. Isa 30:27–28.
30. Jer 23:16–17.

This is a very important point, since the purpose of Jeremiah's prophecies was to prepare the people for judgment, and denying the judgment of God or His power and authority to judge is itself blasphemous. In fact, God commanded His people to submit to the rule of the Babylonians, so that through Nebuchadnezzar, God could punish Judah. Only through this intervention could Judah be put back in the right spot.

> So do not listen to your prophets, your diviners, your dreamers, your fortune-tellers, or your sorcerers, who are saying to you, "You shall not serve the King of Babylon." For it is a lie they are prophesying to you, with the result that you will be removed far from your land, and I will drive you out, and you will perish. But any nation that will bring its neck under the yoke of the King of Babylon and serve him, I will leave on its own land, to work it and dwell there, declares the Lord.[31]

In the end, however, Babylon itself would be judged. While Babylon was an instrument through which Israel would be judged, the point of the Babylonian exile was the redemption of the Jews, not the elevation of Babylon. "Babylon is taken, Bel is put to shame, Merodach is dismayed. Her images are put to shame, her idols are dismayed."[32] But lest the people of Israel view this as vindication for their subjugation, Jeremiah reminds them of the source of their pain: "My people have been lost sheep. Their shepherds have led them astray."[33]

This was not simply a general observation or recommendation. Hananiah, a false prophet, died for telling the Jewish people in Babylon that they would be free within two years. Not only did God punish Hananiah but anyone who listened to Hananiah was punished more harshly than others during their exile.[34] The same held for another false prophet Shemaiah, who presented himself as one of God's anointed messengers. Because of his deceit, Shemaiah and his descendants were punished, for "he has spoken rebellion against the Lord."[35]

Ezekiel also acknowledged the damage caused by false prophets and went to great lengths condemning them:

31. Jer 27:9–11.

32. Jer 50:2.

33. Jer 50:6.

34. The story of Hananiah is found in Jer 28.

35. Jer 29:32.

> Thus says the Lord God, Woe to the foolish prophets who follow their own spirit, and have seen nothing! . . . They have seen false visions and lying divinations. They say, "Declares the Lord," when the Lord has not sent them, and yet they expect him to fulfill their word. Have you not seen a false vision and uttered a lying divination, whenever you have said, "Declares the Lord," although I have not spoken? Therefore thus says the Lord God: "Because you have uttered falsehood and seen lying visions, therefore behold, I am against you, declares the Lord God. My hand will be against the prophets who see false visions and who give lying divinations."[36]

The consequence of false prophecies is the destruction of faith. As the Lord put it to Ezekiel, these false prophecies are "putting to death souls who should not die and keeping alive souls who should not live, by your lying to my people."[37] Lying prophecies and false visions distort God's words, hijacking speech and language for evil purposes. Such behavior's impact on faith is far reaching. True faith is supposed to be a bulwark, a safe haven in the face of evil. But when the language and speech of faith is distorted, it vitiates faith. The truth is co-opted under a veneer of legitimacy. It is an insidious, subtle assault on values that can go unnoticed until it is too late. The Lord knew the dangers of lies and falsehoods and instructed Ezekiel to confront the people with these realities:

> Because you [false prophets] have disheartened the righteous falsely, although I have not grieved him, and you have encouraged the wicked, that he should not turn from his evil ways to save his life, therefore you shall no more see false visions nor practice divination. I will deliver my people out of your hand.[38]

Idolatrous elders and temple leaders, the next target of Ezekiel's wrath, fared no better in the hands of an outraged God. Destroying the core of the Jewish faith through idolatry is equally anathema to the Lord as the perversion of language through the lies of false prophets. "Son of man, these men have taken their idols into their hearts, and set the stumbling block of their iniquity before their faces."[39] The men referred to by Ezekiel in this passage were elders who had so completely absorbed the language of false prophets and idol worship that they were seeking the

36. Ezek 13:3, 6–9.

37. Ezek 13:19.

38. Ezek 13:22–23.

39. Ezek 4:3.

Lord's guidance while openly embracing idols. This reflects the second vision of Ezekiel, in which he sees idols being worshiped in the temple itself. In this vision God instructed Ezekiel to enter the temple "and see the vile abominations that they are committing here." Once in the court, he saw the elders of Judah worshiping idols that had been engraved on the walls of the court of the temple. Even in the inner court, the elders were worshiping the sun, with their backs to the temple. At that point, the Lord ordered the execution of the idolatrous elders,[40] as they are "estranged from me through their idols."[41]

Zephaniah recognized the source of the problem when he declared judgment on Jerusalem and the nations. The very people who should have been leading those under the Law were instead violating it. "Her prophets are fickle, treacherous men; her priests profane what is holy; they do violence to the law."[42] Another generation later, Zechariah prophesied that God would eliminate those who perverted His message:

> And also I will remove from the land the prophets and the spirit of uncleanness. And if anyone again prophesies, his father and mother who bore him will say to him, "You shall not live, for you speak lies in the name of the Lord." And his father and mother who bore him shall pierce him through when he prophesies.[43]

Although Micah prophesied two hundred years earlier than Zechariah, his sarcastic observations on idolatry and false teaching offer a perfect summary to this portion of the conversation. "If a man should go about and utter wind and lies, saying, 'I will preach to you of wine and strong drink,' he would be the preacher for this people!"[44] He further condemned the civil and religious leadership of Judah for their distortion of justice and the hypocrisy of their speech: "Its heads give judgment for a bribe, its priests teach for a price; its prophets practice divination for money; yet they lean on the Lord and say, 'Is not the Lord in the midst of us? No disaster shall come upon us.'"[45]

40. Ezek 8–9.
41. Ezek 14:5.
42. Zeph 3:4.
43. Zech 13:3.
44. Mic 2:11.
45. Mic 3:11

# Chapter 11

# Prophetic Voices: Social Justice, Syncretism and Language

*"You shall not bear false witness against your neighbor."*

Idolatry, false prophets, and false teaching are logical threats to the Creation narrative. They were topics that the Classical Prophets would logically address, as did the patriarchs, judges, kings, and prophets that preceded them. But what role do issues such as social justice and cultural syncretism play in better understanding the distinctions between Creation and other origin myths, and how do these two themes complement other themes that have been discussed?

Social justice in the scriptural context is more nuanced than the idea of social justice in a modern context. As noted earlier, contemporary issues of social justice are derived from grievances, either immediate or historical. Cultural perspectives evolve from generation to generation, and as they change, matters of social justice are revisited. Many of these issues are valid and deserve to be dealt with through social action, government regulation, or legislation. There is a legitimate human interest in eliminating behaviors that are harmful in both their individual and collective capacities.

However, the matter of social justice in the larger Creation narrative is an expression of God's purpose in Creation and His covenantal relationships with mankind. When He created man in His own image, He created humanity according to His moral and ethical nature, for the purposes of governing creation as His stewards. God's intention was that the earth and all its institutions would fully and faithfully reflect His value proposition. Chaos was to be replaced by a well-ordered universe. The period when the Classical Prophets were active was a time of great turmoil and confusion, circumstances quite contrary to Creation intentions. For Creation purposes to be realized, and more immediately, the success of Israel secured, God's order needed to be restored based on His values and the covenants He made with His people. This is what was spoken through the prophets, and these standards have remained unchanged from the beginning. While contemporary issues of social justice are generally not at odds with God's desire for an ordered universe, some may be, and changing cultural standards cannot be relied on to accurately or consistently reflect unshakable Creation standards. Embracing a cultural sense of social justice, to the exclusion of the Creation context, erodes the godly standards necessary for properly ordering the universe.

The question of cultural syncretism, accommodating the habits and practices of competing cultures, can radically change the ethos of one's own culture. For a theocracy such as Israel, that was not an inconsequential concern. But an often-overlooked result of cultural accommodation involves the integrity of a society's language and speech. They are critical to the survival of any given culture. There are numerous instances of societies resisting the intrusion of foreign language in their vocabulary, even to the point of legal or legislative repercussions. Language and speech support the core of a culture's values and norms. Every word, every sentence structure, and every vocal modulation has a semiotic or symbolic significance. They are learned at birth and inculcated through the rituals of growth and development. As soon as accommodations are made to incorporate other words and phrases, modify one's language patterns, or adopt ritual behaviors, these value propositions are diminished, diluted, or even erased. Essentially, the original culture ceases to exist. Hence, from Genesis on, the risks of cultural syncretism are stressed time and again. This is clearly evident in the Classical Prophets.

## *SOCIAL JUSTICE*

It is important to recognize that there was neither the immense bureaucracy nor codified systems of legal precedence for administering justice in the era of the prophets as there are today. There were social pressures on individuals to adhere to the Law, and there was a measure of accountability for failing to strictly follow the Law and its Levitical strictures. Similar circumstances are evident in many tight-knit, often isolated communities today. In ancient Israel, a designated class was identified as both priests and judges. Kings were expected to be obedient to the same set of laws as their subjects, and they were judged accordingly. They were to exemplify God's moral and ethical structure as His servant leaders.

As noted earlier, this was a different pattern from that of their pagan neighbors. As Israeli kingdoms disintegrated and eventually disappeared, the legal structure of compliance eventually fell away, and social pressure was not nearly as effective in the midst of hostile neighbors. It fell to the prophets to remind both individuals and their community leaders, such as remained, that they were called to order their behaviors according to God's will. The prophets could not administer justice, but they were quite clear in their identification and condemnation of injustice, the failure to order society properly, and the outcomes that could be expected from disobedience. And of course, if there remained a remnant of leadership, such as priests or elders, they were more strictly called to account.

There is obviously a close relationship between idolatry and social injustice. It stands to reason that anyone who renounced idols and worshiped according to the Law would be very sensitive to the proper ordering of a just and fair society. Those worshiping idols would be less so. As a result, there is not always a clear demarcation between repudiating idols and calling out injustice. The two often went hand in hand. Nonetheless, there are some very clear expressions of prophetic concerns for correctly ordering a just society that are distinct from the question of idolatry.

This was a particular concern to Amos, who confronted the unethical behavior of the rulers of the northern kingdom. They had overburdened the poor for the benefit of the wealthy and privileged, which turned God's value proposition on its head. His declaration sets the proper tone:

> Hear this, you who trample on the needy and bring the poor of the land to an end, saying, "When will the new moon be over, that we may sell grain? And the Sabbath, that we may offer wheat for sale, that we may make the ephah small and the shekel great and deal deceitfully with false balances, that we may buy the poor for silver and the needy for a pair of sandals and sell the chaff of the wheat?"[1]

1. Amos 8:4–6.

This passage has nothing to do with idols. It has everything to do with fair relationships within the community.

Amos prophesied during the early period after the dissolution of the united kingdom of Israel, while there was still a robust, albeit corrupted, political structure in place. Addressing an audience that included many non-Jews who had migrated to, or were incorporated into, the community through conquest, Amos's condemnation was not limited to injustice against Jews alone but extended to all those living under the aegis of the Israeli kings. As the Creator of the universe, God's ethical norms were universal, and everyone was subject to them. Among the evidence of a right relationship with the Lord was the fair treatment of others, including non-Jews.

But by embracing the secular ethos around him, Jeroboam's leadership became an afront to a jealous God. Amos reminded those who would listen that even when religious practices were scrupulously followed, that alone was not sufficient to justify the unjust treatment of others. Simply going through the motions did not constitute genuine worship, and having mechanically satisfied the language of liturgy did not constitute true worship. Slander, gossip, and false witness could not coexist with genuine adoration and praise for the Lord. Amos reminded the Jews that as covenanted people, they were to be held to the higher standards of a sanctified language and were not exempt from God's judgments just because they went to temple and followed the script.

This issue remained significant even into Jesus' ministry. He was echoing Amos's frustrations when He called His disciples' attention to a wealthy Pharisee in the temple, praying in a loud voice, thanking God that he was not like the tax collector praying on another part of the temple grounds. Meanwhile, the tax collector was so overwhelmed by the enormity of his own sin, he could hardly raise his head to pray.[2] Likewise, with the widow's mite, Jesus asked who was really serving God, the rich man who very conspicuously made his offering, or the poor widow who quietly gave of all she had.[3] This is precisely what Amos confronted when he cried out, "Hear this word that the Lord has spoken against you, O people of Israel, against the whole family that I brought up out of the land of Egypt."[4] Amos was compelled to identify and condemn the false piety and the perversion of justice brought on by Jeroboam and his idolatrous,

2. Luke 18:10–14.

3. Luke 21:1–4.

4. Amos 3:1.

corrupting behavior. In a very poetic turn of phrase, Amos describes this as a famine of hearing, a clear distortion of sanctified speech brought on by the assumption of foreign standards.[5]

Micah echoed many of the same arguments in the southern kingdom that Amos leveled against the northern kingdom. While there was relative calm in Judah during this early period, the people chose to turn from the Lord, and the powerful enriched themselves at the expense of the poor:

> Woe to those who devise wickedness and work evil on their beds! When the morning dawns, they perform it, because it is in the power of their hand. They covet fields and seize them, and houses, and take them away; They oppress a man and his house, a man and his inheritance. . . . The women of my people you drive out from their delightful houses; From their young children you take away my splendor forever.[6]

Social injustice was a perversion of Creation. As the phrase "you take away my splendor forever" indicates, this was an assumption of power reserved for God alone. The leadership of Judah, who "detest justice and make crooked all that is straight,"[7] had completely corrupted the Creation narrative.

Zephaniah was a prophet to the southern kingdom of Judah as well. He shared others' concerns about the integrity of priests and elders, and their role in either maintaining justice or repudiating it. After excoriating sinful behaviors, he reflected upon the characteristics of those who would be qualified to serve as instruments of God's redemption. "They will seek refuge in the name of the Lord, those who are left in Israel [Judah]; they shall do no injustice and speak no lies, nor shall there be found in their mouth a deceitful tongue."[8] In other words, upholding God's value proposition and ordering society in a way that mirrored His moral and ethical standards were as important for salvation as rejecting idols and denying false prophets.

As Jeremiah was grieving for his people, he described the nature of their sin and the root of their disobedience:

5. Amos 8:11–12.
6. Mic 2:1–2, 9.
7. Mic 3:9.
8. Zeph 3:12.

> They bend their tongues like a bow; falsehood and not truth has grown strong in the land; for they proceed from evil to evil, and they do not know me, declares the Lord. Let everyone beware of his neighbor, and put no trust in any brother, for every brother is a deceiver, and every neighbor goes about as a slanderer. Everyone deceives his neighbor, and no one speaks the truth; they have taught their tongues to speak lies; they weary themselves committing iniquity. Heaping oppression upon oppression, and deceit upon deceit, they refuse to know me, declares the Lord.[9]

Zephaniah went on to add, "Her officials within her are roaring lions; her judges are evening wolves that leave nothing till the morning."[10]

The burden and blessing of being made in the image of God is to understand, embrace, and implement His moral and ethical standards as stewards of Creation. Successfully satisfying the various covenantal agreements between God and mankind were predicated on fair and equitable treatment of one another. Being fruitful and multiplying, obeying the Law handed down through Moses, populating the earth after the fall from grace, serving as the ancestral source of a great people and kings, and finally, establishing the lineage that would produce a Messiah all presumed that order would be maintained as originally intended at the Creation. Pursuing justice was, and remains, no small responsibility.

## *SYNCRETISM AND LANGUAGE*

Cultural syncretism was identified as early as Joseph's tenure in Egypt as a destabilizing influence on the Israeli tribes. They had to remain apart if they were not to be subsumed by the much larger and stronger cultures around them. And yet to function in any meaningful way, there had to be a path available for some measure of coexistence. They lived and worked in Egypt for generations, and during the exodus, had occasion to cross paths with other nomadic groups. Patterns of trade, diplomacy, and warfare developed between Israel and neighboring communities on the journey towards Canaan and their sojourn on its border. Clearly, during the conquest of Canaan, it was necessary to settle issues of territory, prisoners, and possessions. All this required some way to communicate and some adjustments to their language. Unfortunately, familiarity on a commercial or political basis often led to intermarriage, which could only

9. Jer 9:3–6.
10. Zeph 3:3.

succeed with one party accommodating the habits and patterns of their partner. In the worst case, there was the wholesale adoption of an entire set of cultural norms. In either event, matters of faith were generally corrupted. Deuteronomic law stated quite clearly, "You shall not intermarry with them, giving your daughters to their sons or taking their daughters for your sons, for they would turn away your sons from following me, to serve other gods."[11]

The issue of syncretism is also closely connected with the integrity of language and speech, since language and speech were the vehicles for passing on the sacred mysteries and obligations of Creation and the Law. In that respect, assimilating the patterns and habits of another culture required the modification of the language of patterns and habits, thereby undermining the ability to sustain and protect the narrative. The prophets knew and understood this, so as they defended the integrity of the narrative and exhorted those who were disobedient, they were also protecting sacred language and speech. The two went hand in hand with holding fast to Jewish heritage, habits, and practices.

Among the concerns Micah addressed was the ritual nature of worship in Judah. Not only did it fail to reflect the covenantal obedience required by God, but merely following ritual without any substance led to injustice, a lack of mercy, and a loss of faith.[12] Under Jotham, Ahaz, and Hezekiah, Judah had developed an upper class, which, in turn, led to an increasingly unjust society. Wealth and power also required Judah to maneuver successfully on a larger regional scale. The compromises and negotiations with neighboring kingdoms resulted in a dilution of Jewish traditions and faith patterns. Specifically, the powerful language and speech of worship lost their vitality. In a bit of historical irony, as the contest for territorial hegemony played out in the region, one small, insignificant, overlooked village under the rule of Assyria, too insignificant to bother negotiating over, would bring forth from a remnant of the faithful the Messiah.[13] The place was home to Naomi, Ruth, and Boaz. It produced the Davidic line and was the birthplace of Jesus. It was called Bethlehem.

Isaiah, who was a contemporary of Micah's, made it very clear the source of Judah's troubles. "For Jerusalem has stumbled, and Judah has fallen, because their speech and their deeds are against the Lord, defying

11. Deut 7:3–4.

12. Mic 6:8.

13. Mic 5:2.

his glorious presence."[14] Later, he continued in the same vein: "For they have rejected the law of the Lord of Hosts, and have despised the word of the Holy One of Israel. Therefore, the anger of the Lord was kindled against this people."[15] A willful and disobedient leadership had permitted, by their laxity, the appropriation of sanctified speech. This, in turn, led to the demise of the nation: "The prophet who teaches lies, . . . those who guide this people have been leading them astray, and those who are guided by them are swallowed up . . . everyone is godless and an evildoer, and every mouth speaks folly."[16]

As noted earlier, in speaking directly to the leadership and the people of Judah, Isaiah reconfirmed the power of speech in very plain terms. "And he shall strike the earth with the rod of his mouth, and with the breath of his lips he shall kill the wicked."[17] "The rod of his mouth" is the truth of His holy word. Isaiah's narrative to his contemporaries constantly warned of resorting to cavalier and distorted speech, whether it be through the profanity of appropriating the language of unbelievers for worship or twisting the truth through false prophets and false witnesses. The residents of Judah consciously chose to embrace the norms and behaviors of their secular world, wishing to "leave the way, turn aside from the path, let us hear no more about the Holy One of Israel."[18] Furthermore, they perverted sacred covenant language by undermining the authority of God and bearing false witness to crush the oppressed and reinforce the position of the wealthy. "For the ruthless shall come to nothing and the scoffer cease, and all who watch to do evil shall be cut off, who by word make a man out to be an offender, and lay a snare for him who reproves in the gate, and with an empty plea turn aside him who is in the right."[19]

As his focus shifted to the generation of exiles in Babylon who chose not to follow the Lord, Isaiah made it clear that the Lord still controlled the destiny of His people, even if He now must speak through the voice of the conquerors. The fact that both Israel and Judah had fallen victim to foreign invaders did not mean that God had abandoned His people or broken His covenant vows. But if the people of Judah refused to listen to

14. Isa 3:8.

15. Isa 5:24–25.

16. Isa. 9:13–17.

17. Isa 11:4.

18. Isa 30:8–14.

19. Isa 29:20–21.

the language the Lord spoke, then He would demonstrate His command over history by means of other languages. "For by people of strange lips and with a foreign tongue the Lord will speak to this people."[20] Some will repent, chastened by their exile experience. Others will choose to continue following the words of false prophets and will not be saved. Harkening back to the northern tribes, they clearly chose the latter, and they were completely absorbed into the Assyrian empire. Samaritans and Jews became a separate people. The obedient remnant of Judah would eventually rejoice at the time of their release from exile and would remember their circumstances in a way vaguely reminiscent of the punishment God meted out to His recalcitrant followers at Babel: "You will see no more the insolent people, the people of an obscure speech that you cannot comprehend, stammering in a tongue that you cannot understand."[21]

Interestingly, these two passages pair rather nicely with Paul when he speaks to the Corinthians about prophesying and speaking in tongues. "There are doubtless many different languages in the world, and none is without meaning, but if I do not know the meaning of the language, I will be a foreigner to the speaker and the speaker a foreigner to me."[22] Paul was reminding the Corinthians that words have meaning and purpose, and if one speaks in tongues that are unintelligible to the hearer, they are not speaking to the body, but to themselves. Isaiah invited the listener to become one with the Creator and embrace the redeeming language of God. This can only occur if one is wholly obedient to the Word of God, spoken through the prophets. Language is a holy instrument, capable of unifying and edifying or, as in the case of false teachers and prophets, of causing destruction and division.

God's covenants had been declared for all mankind, not just reserved for the descendants of Abraham, and they are to continue until the end of time. The covenantal language of God will be sustained through history. "My spirit is upon you, and my words that I have put in your mouth, shall not depart out of your mouth, or out of the mouth of your offspring, or out of the mouth of your children's offspring . . . from this time forth and forevermore."[23] "The nations shall see your righteousness, and all the kings your glory, and you shall be called by a new name that the mouth

20. Isa 28:11.

21. Isa 33:19.

22. 1 Cor 14:10–11.

23. Isa 59:21.

of the Lord will give."[24] God alone has the power to name and define the character and destiny of His people. The new name will be reserved for all those who choose to be obedient.

Nahum, Zephaniah, and Habakkuk were all active at about the same time, and Zephaniah and Habakkuk were contemporaries. This was a period of great political uncertainty in the region. The northern kingdom of Israel had collapsed with the fall of Samaria, its capital, in 722 BCE. The Assyrian Empire had grown, but its authority was being challenged by Babylon. Judah was a vassal state to the Assyrian Empire, notwithstanding the Babylonian threat to Assyria. Until the return of the exiles in the fifth century BCE, and the last of the prophets in Malachi, the constant churning of great power contests in the region defined the unstable and frightening atmosphere within which the prophets following Isaiah operated.

When Nahum began his prophesying, Nineveh had replaced Samaria as the capital of the Assyrian Empire. Nahum's mission was to denounce the behavior of the people and their leaders and warn them of eternal damnation if they did not change their ways. Nahum predicted that Nineveh would fall, despite its extraordinary status and power, because of the enormity of its sin. "Woe to the bloody city, all full of lies and plunder—no end to the prey."[25] The city was the center of Assyrian idolatry and exported that idolatry to other nations. Its sin was compounded by its role in the syncretic corruption of all around it. "And all for the countless whorings of the prostitute, graceful and of deadly charms, who betrays nations with her whorings, and peoples with her charms."[26] Nineveh was the antithesis of the moral structure of Creation, and its lies had corrupted the language of those Jews who remained in the region. Its "whorings" represented the wholesale adoption of Assyrian cultural patterns and habits, the same issue and representation identified by Jeremiah.

A decade or so later, Habakkuk offered a similar opinion of those in the southern kingdom living under the authority of the Assyrian Empire. "So the law is paralyzed, and justice never goes forth. For the wicked surround the righteous; so justice goes forth perverted."[27] It is not simply a matter of unjust behavior, it is the application of a distorted system of

24. Isa 62:2.

25. Nah 3:1.

26. Nah 3:4.

27. Hab 1:4.

justice that turned the order of Creation into chaos. To administer a foreign justice system through the language and rituals of faith completely repudiated God's value structure. It involved false oaths, deceitful speech that betrayed confidences and faith, false prophets and teachers, and the language of cultural accommodation. The law to which Habakkuk referred was the Law given by Moses and the promises of covenantal relationships, not the misbehavior of a conquering people. The conquerors are not expected to know or obey God's laws, but faithful leaders of Judah were and did not need to bend over backwards to embrace the language of disobedience. God would take care of the sinful in His own way and time, but that did not obviate the need for the faithful to remain faithful and wait on Him.

Zephaniah, Habakkuk's contemporary, targeted the matter of cultural accommodation specifically. "I will punish the officials and the king's sons and all who array themselves in foreign attire."[28] Once again, this is not simply a matter of adopting social practices and habits of those inimical to God's will, but the deleterious impact such behavior has on faith when the Creation system is allowed to be eroded by outside influences. Eventually God's people will be redeemed, and speech is one of the key ingredients in the redemptive process. The relationship between speech and social acclimation is made quite clear. "For at that time [the redemption of Judah and Jerusalem] I will change the speech of the peoples to a pure speech, that all of them may call upon the name of the Lord and serve him with one accord."[29]

Jeremiah, following a couple of decades later, identified cultural syncretism as the heart of the matter. In passages cited in the last chapter, the sins of idolatry that Jeremiah called out were also symptomatic of cultural accommodations: "You rebelled against the Lord your God and scattered your favors among foreigners under every green tree."[30] Under the pressure of a disintegrating Assyrian presence and the ascendance of Babylonian and Egyptian Empires, the Jewish people had been indiscriminate in their associations with other cultures, denigrating the favors and grace of God by polluting His message with local practices and behaviors. Judgment was swift and unequivocal. "I am making my words in your mouth a fire, and this people wood, and the fire shall consume

28. Zeph 1:8.

29. Zeph 3:9.

30. Jer 3:13.

them."[31] Later, God added that He would bring a nation to conquer Judah, "a nation whose language you do not know, nor can you understand what they say."[32] Just as Isaiah harkened back to Babel, so did Jeremiah. Language and speech became tools of confusion and discord, part and parcel of the punishment for rejecting the divinity of the Lord's holy words. "And you shall say to them, 'This is the nation that did not obey the voice of the Lord their God, and did not accept discipline; truth has perished; it is cut off from their lips.'"[33]

The Jewish community had become so enmeshed in local social and cultural practices that they could not even understand why God would judge so harshly. "Who is the man so wise that he cannot understand this? To whom has the mouth of the Lord spoken, that he may declare it? Why is the land ruined and laid waste like a wilderness, so no one passes through? . . . Because they have forsaken my law" and "have stubbornly followed their own hearts and gone after the Baals."[34]

Jeremiah continued with a long passage dealing with the differences between idols and the living God. The starting point for this descent into apostasy is stated clearly at the outset: "Learn not the way of the nations, nor be dismayed at the signs of the heavens because the nations are dismayed at them."[35] In other words, other nations do not get it. They do not understand the ways of the Lord (signs of the heavens), so they are disturbed and upset by them. The Lord is telling the people through Jeremiah that the beginning of disobedience and disbelief is to accept the foundational fears and reactions of other cultures and faiths, and to adopt their standards for assessing right from wrong. The images the Jews are embracing are false: "There is no breath in them. They are worthless, a work of delusion."[36]

Looking at Daniel, again from our narrow perspective, his faithfulness serves as a model of how to avoid cultural accommodations. While the rejection of idols is clearly part of his larger message, the apocalyptic imagery of his prophesy is more instructive in the abstract than practical in its specific guidance. But Daniel, along with Shadrach, Meshach, and Abednego, offer a very dynamic and powerful example of rejecting

31. Jer 5:14.
32. Jer 5:15.
33. Jer 7:28.
34. Jer 9:12–13.
35. Jer 10:2.
36. Jer 10:14–15.

the whole notion of cultural syncretism. They would not eat of the king's table or bow down to his gods. This was the very essence of their prophetic message. Acculturation brings with it a surrender of linguistic sovereignty and the erosion of holy speech. Only through the active rejection of foreign standards could God work through the ephemeral nature of human understanding. The four of them not only guarded their heritage, they also very visibly celebrated it.

The Spirit called upon Ezekiel to confront "men who devise iniquity and who give wicked counsel in this city."[37] This reference is to civic rather than priestly leadership, but their words and deeds brought great misfortune on the people, and judgment was warranted. Here, Ezekiel testifies to the complicity of civic leadership in furthering the erosion of uniquely Jewish virtues and beliefs. Such complicity created a climate of disobedience and rebellion, which contributed to the moral decline of faith. The connection is clearly identified. "For you have not walked in my statutes, nor obeyed my rules, but have acted according to the rules of the nations that are around you."[38]

The sins of those idolatrous elders and temple leaders of Ezekiel's second vision[39] went beyond the matter of apostate elders worshiping idols. It was a case of the very leaders of the community appropriating the temple itself, the house of God, for practices that mimicked the patterns of pagan worship. It exposed the dangers of contaminating cultures and permitting local practices and beliefs to infiltrate and infest the core values of the Jewish community. It was not the result of being forced by conquerors or tyrants to accept prevailing social practices but the willing adoption by the leadership of the community of the language of idolatry. Jewish leadership during Jesus' ministry was more concerned with maintaining relationships with the Romans, even though it meant sacrificing some of their liturgical and theological integrity, than protecting the purity of the Law.

"Although the exilic setting is not required to explain the idolatry of these elders, the new cultural setting and dislocation could promote unthinking syncretism."[40] This is precisely the risk identified as far back as Moses and Joshua. It is more than merely acceding to the laws of those communities within which the Jews found themselves. Many of these

37. Ezek 11:2.

38. Ezek 11:12.

39. Ezek 8–9.

40. ESV, 1517; Ezek 14:1–11, note.

foreign standards and morés, such as those concerning murder, theft, and civil disobedience, were perfectly compatible with the well-ordered society the Jews themselves sought. But deeply inculcating beliefs that are inimical to the soul of the community, and embracing the language required to communicate these value systems insures total annihilation.

> Therefore thus says the Lord God: Like the wood of the vine among the trees of the forest, which I have given to the fire for fuel, so have I given up the inhabitants of Jerusalem. And I will set my face against them. . . . And I will make the land desolate, because they have acted faithlessly, declares the Lord.[41]

The situation had deteriorated to the point that even God's name was at risk. Israel was willing to exchange the holiness of His name for advantageous working relationships with other nations.

> So I poured out my wrath upon them for the blood they had shed in the land, for the idols with which they had defiled it. . . . But when they came to the nations, wherever they came, they profaned my holy name. . . . But I had concern for my holy name, which the house of Israel had profaned among the nations to which they came.[42]

This passage in Ezekiel underscores what was actually at risk. The profanity of the house of Israel, which was condemned so thoroughly by the Lord, occurred "among the nations to which they came." The nature of that sin that God found so abominable was the appropriation of faith language, which was to reflect the unique, chosen status of the Jews, for purposes of accommodating foreign cultures and practices. The remnants of Israel, as a captive and exiled community, were in no position to impact their captors. They could not overthrow the authorities, wage destructive war, or destroy the physical representations of power. But they felt they could fit in and avoid the consequences of conquest by adapting their faith language to local custom. This, simply put, denied the holiness of God. His powerful words, the source of Creation, were put to use placating their conquerors.

These conversations did not end with the period of the Classical Prophets. Paul's letter to the Colossians, as an example, touches upon every concern expressed by the prophets. He speaks to a people "who once were alienated and hostile in mind," praying that they remain "stable and

41. Ezek 15:6–8.

42. Ezek 36:18, 20–21.

steadfast, not shifting from the hope of the gospel that you heard." Paul proclaims his "stewardship from God" to make known "the mystery hidden for ages and generations but now revealed."[43] "See to it that no one takes you captive by philosophy and empty deceit, according to human tradition,"[44] which "have indeed an appearance of wisdom in promoting self-made religion."[45] The pattern by which Christ orders His relationship with the church, His bride, is to be the pattern for ordering earthly relationships. All the themes of the prophets, idolatry, false teaching, ordering Creation, and protecting the narrative are summed up in this one short letter from Paul. They were vital reminders of Creation, and they remain vital to this day.

43. Col 1:21, 23, 25–26.

44. Col 2:8.

45. Col 2:23.

# Chapter 12

# The End of an Era

*"The exiles of this host of the people of Israel shall possess the land."*

When Jerusalem fell in 586 BCE, the treasures of the city were removed to Babylon along with many of its more accomplished citizens. What remained was an inconsequential outpost with no significant infrastructure. The remaining residents of the once powerful kingdom were itinerants, shepherds, and erstwhile residents of the city eking out a living. There were few, if any, individuals of consequence, save for the possibility of a successful herder or trader. Any remaining presumptions about the viability of an independent kingdom had been dashed.

The focus of the prophets up to this point had been dealing with a hollow facsimile of a great kingdom, as corrupted as it may have been, with at least the trappings of a religious and political structure. The prophets were addressing a society with some semblance of structure but no substance, appealing for repentance and a return to obedience. The message, both implicit and explicit, included the promise that repentance would bring a restoration of the relationship between God and His people. Warnings were abundant and predictions were dire, but there was a clear intention to redeem God's chosen people. For all their warnings and condemnations, the prophets had a unique ability to clearly see the future. But unlike the diviners and seers of pagan societies, who simply predicted what would happen next, the prophets of Scripture saw the completion of Creation and instructed the people accordingly.

No one can refer to the Classical Prophets as a particularly hopeful bunch, but nonetheless, reading the prophets from Amos to Ezekiel reveals a measure of hope, especially for Judah, if only they would return to the Lord and scrupulously follow the Law. There was always the promise of a future hope, but there was a sense of immediacy that suggested hope in the present was not beyond the realm of possibility. All that ended with the collapse of Jerusalem. For the prophets Haggai, Zechariah, and Malachi, along with the efforts of Ezra and Nehemiah, that scant measure of hope was gone. Now the matter at hand was rebuilding the temple and reestablishing patterns of living and worship that bore some relationship to what had existed a couple of generations earlier.

With this shift in emphasis came a similar shift in the tone of prophecy. Clearly, idolatry remained a huge concern for anyone seeking a new temple and a society ordered along the lines of the Law, but from a policy standpoint, the work of rebuilding a society meant that certain realities had to be addressed dramatically. A fragile and weak community needed protection from neighbors who were none too pleased to see Jerusalem rebuilt, as well as guarding against falling back into the syncretic patterns that doomed the nation in the first place. Enforcing strictures against idols required creating a secular and theological structure with sufficient authority to demand compliance, and the physical resources to enforce the administration of the Law. While that was important, the matters of social justice and cultural syncretism were far more immediate. To successfully restore Jerusalem, there had to be an ordered society that consciously remained apart. This was the necessary antecedent for an obedient and faithful practice of Judaism and recentering of the temple in the life of the community.

The subtitle for this chapter might also have been "What Happened to Poor Obadiah?" Obadiah was present as Jerusalem was sacked and its inhabitants sent into exile. In that sense, he shared the bleak vision of an unrepentant and disobedient Judah with those prophets who preceded him. At the same time, seeing the Jewish people clearly in disarray and utterly defeated, there was little sense in merely foretelling doom. What was left for Obadiah was to remind the Jewish people that God had not abandoned them. While they were being punished for their sins, the time would come when Jerusalem would be restored. Their oppressors would also suffer in time, and they would have no hope for salvation. But Obadiah did foretell of a time when God's order would be established for all of eternity, "and the kingdom shall be the LORD's."[1] For that reason, Obadiah should get some well-deserved billing after all.[2]

By the time Haggai and Zachariah began their ministry, the Babylonian Empire had been supplanted by the Persians. Kings Cyrus and Darius permitted the exiled community to return to Jerusalem and begin rebuilding the temple. The temple became an important focus because it was the Lord's house, and rebuilding a holy place of worship would signal a return to orthodoxy and a rejection of other cultural patterns. Zerubbabel was chosen by Darius as the governor of Yehud province (essentially Judah), tasked with leading the exiles back to Jerusalem and rebuilding the temple. Zerubbabel was not only a provincial governor in the Persian Empire, but he was also the grandson of Jehoiachin, the king of Judah at the time of Jerusalem's fall. Jehoiachin was dethroned by Nebuchadnezzar and taken into captivity. That places Zerubbabel in the Davidic line. Ironically, the name Zerubbabel was of Babylonian origins, signaling how closely assimilated Zerubbabel was within the Babylonian power structure.[3] He was from the House of David while also serving as a living example of the dangers of cultural syncretism to God's chosen ones.

But this was clearly God's will: "The word of the Lord came by the hand of Haggai the prophet to Zerubbabel"[4] to rebuild the temple. The people, through Haggai, were given assurances that compliance would be the first step in restoring Jerusalem to its former position, and faithfulness would be rewarded. The physical work of restoring the temple, in a sense, became a sign of penance. Putting the work of the Lord above all else was an important step in the redemption of the people. It was, however, slow in coming. Haggai stressed the importance of the Lord's work. Zechariah was called to encourage the returning exiles with visions of salvation and to remind them of God's faithfulness in the past.

Haggai had used the analogy of ritual uncleanliness to underscore the need to purge the sins of the people through the restoration of the temple. The ruins of the temple were like a corpse, polluting all around

1. Obad 21.

2. Obad 20.

3. It should be noted that when Daniel and his companions were exiled to Babylon, they were given Babylonian names as well. In Daniel's case, it was Belteshazzar. While Zerubbabel accepted his syncretic renaming, Daniel, Hananiah, Mishael, and Azariah (Belteshazzar, Shadrach, Meshach, and Abednego, respectively), apparently never did.

4. Hag 1:1.

it. Rebuilding the house of the Lord was an act of purification for the returning exiles as well as the temple itself.[5] It represented the restoration of order and the rejection of the idea that the path to success was through relationships with surrounding nations. The only relationship that mattered to Haggai was the relationship between God and His people. He continued to remind the returning exiles that the nations are also subordinate to the Lord,[6] and if they carefully considered the defilement occasioned by absorbing the patterns of other nations, they would see the futility and danger of cultural accommodations.

Zechariah continues the analogy when, in one of his visions, he speaks to a fountain in the house of David, which will serve to purify and cleanse the people. Zechariah places idolatry, the language of disobedience, at the center of their sinful state. He refers to the Lord, against whom they have sinned by their worship of idols, as "him whom they have pierced,"[7] a metaphorical reference clearly anticipating the death of Jesus. Once the people have been purified and cleansed, the Lord "will cut off the names of the idols from the land, so that they shall be remembered no more."[8] Similarly, He will eliminate the agents who distort and pervert the language of the Lord, as first causes of disobedience and rebellion. "And also I will remove from the land the prophets and the spirit of uncleanness. And if anyone again prophesies, his father and mother who bore him will say to him, 'You shall not live, for you speak lies in the name of the Lord.'"[9] Using the image of Zech. 12:10, "And his father and mother who bore him shall pierce him through when he prophesies."[10]

In the context of rebuilding the temple and restoring obedience to the Law, rejecting idols was far more than simply turning away from them.[11] These references to idolatry were materially different from that of the previous prophets. They precede a long passage on the coming day of the Lord, which is filled with visions of an entirely new order, the redemption of Creation according to God's value proposition. What had come before, allures of competing cultures that so seduced the people of Israel, would be utterly destroyed. The temptations of other cultures

5. Hag 2:14, note.
6. Hag 2:6–8.
7. Zech 12:10.
8. Zech 13:2.
9. Zech 13:2–3.
10. Zech 13:3.
11. Zech 12:10, note.

would become the spoils of those faithful gathered in Jerusalem. Idols no longer existed, temptations were eliminated, and chaos was replaced by order.

Malachi was, indeed, the last prophet of the Classical Period. To best understand the end of the Old Testament, Malachi should be examined in conjunction with Ezra and Nehemiah. The latter two are not prophets, but in many ways, Malachi, Ezra, and Nehemiah served as a triumvirate, closing out the Old Testament period of history.

There remain a number of differing perspectives on Ezra and Nehemiah. Most scholars seem to agree that the author of Ezra probably wrote most, if not all, of Nehemiah. During the formative years of the canon and Christian doctrine, the two books were treated as one. There were even suggestions that Ezra, Nehemiah, and the author of Chronicles were the same. We do know that Ezra was sent to Jerusalem by King Artaxerxes I to reestablish the fundamentals of Mosaic and covenantal law as the basis for the Jewish faith. He was described as a scribe or a learned man, and he arrived c. 458 BCE. His principal obligation was theological. Nehemiah was an official in Artaxerxes's court and was commissioned by the king to go to Jerusalem as its governor and assist in the rebuilding of the city walls. Nehemiah followed Ezra by roughly thirteen years, and it is clear that they not only knew one another but cooperated in their mission.

Both found the situation in Jerusalem troubling. Ezra was outraged by the apostasy of the Jews and their seeming unwillingness to reengage the tenets of their faith. Nehemiah's task was compounded by the recalcitrance of the local population and the resistance of the neighboring communities. The Samaritans, many of whom were descendants of the northern kingdom of Israel, and who now had official standing in both the Assyrian and Persian Empires, were especially committed to seeing that their erstwhile brethren not reemerge as a local power. Both Ezra and Nehemiah took drastic and unpopular steps to achieve their objectives, having to overcome strong internal and external opposition in the process to do so.

Malachi was a contemporary of both Ezra and Nehemiah, ministering in Jerusalem while both were active. All three faced a community that was discouraged by what appeared to be the indifference of God to their plight, both materially and spiritually. What the three saw was less godly indifference than an almost studied unwillingness of the Jews to repudiate their sinful ways and return to faithful practices. It had been roughly eighty years since Haggai and Zechariah had been active. The hope and promise of their testimonies and the initial excitement of returning and rebuilding had worn off. However, now Jerusalem had an authentic prophet, a faithful teacher, and a godly governor operating simultaneously and courageously. All three reinforced the messages of the others, and fears of surrendering the tenets of faith under the pressure of neighboring cultures are featured heavily in the interplay amongst the three.

Malachi opens with a graphic description of the state of the priestly caste. "For my name will be great among the nations, says the Lord of hosts. But you profane it when you say that the Lord's table is polluted, and its fruit, that is, its food may be despised."[12] The Lord had established a covenant with the priestly class of the Levites, and in turn, Levites feared the Lord and followed His commands. And here is the point: "True instruction was in his mouth, and no wrong was found on his lips."[13] The state of the priestly class during Malachi's time was not simply a matter of poor behavior or lazy disregard for the specifics of priestly duties. It was a matter of false teaching. The example priests were supposed to set was not merely one of artful practice but of sound teaching, the language of obedience and faith. "For the lips of a priest should guard knowledge, and people should seek instruction from his mouth, for he is the messenger of the Lord of hosts. . . . You have caused many to stumble by your instruction. You have corrupted the covenant of Levi."[14] These were not ignorant men, new to the faith. These were learned individuals who were supposed to know better. To ignore what they knew to be the truth constituted wanton disregard for the Lord. In God's words, they have shown "partiality in your instruction." In other words, they chose to knowingly teach something contrary to God's truth in favor of something more in line with the communities around them. This behavior was branded as cowardly and profane. It mocked the just order of Creation. From Malachi's standpoint, Judah had boldly and clearly rejected the Law and covenants.

In his third disputation, Malachi condemns those who continue to marry outside of their faith as infidels.[15] Here, he is specifically challenging the difficult question of cultural syncretism in the harshest of language. Similar concerns are expressed by Ezra when he discovered

12. Mal 1:11–12.

13. Mal 2:6.

14. Mal 2:7–8.

15. Mal 2:10–16.

that even the priests had violated the covenant,[16] a disconcerting fact that Nehemiah confronted as well. "Remember them, O my God, because they have desecrated the priesthood and the covenant of the priesthood and the Levites."[17]

The language of the three focused on the seriousness and immediacy of intermarriage, since that exposed the faithful to the abominations of idolatry and the language of disobedience. It is difficult in this day and age to completely understand the enormity of the problem to Old Testament leaders. It might appear, on the surface, as though God were encouraging an arrogant exclusiveness. In one sense, that is true. The people of Israel were supposed to be set apart, examples of God's virtues. But the purpose was not to set a people above others but to demonstrate the magnificence of God's power, mercy, and grace. At all times, people of other nations were invited to become one with the Jews in their worship of the true God. They were not to be separated if they chose to follow God. Indeed, they were welcomed. The difficulties arose when interactions with other nations led to a diminution of faith, a negotiation and compromise of the exacting standards God demanded. The Jews could no longer be examples if they surrendered or diluted their faith. Some of this tension continued even after the ascension, when some early church leaders argued that gentiles must first become Jews before they could convert.

Shortly after returning to Jerusalem with a number of exiles and offering sacrifices of thanks, a group of officials sat down with Ezra and confessed that "the people of Israel and the priests and the Levites have not separated themselves from the peoples of the lands with their abominations."[18] Once again, the putative leaders of the community were among the worst offenders. "For they have taken some of their daughters to be wives for themselves and for their sons, so that the holy race has mixed itself with peoples of the lands. And in this faithlessness the hand of the officials and chief men has been foremost."[19]

After reminding the returning exiles of God's commandments regarding intermarriage,[20] Ezra cried out to God in prayer, saying "shall we break your commandments again and intermarry with the peoples who

16. Ezra 9:1.
17. Neh 13:4–9, 29.
18. Ezra 9:1.
19. Ezra 9:2.
20. Ezra 9:10–12.

practice these abominations?"[21] Ezra is asking for the Lord's guidance on whether breaking the Lord's commandments against divorce is justified in light of His other commandments about intermarriage. Specifically, in his disputation concerning intermarriage, Malachi identified the same dilemma facing Ezra. Marriage to idolators was an abomination, but so too was divorce from a legitimate marriage "to the wife of your youth."[22] "Did he not make them one, with a portion of the Spirit in their union? And what was the one God seeking? Godly offspring."[23] This was the crux of the matter. Only godly offspring could continue to grow the faith. In the end, Ezra acknowledged the distinction and demanded that all faithful Jews in Jerusalem put away their spouses and separate from their children and families rather than continue to accommodate the secular practices of those outside the faith.[24]

Nehemiah insisted on a general confession and a covenant attested by the Jews in Jerusalem, committing themselves to following the dictates of earlier covenants and the Law, including the commandment not to intermarry.[25] Later, as he is reflecting upon the state of affairs when he first arrived in Jerusalem, Nehemiah remarks, "In those days also I saw Jews who had married women of Ashdod, Ammon, and Moab."[26] Here Nehemiah echoes Malachi: "And half of their children spoke the language of Ashdod, and they could not speak the language of Judah, but only the language of each people."[27] Unlike Ezra who rent his garments and pulled out his hair, Nehemiah physically beat the offenders and pulled out their hair. He made them take an oath not to intermarry. "Thus I cleansed them from everything foreign."[28]

In all of this, the prophet Malachi concurred. "For Judah has profaned the sanctuary of the Lord, which he loves, and has married the daughter of a foreign god."[29] The language and speech of God is of vital importance. It is the vehicle through which Creation occurred, and it is the mechanism for continuing Creation. It is at the core of faith. If

21. Ezra 9:14.
22. Mal 2:14–15.
23. Mal 2:15.
24. Ezra 10.
25. Neh 10:30.
26. Neh 13:23.
27. Neh 13:24.
28. Neh 13:30.
29. Mal 2:11.

faith cannot be translated to one another and to following generations, then it cannot succeed as an instrument of redemption and salvation. From the standpoint of reclaiming Creation, language and speech cannot be divisive. They cannot be allowed to separate mankind from God and His intentions for His Creation. They are not tools to set one apart from another or elevate the status of one while diminishing the status of another. Language and speech are to bind one another together under the godhead of the victorious King of Kings.

# Chapter 13

# The New Testament

The New Testament introduces the creative Word into time, space, and matter. The Law is not set aside but is transformed into a vital, animating, living embodiment of faith. The transformation of the Law began with the disintegration of the united kingdom of Israel and was completed with the resurrection and ascension of Jesus.

It is important to understand the arc of this process. The abandonment of the Law by the rulers of both the northern and southern kingdoms undermined the social and political authority of the Law and contributed to the growing apostasy of Israeli society and worship. God's response was to send forth the Classical Prophets. During this period, as we saw, many non-Jews heard the prophetic messages, and by their physical association with the exilic community, were invited to participate in the Law. This was not necessarily a new development, since throughout the Old Testament, non-Jews often became Jews. Ruth is a very prominent example. But there was now greater urgency to the prophetic message. It entailed the survival of Judaism as a cohesive social and theological community.

But the personal, social, and theocratic relationships defined in the Law were static. They were rigorously defined and set out. From the giving of the Law until its completion in Jesus, the Law may have been restated, but its essential nature and substance were unaltered. This was not to be confused with the physical expansion of the nation. This was designed to broaden the reach of Judaism as reflected in the Law and protect its integrity from outside influences. It was not overtly committed to converting non-Jews to Jews. The Law motivated Jews to obey God, which included geographical expansion, but not to actively proselytize and expand a community of faith. Indeed, nearly every conquest involved utter destruction of the conquered, not an invitation to join. Prior to the exile, Jews were operating within a network of highly structured relationships. There was even a special class of non-Jews who were admitted as sojourners but were accorded that status only by obeying all the tenets of the Law. All the mechanisms were present and available to support a very strict set of conditions. During the exile, those structures were missing or, at the very least, severely weakened. Even as the temple was being rebuilt, it was a whole new world for the post exilic generations of Jews and those who might have been inclined to convert.

Between the days of Ezra, Nehemiah, and Malachi and the birth of Jesus, the temple was eventually rebuilt. During that interlude, there was a short-lived period of independence under the Hasmoneans (140–37 BCE). Excepting that stretch, the sources of power and authority associated with the temple were now far more imperial than the days of Saul, David, and Solomon, when God made the temple His home. Rabbis then, and probably now, would argue, but the fact remained that the rebuilt temple could not sustain its position in Jewish culture and theology without the support, either implicit or explicit, of more dominant political enterprises. Even the rebuilding of the temple itself relied on the support of Cyrus and the Persians. The temple, and the Jewish ruling class, existed at the pleasure of others.

That was the state of affairs when Jesus was born. The Caesars tolerated Judaism as long as it was useful to the Roman Empire. The political terms were clearly evident at the time Jesus was tried and convicted and reflected the changed the nature of the Law. It was no longer both a cultural and religious authority. It was implemented only to the extent that it did not intrude upon Roman political authority. For a faithful Jew, this meant keeping one eye on the chief priest and the other on the imperial governor.

The Law was the creative Word given by God. It was the embodiment of God's moral and ethical value propositions. The Law represented the standards for ordering the universe as intended at Creation. It provided guidelines for governing all behaviors, secular and divine, and its purpose was to replicate, as closely as possible, the perfection of the initial human-divine relationship. But it was rigid and unchanging, inflexible and unforgiving. There was no room for error, and on its own merits, the Law was incapable of accommodating the weakness and frailty of humanity.

With the birth of Jesus, the Law became a living thing. It was not merely a codified set of rules and regulations; it was alive in the Word made flesh. With Jesus, the incarnate Word, the Law embraced the fallen nature of humanity. This was something that it could not do under Old Testament circumstances. The Law was not suited for those purposes. But it was never God's intention that the Law would be replaced. As God's Word, it could not be imperfect or inadequate. It simply needed to be finished as Jesus Himself acknowledged. "Do not think that I have come to abolish the Law or the Prophets; I have not come to abolish them but to fulfill them. For truly, I say to you, until heaven and earth pass away, not an iota, not a dot, will pass from the Law until all is accomplished."[1] Accomplishment was defined as the redemption of Creation at the end of time.

Both the Old and the New Testaments are part of a seamless narrative of Creation, redemption, salvation, and the realization of a new kingdom. In the person of Jesus, the Law was completed, the kingship of Christ was established, and the relationship between God and humanity was once again perfected. With the New Testament, the creative Word became the incarnate Word; and in the incarnate Word, the authentic narrative became a living narrative, a divine-human project began but not yet completed.

The Gospel of John most effectively presents the nexus for understanding and embracing the relationship between the creative Word and the incarnate Word. The Gospel opens with, "In the beginning was the Word, and the Word was with God, and the Word was God."[2] John used the Greek *logos* for "Word." The *logos* "is the divine word, a self-communicating divine presence that existed with God and was uniquely manifested in Jesus Christ."[3] Continuing with that thought, "Wisdom or Word was God's creative presence through which the world came into being."[4] This divine presence was "fully and uniquely" present in Jesus, "necessary because the world had rejected the original creative presence."[5] The animating force, the agency of Creation, the "Word" became real and immediate with the birth of Jesus.

1. Matt 5:17–18.
2. John 1:1.
3. Metzger and Coogan, *Oxford Companion*, 463.
4. Metzger and Coogan, *Oxford Companion*, 463.
5. Metzger and Coogan, *Oxford Companion*, 463.

The magnificence of this incarnation cannot be overstated. The "Word" is the animating force behind God's intentions and motivations in creating the universe. It represents a life lived in absolute harmony with Him, fully imbued with the values and ethics of the Creator God. And now it existed in human form, subject to the entire range of human experience. From that moment on, the creative Word was the incarnate Word, not simply speaking to us through carefully selected intermediaries but walking among us as the Creator had originally walked among His Creation at the beginning of time. The gift of language and speech present within the "Word" had become the good news of an active narrative designed to deliver humanity to a perfected conclusion, just as it had been intended at the outset.

At its most basic, the word "incarnation" simply means to be made flesh. For something to be made flesh, it had to have existed previously and in some other form. If it was the "Word" made flesh, and the "Word" was God and was with God, the only logical conclusion is that Jesus was with God and in God prior to the Creation. Since nothing preexisted Creation, then it further follows that Jesus and God have an eternal existence as one. The concept of the Trinity is an altogether different subject, but from the perspective of the "Word" made flesh, it is now possible to see the continuity of the Creation. By becoming flesh, the pattern and purpose of Creation is made real. Creation did not simply end at the fall but is central to God's continuing efforts to redeem and save mankind. The "Word" is the creative God the Father, the creative Son made flesh, and the creative Spirit left for us at the Pentecost, all committed to the ongoing reclamation of Creation and the salvation of the created. Looked at from a different standpoint, the Trinity might also be understood as the created Word (God the Father), the incarnate Word (God the Son), and the everlasting Word (God the Holy Spirit).

John expands upon the theme of the Incarnate Word in his first epistolary letter:

> That which was from the beginning, which we have heard, which we have seen with our eyes, which we looked upon and have touched with our hands, concerning the word of life—the life was made manifest, and we have seen it, and testify to it and proclaim to you the eternal life, which was with the Father and was made manifest to us—that which we have seen and heard we proclaim also to you, so that you too may have fellowship with us; and indeed our fellowship is with the Father and with

> his Son, Jesus Christ. And we are writing these things so that our joy may be complete.[6]

In his letter, John is testifying to the reality of Jesus in human form: the living, experiential Word. "The repetition of *made manifest* (publicly seen and known) stresses the revelatory nature of Christ's coming; he was sent from and revealed by God."[7] To be revealed is to be made known in a very personal way. By contrast, Moses, the patriarchs, and the prophets were all sent from God but did not reveal the personal nature of God.

John directly participated in the fellowship of the Father and the Son. The immediate fellowship of the apostles was given to those who knew Christ in the flesh in order that fellowship could be shared with hearers of the word, that is, later Christians. This is the significance of apostolic succession, a confirmation of the authenticity of the Creation narrative. Furthermore, that fellowship is far more profound than any human relationship could ever be. It is a real relationship with God made possible through the incarnation of the Word in His Son. The Word made flesh cannot have fellowship with anyone who denies the truths of Creation. Anyone who does so cannot be considered a faithful witness. The fact that the apostles lived that witness makes their testimony totally reliable, as truthful as the words of God passed on through the prophets. Just as Moses seeing and speaking to God "face to face" established the legitimacy, provenance, and sanctity of Moses' Law, the testimony of the apostles and those having seen and spoken with Jesus "face to face" are equally legitimate and sanctified. The testimony and fellowship of the apostles given through the incarnate Word continues to be manifest for all of mankind after the ascension in the form of the everlasting Word, the Holy Spirit. The "Word" remains unbroken from Creation to the end of time.

John's first letter moves quickly and significantly to the matter of relating the Creation narrative truthfully. John speaks to walking in the light, "that God is light, and in him is no darkness at all. If we say that we have fellowship with him while we walk in darkness, we lie and do not practice the truth."[8] Light, of course, is goodness and darkness represents evil; light and darkness are truth and falsehood. It is crucial to John's testimony and commission that he experienced the light and the dark in

6. 1 John:1–4.

7. ESV note, 2430.

8. 1 John 1:5–6.

real time, in the presence of the author of light. Very simply put, as John is "writing these things so that our joy may be complete," what he proclaims for the generations to follow must be in the light, that is, truthful. It reiterates the importance of our maintaining the integrity of the Word now that it has been delivered in its incarnate form. Jesus confirms the continuation of Creation when he proclaimed in Matthew, "I will utter what has been hidden since the foundation of the world."[9]

Paul's opening greeting to Titus makes the same point:

> Paul, a servant of God and an apostle of Jesus Christ, for the sake of the faith of God's elect and their knowledge of the truth, which accords with godliness, in hope of eternal life, which God, who never lies, promised before the ages began and at the proper time manifested in his word through the preaching with which I have been entrusted by the command of God our Savior.[10]

The old sins of idolatry, false teaching, false prophets, and cultural assimilation remain, but the New Testament is all about testifying to a new reality. The good news is the reenergized narrative of Creation, now fully embodied in the person of Jesus. Language and speech become preeminent. Hence, warnings, instructions, and admonitions regarding language and speech in the New Testament now take on a new dimension. While God's Word in the Old Testament was authoritative, indisputable, powerful, and intentional, God's Word in the New Testament is not merely spoken; it is alive. Once Christ walked the earth and God's words became part of the bodily fabric of people's lives, they had a new intensity and urgency. The advent of the new kingdom was at hand, and humanity was now invited to directly participate in the completion of Creation with Christ Himself.

Once again, it is Paul who frames the argument post-ascension, and one of the best examples of this new urgency is in his first letter to the Corinthians. Here he deals with matters not unfamiliar to the modern church. The Corinthian church had devolved into division, apostasy, immorality, false teaching, and social snobbery. Paul opens with giving thanks to God for the gifts of speech and knowledge, which the Corinthians treasured but misused: "Because they had used these gifts in

9. Matt 13:35.

10. Titus 1:1–3.

wrong and improper ways, the exercise of the gifts led to disunity."[11] The substitution of false narratives put the salvation of those weak in faith at real risk.[12]

These sins were certainly not unique to the Corinthians, or unique to that moment in time, but what makes this different now is laid out by Paul. The new kingdom had been established at Jesus' ascension and was active in time and space. After the ascension, the everlasting Word—the Holy Spirit—remained an integral and inseparable extension of both the creative Word and the incarnate Word, imbedded in the hearts and souls of believers. Whereas the Old Testament faithful waited for a Messiah, the New Testament faithful had an unimpeachable record of the King of Kings living and interacting directly with mankind. The apostles were not prophets, chosen by God to relay His commands; they were the new patriarchs of the living Word helping prepare the way to salvation. This made matters of speech and language far more significant and immediate. The new kingdom was no longer theoretical or mysterious, the domain of priests and prophets. It was at hand, and all were invited to become members. "Therefore, my beloved brothers, be steadfast, immovable, always abounding in the work of the Lord, knowing that in the Lord your labor is not in vain."[13]

## *THE GOSPELS, THE INCARNATE WORD*

The Gospels focus on the life of Jesus, while the remainder of the New Testament focuses on the ministry of Christ as taught through the words and actions of His followers. His followers include not only the apostles, who had directly experienced Christ, but others who were teaching and testifying to the powerful Word of God. Jesus knew His time on earth was limited. Therefore, He had to rely on His followers and subsequent believers to protect the sanctity and the integrity of His message. While Jesus certainly spoke to the entire range of sin and disobedience, He was constantly stressing the importance of passing these lessons on unerringly.

Both the Gospels and the epistles offer a testimony to the power of language and speech when the good news is faithfully and fervently embraced by those who become hearers and doers of the word. The linkage

11. ESV note 1:5, 2192.

12. 1 Cor 8:9–13, 10:1–22.

13. 1 Cor 15:58.

of language and speech to Creation in the Old Testament is God speaking to and through others. The Gospels establish the linkage by way of God speaking directly to all of humanity through the ministry of Jesus, while the epistles link language and speech with Creation through the words of the faithful, now informed and sustained by the Holy Spirit. At the risk of overstating the case, the New Testament does not minimize the fallen nature of mankindor the struggle to maintain and protect the Law, but it emphasizes the greater urgency of spreading these truths accurately. This became the good news of the Bible.

There is sound reasoning behind distinguishing the newness of this testimony from the style and characteristics of the old. When the essential nature of the Law moved from a static set of rules and regulations to an active set of instructions for completing the work begun at the Creation, Old Testament concepts such as authority, judgment, and witness (maintaining the integrity of the narrative) took on a different quality as well. In the Gospels, Jesus stresses the importance of the gift and responsibility of ordering Creation as His stewards. Everything He said is stated in the active tense, often through metaphors that employ living things, such as what would be found in very familiar, natural settings. The new kingdom is at hand. Obeying the Law now means doing, building, and growing, not merely protecting and condemning. The same holds for the epistles, with the addition of a helper, the Holy Spirit, the everlasting Word.

Language and speech are the mechanisms by which the *authority* of God is given to His Son, and through His Son, extended to His followers for the purposes of acting on His behalf. The words spoken through His Son expanded the scope of the Law and become the new standard for *judgment,* based on promoting Christ's kingship and a commitment to the task of building the new kingdom. Language and speech, imbued with His authority, no longer the exclusive purview of a selected few, are an energized *witness* attesting to the authenticity and vitality of the Creation narrative. In the epistles, we see the active participation of the *everlasting Word* (Holy Spirit), given at the Pentecost, promised for all time, readily available to the end of time for the support and sustenance of the faithful.

Beginning with the Gospels, Jesus' authority is established early on, while teaching in the Tabernacle at roughly twelve years of age. "And he was teaching them on the Sabbath, and they were astonished at his teaching, for his word possessed authority."[14] It is clear that this was not merely

14. Luke 4:31–32.

worldly authority or a desiccated display of intellectuality, displayed at an unusually young age. Those who heard Jesus speak understood that His level of understanding could only proceed from a much higher authority than that of mere mortals. He exhibited far greater learning than the rabbis and scribes. Coupled with later miracles, where He cast out demons, healed the sick, and raised the dead, Jesus' words pointed to a relationship with the Father that was beyond the comprehension of mere human understanding.[15] It was a message that Jesus reinforced time and again. When addressing a group of apostles towards the end of His ministry, Jesus asks, rather pointedly, "Do you not believe that I am in the Father and the Father is in me? The words that I say to you I do not speak on my own authority, but the Father who dwells in me does his works."[16] This was an authority that called followers to action in a way that eventually ran afoul of both the Romans and the Jewish hierarchy.

Language and speech as agents of judgment are equally clear. Jesus' description of the one unforgiveable sin is not one of action or behavior; it is one of speech. "And whoever speaks a word against the Son of Man will be forgiven, but whoever speaks against the Holy Spirit will not be forgiven, either in this age or in the age to come."[17] Language alone is capable of a sin so egregious that it cannot be forgiven. In Mark, Jesus again addresses the unique power language has to separate humanity from the Creator, and by so doing, bring upon the speaker eternal judgment. "For whoever is ashamed of me and of my words in this adulterous and sinful generation, of him will the Son of man also be ashamed when he comes in the glory of his Father with the holy angels."[18] The idea of being ashamed took on a much more ominous meaning in the Old Testament context, more a matter of condemnation than the sense of embarrassment in its current use. There are no references in the New Testament to the Father and the Son being ashamed of humanity except when it was a matter of rejecting the Word of God manifested in His Son. But the point here is that the Son was called to deliver humanity from sin and despair, and when the power, authority, and obligations of language and speech are ignored or dismissed, the whole process of redemption is at risk.

In the Old Testament, the words of God were from God, hence ignoring or corrupting them was blasphemous. In the New Testament,

15. Matt 5:22, 8:16.

16. John 14:10.

17. Matt 12:32; Luke 12:8–10.

18. Mark 8:38; Luke 9:26.

the words were not just from God, they were God. The Old Testament provides the history of a chosen people seeking a Messiah, awaiting a divine promise they could not entirely comprehend. Then the Messiah arrived. Rejecting God's Word in the Old Testament was not the same as rejecting God in the flesh. Doing so in the New Testament context was to deny the existence of God Himself, face to face. In John, Jesus makes the judgmental nature of holy language very clear. "The one who rejects me and does not receive my words has a judge; the word that I have spoken will judge him on the last day."[19] That is the urgency of the post-ascension world of the New Testament.

The power of language and speech as tools for judgment is clear, but why was judgment so severe? The answer lies in the larger role language and speech have in sustaining the vitality of the Creation narrative, what is referred to as witness. The word "witness" in the scriptural context is based on two very important components. In the first instance, the context in which the modern church uses the term, witness means to testify to the personal acceptance of the Savior and to declare that acceptance to others through both speech and action. The second sense of the word, a more Old Testament driven perspective, is the importance of having two people attest to the truth of an issue. This is referenced repeatedly, especially in the Law. The modern church has moved away from this understanding, to its detriment. It is as important to corroborate a truth through the testimony of at least two people as it is to declare one's beliefs. This is the strength of the New Testament, that the accuracy of the apostles' testimony was corroborated by others. This is what John was addressing in the Gospel reference cited earlier, and this gives the narrative its authenticity and accuracy. Faith is communal, not merely personal, and collective testimony is a critical piece of individual testimony.

The point has been made repeatedly that the power of misusing language and distorting God's Word rests in the influence it exercises over those beyond the speaker. Bodily harm, theft, and conspiracy, for example, corrupt the initiator of the sin, but the victim who does not chose to live in a constant state of victimhood does not become a sinner. When one perverts the narrative, distorts Creation, or manipulates God's words for a purpose not intended by the Creator, the speaker can perpetuate falsehoods for generations that, as Paul said, destroy the faith of families and communities. This can be seen today in the long-lasting and

19. John 12:48.

destructive impact cults have, not only on their immediate members but on the generations that follow. That is why false prophets, teachers, and those who trade in the currency of lies and deceit are the subject of more condemnation throughout the Scriptures than any other group.

When Jesus was dressing down the Pharisees and scribes, He made this connection between core beliefs in the heart, the expression of corruption, and ultimate judgment:

> You brood of vipers! How can you speak good, when you are evil? For out of the abundance of the heart the mouth speaks. The good person out of his good treasure brings forth good, and the evil person out of his evil treasure brings forth evil. I tell you, on the day of judgment people will give account for every careless word they speak, for by your words you will be justified, and by your words you will be condemned.[20]

This theme of witness and the spiritual welfare of community is revisited frequently by Jesus in the Gospels. Referencing the words of Isaiah, "This people honors me with their lips, but their heart is far from me; in vain do they worship me, teaching as doctrines the commandments of men."[21] Words carry the promise of life and the risk of death. Jesus used the analogy of a tree and its fruit to convey this reality. "The good person out of the good treasure of his heart, produces good and the evil person out of his evil treasure produces evil, for out of the abundance of the heart his mouth speaks."[22] Truth is the source of lightness and life, and falsehood brings forth only darkness and death. "Man shall not live by bread alone, but by every word that comes from the mouth of God."[23] The idea of witness becomes an active verb, used to draw in and sustain new generations of believers. Obeying the faithful narrative transmitted through the Law was replaced by an active narrative, an invitation to build a new kingdom. Obedience no longer meant just following rules; it now meant actively participating as partners with the King of Kings.

As Jesus was facing crucifixion and death, He promised to leave behind a guide and comforter, the Holy Spirit, an everlasting Word, that would sustain all faithful believers until the end of time. The everlasting Word carried all the authority of the Creator Word and the incarnate

20. Matt 12:34–37.

21. Matt 15:8–9; Mark 7:6.

22. Luke 6:45; Matt 7:15–20.

23. Matt 4:4.

Word and would remain uninterrupted through eternity. There were no gaps in the Creation narrative; the living Word was constant and consistent, through the Father and the Son, and ultimately the Holy Spirit. Jesus' proclamation of the truth of this reality is recorded in each of the synoptic Gospels. "Heaven and earth will pass away, but my words will not pass away."[24] Jesus tells His disciples that they will suffer and be persecuted for passing on His words, but He reinforces the sanctity of language and the reliability of the Holy Spirit. The words will be there, the witness will be genuine, and the language that is supplied by the Holy Spirit is trustworthy and not to be second-guessed. "This will be your opportunity to bear witness. Settle it therefore in your minds not to meditate beforehand how to answer, for I will give you a mouth and wisdom, which none of your adversaries will be able to withstand or contradict."[25] "It is the spirit who gives life; the flesh is no help at all. The words I have spoken to you are spirit and life."[26]

In a poignant moment just prior to His betrayal and arrest, Jesus reaffirms the essential unity of Creation, the significance of His relationships on earth, and God's commitment to the salvation of humanity. In an emotionally rich and complex high priestly prayer, Jesus lifts up three prayers: for Himself as His ministry is about to come to a close, for His disciples, and for all those who will later come to believe. His first prayer establishes Jesus' existence from the beginning and the authority under which Jesus' earthly ministry was conducted. Through God, Jesus has the authority to give eternal life to all believers. The authority to confer eternal life includes, by logical extension, an element of judgment that will become manifest at the end of time. This is a firm affirmation that conditions under the Law have indeed changed. The ability to confer eternal life would be of no value if Jesus could not also forgive sins. In addition, Jesus, by His humanity, represents the one true path to knowing the Father at an immediate, intimate, and personal level.[27]

In the second part of the prayer, Jesus prays specifically for His disciples, those who have known Him, loved Him, and would sacrifice themselves for Him. Jesus confirms the authority of language. "For I have given them the words that you gave me, and they have received them and have come to know in truth that I came from you; and they have believed

24. Matt 24:35; Mark 13:31; Luke 21:33.

25. Luke 21:13–15.

26. John 6:63.

27. John 17:1–5.

that you sent me."[28] God's words, which formed the universe, had been given to the Son, who in turn shared them with His disciples. They have accepted the truth of these words and become witnesses of the authentic narrative of Creation—not only witnesses of Creation but participants and stewards, as initially intended. They have cherished the language of light and truth, have protected the integrity of speech, and are now justified by them. "I have given them your word, and the world has hated them because they are not of the world, just as I am not of the world."[29] Jesus asks that they not be taken from the world but remain as faithful witnesses to Creation.

In the final section of His prayer, Jesus shifts emphasis to those in the future who "will believe in me through their word."[30] There are elements of both judgment and the everlasting Word in this part of His prayer. In praying that God sustain all believers, Jesus is acknowledging the authority and power of the Holy Spirit to continue moving the Creation and salvation narrative forward. In praying that future believers be with Him through the end of time, Jesus presages final judgment and the end of time.

## *THE EPISTLES, THE EVERLASTING WORD*

The pivotal event in the epistles is Pentecost. This is the final reclamation of language and speech. Here, the confusion and chaos represented by the tower of Babel is reversed. At Babel, language and speech were confused as punishment for sin and disobedience, and they remained confused and chaotic until the world could be freed from sin. With Christ's resurrection, death was conquered, and language and speech were redeemed. Now language and speech were triumphant. Freed from sin, all languages were now capable of presenting and spreading good news, the perfected gift of language and speech. The miracle of Pentecost is that the language of the completed Law was now available to all, and the narrative was not constrained by parochial boundaries of speech. When Paul was cautioning the Corinthians about speaking in tongues, he was essentially warning them not to fall back into the sins of Babel. The authority inherent in the gifts of language and speech, the tools for ordering Creation, had

28. John 17:8.
29. John 17:14.
30. John 17:20.

been reestablished at Pentecost, and these gifts were to be used for building the kingdom, not confusing the effort.

After Pentecost, the questions of authority, judgment, and witness assumed greater importance since they were the means by which Jesus' ministry on this earth was to be completed. The Holy Spirit, the everlasting Word, the manifestation of both the Creator Word and the incarnate Word, was essential to completing this task. Just before His betrayal, Jesus told His disciples:

> It is to your advantage that I go away, for if I do not go away, the Helper will not come to you. But if I go, I will send him to you. And when he comes, he will convict the world concerning sin and righteousness and judgment: concerning sin, because they do not believe in me; concerning righteousness, because I go to the Father, and you will see me no longer; concerning judgment, because the ruler of this world is judged.[31]

These are the very themes identified in the Gospels as the imperatives of language and speech, but now they are much more than the unique authority, judgment, and witness inherent in Jesus' ministry; they are the qualities upon which the new kingdom will be built.

When Paul left Titus in Crete to support the newly planted churches there, he insisted on adherence to the true word as a sign of authority. Elders, for example, "must hold firm to the trustworthy word as taught, so that he may be able to give instruction in sound doctrine and also rebuke those who contradict it."[32] Establishing the line of authority back to the unimpeachable Word of God as taught and as incarnate in Christ was essential, since "there are many who are insubordinate, empty talkers and deceivers," and "they are upsetting whole families."[33] Again, Paul stresses to Titus, "Show yourself in all respects to be a model of good works and in your teaching show integrity, dignity, and sound speech that cannot be condemned."[34] In writing to the Ephesians, Paul warns, "Let there be no filthiness nor foolish talk nor crude joking. . . . Let no one deceive you with empty words, for because of these things the wrath of God comes upon the sons of disobedience."[35] Peter also insisted that human author-

31. John 16:7–11.
32. Titus 1:9.
33. Titus 1:10–11.
34. Titus 2:7–8.
35. Eph 5:4,6.

ity could only be legitimate if it flowed from the source of Creation and through Jesus. Jesus was the only sound example. "He committed no sin neither was deceit found in his mouth."[36] Followers of Christ must be imitators of Christ and be disciplined in speech and language. "When he was reviled, he did not revile in return."[37] The only path to salvation was obedience. Quoting Isaiah, Peter says, "For 'Whoever desires to love life and see good days, let him keep his tongue from evil and his lips from speaking deceit.'"[38]

Authority and judgment are inextricably connected, particularly when it comes to representing the narrative of Creation and salvation accurately. Since managing language and speech were essential components of authoritative teaching and worship, judgment was particularly harsh for those who taught or led worship without legitimacy or authority. James was particularly pointed in his remarks on controlling language and speech, and the deleterious consequences to those who misled others with their words. "Not many of you should become teachers, my brothers, for you know that we who teach will be judged with greater strictness."[39] He went on to add, "How great a forest is set ablaze by such a small fire! And the tongue is a fire, a world of unrighteousness. The tongue is set among our members, staining the whole body, setting on fire the entire course of life, and set on fire by hell, . . . no human being can tame the tongue. It is a restless evil, full of deadly poison. . . . From the same mouth come blessing and cursing."[40] For James, "a person's words reflect his character and thus are a key to his whole being. . . . The tongue turns upside down every aspect of life in the community as well as in the individual."[41]

The theme of judgment for distorting and perverting language and speech, whatever the motivation, is constant throughout the New Testament. The message is clear and unequivocal. Anything said that does not glorify God or acknowledge His Son, no matter how seemingly trivial, is blasphemous and warrants severe judgment.

36. 1 Pet 2:22.

37. 1 Pet 2:23.

38. 1 Pet 3:10.

39. Jas 3:1.

40. Jas 3:5–10.

41. ESV note, 2395.

> Behold, the Lord comes with ten thousands of his holy ones, to execute judgment on all and to convict all the ungodly of all their deeds of ungodliness that they have committed in such an ungodly way, and of all the harsh things that ungodly sinners have spoken against him. These are grumblers, malcontents, following their own sinful desires; they are loud-mouthed boasters, showing favoritism to gain advantage.[42]

In this passage, Jude is reaching back to the prophecies of Enoch in the Old Testament. Enoch was calling out the blasphemous ways of the ungodly, which, in Jude's day, were those who denied Jesus. "But you must remember, beloved, the prediction of the apostles of our Lord Jesus Christ. They said to you, 'In the last time there will be scoffers, following their own ungodly passions.' It is these who cause divisions, worldly people, devoid of the Spirit."[43]

Peter reflects Jude's warnings about scoffers, grumblers, and malcontents: "Knowing this first of all, that scoffers will come in the last days with scoffing, following their own sinful desires."[44] A scoffer was one who refused to abandon their evil ways and in their sinfulness derided biblical truth by cynicism and tedious argumentation.

Peter commits an entire section of his second letter to the terrible judgment that will fall on false prophets and teachers who "secretly bring in destructive heresies, even denying the Master who brought them . . . exploit you with false words, . . . and because of them the way of truth will be blasphemed."[45] Peter minces no words in describing the enormity of their sin or the magnitude of their punishment. Paul is equally adamant that irreverent, intemperate speech will result in a tragic judgment for those who profane and blaspheme:

> For such men are false apostles, deceitful workmen, disguising themselves as apostles of Christ. And no wonder, for even Satan disguises himself as an angel of light. So it is no surprise if his servants, also, disguise themselves as servants of righteousness. Their end will correspond to their deeds.[46]

42. Jude 14–16.
43. Jude 17–19.
44. 2 Pet 3:3.
45. 2 Pet 2:1–3.
46. 2 Cor 11:13–15.

Paul makes it clear that the only path to salvation during "this present darkness" is through the word and the truth of the Creation narrative. Letters to the Ephesians, the Colossians, and the Romans all reiterate the message. "Take the helmet of salvation, and the sword of the Spirit, which is the word of God, praying at all times in the Spirit, with all prayer and supplication."[47] To the church in Colossae, Paul charges them to put on the new self and avoid those things which will earn eternal condemnation and the "wrath of God": "But now you must put them all away: anger, wrath, malice, slander, and obscene talk from your mouth. Do not lie to one another, seeing that you have put off the old self."[48] Paul makes reference to the Creation itself, in words that God used when He called the universe into being: "Put on the new self, which is being renewed in knowledge after the image of its creator."[49] Anticipating the possibility of a visit to the faithful in Rome, Paul lays out the path to salvation, and it is through the proclaiming of the word and the truths behind the incarnate Word. In speaking of the righteousness of faith, he says:

> But what does it say? "The word is near you, in your mouth and in your heart" (that is, the word of faith that we proclaim); because, if you confess with your mouth that Jesus is Lord and believe in your heart that God raised him from the dead, you will be saved. For with the heart one believes and is justified, and with the mouth one confesses and is saved.[50]

In addition to dealing with matters of authority and judgment, which are necessary components of faith, the epistles also address the qualities of witness and the power of the Holy Spirit. There are far more references to these topics, which makes absolute sense. Faith is not essentially authority and judgment, no matter how important it is to understand and accept their consequences. Faith is far more essentially the good news. The dynamic source of real joy is found in the obligation to proffer true and faithful witness, both to one's own beliefs as well as in support of the testimony and faith of others' beliefs. These are the ordained tools for spreading the gospel message and finding strength in the midst of darkness and despair. There was an underlying tension within Christian communities in the first century CE that the Lord's return was

47. Eph 6:17–18.

48. Col 3:8–9.

49. Col 3:10.

50. Rom 10:8–10.

imminent. Hence, there was a heightened sense of urgency to take care that language and speech properly and accurately represented the narratives of faith and that false prophets and teachers were forestalled in their efforts to distort and pervert tenets of belief before it was too late.

Witness, in the New Testament context, is not merely accurately reciting and following the Law. Witness is essential for representing the good news, increasing and growing the faith, and supporting the validity of the narrative. In other words, it was a crucial tool for the task at hand, and one's witness, both in the Old and New Testament context, must therefore be unimpeachable. In this regard, the epistles speak to three essential characteristics of witness: the personal discipline of the one witnessing; any evidence that one could not provide effective witness to their own or others' testimony; and the credibility of those professing to offer community witness, that is, those who teach or prophesy in the name of the Lord.

James makes the first point quite clearly: "If anyone thinks he is religious and does not bridle his tongue but deceives his heart, this person's religion is worthless."[51] There is no subtlety or nuance to sort through with James. Paul is equally blunt with the Ephesians: "Let no corrupting talk come out of your mouths, but only such as is good for building up, as fits the occasion, that it may give grace to those who hear."[52] When offering guidance to Timothy, Paul expands on the theme of personal discipline when it comes to language and speech:

> Remind them of these things, and charge them before God not to quarrel about words, which does no good, but only ruins the hearers. Do your best to present yourself to God as one approved, a worker who has no need to be ashamed, rightly handling the word of truth. But avoid irreverent babble, for it will lead people into more and more ungodliness, and their talk will spread like gangrene.[53]

Paul reminded those to whom he ministered that he remained strictly committed to that principle. "We put no obstacle in anyone's way, so that no fault may be found with our ministry, but as servants of God we commend ourselves in every way."[54] He goes on to list a series of ex-

51. Jas 1:26.
52. Eph 4:29.
53. 2 Tim 2:14–17.
54. 2 Cor 6:3–4.

periences and behaviors that include "truthful speech, and the power of God."[55]

Paul's letter to the churches in Rome was designed to address, among other things, tensions between resident Jews, diasporic Jews, and gentiles in matters of faith and worship. Paul describes the conditions of those in a state of sin with respect to matters of language and speech:

> For although they knew God, they did not honor him as God or give thanks to him, but they became futile in their thinking, and their foolish hearts were darkened. Claiming to be wise, they became fools, and exchanged the glory of the immortal God for images resembling mortal man and birds and animals and creeping things . . . they exchanged the truth about God for a lie and worshiped and served the creature rather than the Creator.[56]

To Paul, "the essential sin is idolatry, the devotion to something as god that is not God."[57] Teaching idolatrous behavior as the true Word of God created the greatest risk within the young Christian community. He goes on in the verses following to describe the abominations that grew out of exchanging "the truth about God for a lie."

> They are gossips, slanderers, haters of God, insolent, haughty, boastful, inventors of evil, disobedient to parents, foolish, faithless, heartless, ruthless. Though they know God's righteous decree that those who practice such things deserve to die, they not only do them but give approval to those who practice them.[58]

It is the endorsement of the behavior that is the most galling to Paul. Finally, in a more dramatic fashion, Paul excoriates the sins of language and speech. "Their throat is an open grave; they use their tongues to deceive. The venom of asps is under their lips. Their mouth is full of curses and bitterness."[59] This passage echoes Ps 5:9: "For there is no truth in the mouth; their inmost self is destruction; their throat is an open grave; they flatter with their tongue." The references to "grave" are a sign of corruption, sin, and death, and the venom of an asp associated with the tongue certainly refers to the poisonous effects of speech.

55. 2 Cor 6:7.

56. Rom 1:22–25.

57. Barton and Muddiman, *Oxford Bible Commentary*, 1098.

58. Rom 1:28–32.

59. Rom 3:13–14.

The risks created by false prophets, teachers, and priests assume a greater urgency, since now the language and speech being distorted or perverted is living language and speech. While it was certainly sinful and disobedient to blaspheme or profane God's words given through the prophets, the prophets were representing the Word; they were not the Word itself. Paul's writings are replete with warnings to avoid such persons and constantly test the accuracy of what is being taught by balancing their words against God's. "For we are not, like so many, peddlers of God's word, but as men of sincerity, as commissioned by God, in the sight of God we speak in Christ."[60] "But we have renounced disgraceful, underhanded ways. We refuse to practice cunning or to tamper with God's word, but by the open statement of the truth we could commend ourselves to everyone's conscience in the sight of God."[61]

In both his letters to Timothy, Paul stresses diligence and a keen awareness of deviations from holy speech. "Now the Spirit expressly says that in latter times some will depart from the faith by devoting themselves to deceitful spirits and teachings of demons," as Paul wrote in his first letter, "through the insincerity of liars."[62] Later in the same letter, he warns:

> Teach and urge these things. If anyone teaches a different doctrine and does not agree with the sound words of our Lord Jesus Christ and the teaching that accords with godliness, he is puffed up with conceit and understands nothing. He has an unhealthy craving for controversy and for quarrels about words, which produce envy, dissension, slander, evil suspicions and constant friction between people who are depraved in mind and deprived of the truth.[63]

Writing a second time, he continues, "For the time is coming when people will not endure sound teaching, but having itching ears they will accumulate for themselves teachers to suit their own passions, and will turn away from listening to the truths and wandering off into myths."[64] This was a serious issue. The destruction that a distorted and twisted narrative can inflict on a faith community is almost incalculable. More

60. 2 Cor 2:17
61. 2 Cor 4:2.
62. 1 Tim 4:1–5.
63. 1 Tim 6:2–5.
64. 2 Tim 4:3–5.

than anything else, profaning and perverting the language and speech of Creation is an intolerable sin, against which the leaders of the faithful must be constantly on guard. After all his advice to the Romans, Paul's final instructions return to this message:

> I appeal to you, brothers, to watch out for those who cause divisions and create obstacles contrary to the doctrine that you have been taught; avoid them. For such persons do not serve our Lord Christ, but have their own appetites, and by smooth talk and flattery they deceive the hearts of the naïve.[65]

In many respects, the gift of the Holy Spirit is the sustaining reality of the New Testament. The Old Testament was defined by the Word of God to His people through patriarchs and prophets for their immediate instruction. However, there were significant periods when the Word of God was silent: between the end of the judges and the call to Samuel, and the prophecy of Malachi to the birth of Jesus. When the Word became incarnate, during the three years of His mission and ministry, creative and holy speech was conveyed by Jesus to His followers in real time, space, and matter. After His crucifixion, resurrection, and ascension, the creative Word still remained active in the form of the Holy Spirit given at the Pentecost. It has not been interrupted and will never be interrupted. This was, and continues to be, the living hope to which we have been born anew. It is the language of the new kingdom, active in time and space. It is the support structure for the faithful until the end of time. After Jesus had identified the twelve, He warned them that they would be sorely tested and persecuted for their role in His ministry. But Jesus assured them that they would not be left to their own devices. "When they deliver you over, do not be anxious how you are to speak or what you are to say, for what you are to say will be given to you in that hour. For it is not you who speak, but the Spirit of your Father speaking through you."[66]

These words are full of meaning for the faithful. Believers will be given the right things to say, and they will be speaking the words of the Father through the Holy Spirit. In a very real sense, they will be the heirs to the prophets. "And we also thank God constantly for this, that when you received the word of God, which you heard from us, you accepted it not as the word of men but as what it really is, the word of God, which is

65. Rom 16:17–18.

66. Matt 10:19–20.

at work in you believers.[67] This is the sacrifice pleasing to God that was the intended relationship between humanity and its Creator in the beginning. "Through him then let us continually offer up a sacrifice of praise to God, that is, the fruit of lips that acknowledge his name."[68] This is the gift of speaking wisely that Paul describes in his first letter to the Corinthians: "For to one is given through the Spirit the utterance of wisdom, and another the utterance of knowledge according to the same Spirit."[69] Finally, as Paul wrote in Rom 10:17, it is the source of faith. "So faith comes from hearing, and hearing through the word of Christ"—words that would faithfully and accurately protect the authentic narrative of Creation for future generations, provided by the Holy Spirit, the everlasting Word.

## *THE REVELATION TO JOHN, THE CREATED WORD TRIUMPHANT*

"In the beginning was the Word, and the Word was with God, and the Word was God."[70] This is where it all started: a powerful Word that brought into being the entire physical universe. The ability to create must logically include the ability to be stronger than that which was created, to be more physical than that which has been created physical. The Word, the agency of Creation, is the immediate, real, and physical manifestation of language and speech. The Word is creative, incarnate, and everlasting. The Word is revealed to John in both its individual capacities and collectively as the Trinity. The Revelation is a rich, dynamic, and lyrical vision of the end of time, and the power of speech is evident in its greatest glory. Language with the power to create also has the power to destroy, and that power is on full display in Revelation. "And then the lawless one will be revealed, whom the Lord Jesus will kill with the breath of his mouth and bring to nothing by the appearance of his coming."[71]

John describes the one who delivered this revelation vision as terrifying, with various physical attributes, and "from his mouth came a sharp two-edged sword."[72] That same imagery is used in the letter John

67. 1 Thess 2:13.
68. Heb 13:15.
69. 1 Cor 12:8.
70. John 1:1.
71. 2 Thess 2:8.
72. Rev 1:16.

is to send to the church in Pergamum: "Therefore repent. If not, I will come to you soon and war against them with the sword of my mouth."[73] The Scriptures require two witnesses to confirm any testimony, and the two witnesses accompanying the one with the vision are armed with the destructive powers of God's words as a judgment. "And if anyone would harm them, fire pours from their mouth and consumes their foes."[74] The "name by which he [the rider on the white horse, the Redeemer] is called is the Word of God," and a sharp sword is in his mouth with which to strike down the nations. The beast and the false prophet are cast into the lake of fire, and those enemies remaining are "slain by the sword that came from the mouth of him who was sitting on the horse."[75] This allegorical sword is the one the faithful were provided through the Holy Spirit to be witnesses in both the individual and communal sense.

The power of profane and perverted speech to undermine the witness of the faithful, a theme throughout the Scriptures, is also evidenced in John's vision. In a symbolic reference to Eve in the garden, and the immaculate birth of Jesus to a woman, falsehoods flow from the mouth of evil in an attempt to destroy. "The serpent poured water like a river out of his mouth after the woman, to sweep her away with a flood."[76] Further on, the vision revealed that "the beast was given a mouth uttering haughty and blasphemous words, and it was allowed to exercise authority for forty-two months. It opened its mouth to utter blasphemies against God, blaspheming his name and his dwelling."[77] Echoing the plagues of Egypt and warnings to prepare for the coming of the Lord, the sixth angel prepares the setting for the impending battle.

> And I saw, coming out of the mouth of the dragon and out of the mouth of the beast and out of the mouth of the false prophet, three unclean spirits like frogs. For they are demonic spirits, performing signs, who go abroad to the kings of the whole world, to assemble them for battle on the great day of God the Almighty. (Behold, I am coming like a thief! Blessed is the one who stays awake, keeping his garments on, that he may not go about naked and be seen exposed!)[78]

73. Rev 2:16.
74. Rev 11:5 and note.
75. Rev 19:11–21.
76. Rev 12:15.
77. Rev 13:5–6.
78. Rev 16:13–15.

This, as opposed to the faithful, "and in their mouth no lie was found, for they are blameless."[79]

As Revelation closes, John reminds his readers of the completeness and sufficiency of God's Word:

> I warn everyone who hears the words of the prophecy of this book: if anyone adds to them, God will add to him the plagues described in this book, and if anyone takes away from the words of the book of this prophecy, God will take away his share in the tree of life and in the holy city, which are described in this book.[80]

~

In a sense, although not completed, Creation had come full circle in the New Testament. From the Word in the beginning, God guided Creation history through the fall, the flood, the exodus, the judges and kings, and finally, the era of the prophets. The principles underpinning the narrative were outlined very specifically in the Law, and the importance of speaking to the truth of the Law is continuously reinforced throughout the Old Testament.

With the ascension of Christ and the advent of the new kingdom, believers were presented with the new realities of the Law. Being freed from the old version of the Law meant being beyond condemnation. The Old Testament version of the Law could not contemplate eternal life and the forgiveness of sins except in the abstract, since followers of the Law still awaited their Messiah. For those accepting Jesus, however, this was no longer the case. Believers were no longer bound to the prior version of the Law, instead living according to the Spirit. Paul describes this new life in the Spirit in some detail in his letter to the Romans. "There is therefore now no condemnation for those who are in Christ Jesus. For the law of the Spirit of life has set you free in Christ Jesus from the law of sin and death. For God has done what the law, weakened by the flesh, could not do."[81] This was not a description of a future state; it was the present reality. "But if Christ is in you, although the body is dead because of sin, the Spirit is life because of righteousness. If the Spirit of him who raised Jesus

79. Rev 14:5.

80. Rev 22:18–19.

81. Rom 8:1–3.

from the dead dwells in you, he who raised Christ Jesus from the dead will also give life to your mortal bodies through his Spirit who dwells in you."[82]

This Spirit is the everlasting Word, which, along with the Creator Word and the incarnate Word, has existed from the beginning of time and remains eternal. This is the language and speech that brought the universe into being in the Old Testament and is now reordering Creation in the New Testament. Again, Paul makes the point:

> For creation waits with eager longing for the revealing of the sons of God. For the creation was subjected to futility, not willingly, but because of him who subjected it, in hope that the creation itself will be set free from its bondage to corruption and obtain the freedom of the glory of the children of God. For we know that the whole creation has been groaning together in the pains of childbirth until now. And not only creation, but we ourselves, who have the firstfruits of the Spirit, groan inwardly as we wait eagerly for adoption as sons, the redemption of our bodies.[83]

This whole process of salvation was never about individuals, but the "whole creation." Humanity was never the center of the universe. Salvation is about redeeming all of Creation as ordained in the beginning.

> Then I saw a new heaven and a new earth, for the first heaven and the first earth had passed away, and the sea was no more. And I saw the holy city, new Jerusalem, coming down out of heaven from God, prepared as a bride adorned for her husband. And I heard a loud voice from the throne saying, "Behold, the dwelling place of God is with man. He will dwell with them, and they will be his people, and God himself will be with them as their God."[84]

And the Creator Word and the incarnate Word left a memorial of Creation with us in the everlasting Word.

This was the second time God gave mankind the gift of language and speech. At the Creation, God gave Adam the gift of speech to name and order His Creation. At Pentecost, this gift was given again in the form of the Holy Spirit. The purpose, however, remained the same: to be

82. Rom 8:10–11.

83. Rom 8:19–24.

84. Rev 21:1–3.

God's agents serving Him in the ordering of Creation. While the individual, as a part of the larger reclamation of Creation, is the beneficiary of this process, reclaiming and redeeming Creation is not for humanity's well-being. It is to fulfill the original purpose of Creation, which was to center on the fullness of God in an attitude of complete subjection, worship, and praise. We are blessed to be invited to participate.

Sanctified language and speech are even more critical in the New Testament context because the kingdom is at hand and death has been conquered. The authentic narrative must be even more carefully guarded, lest it destroy authority and witness and trigger sin, judgment, and eternal damnation.

> Likewise the Spirit helps us in our weakness. For we do not know what to pray for as we ought, but the Spirit himself intercedes for us with groanings too deep for words. And he who searches hearts knows what is the mind of the Spirit, because the Spirit intercedes for the saints according to the will of God.[85]

Like Moses, we are now able to speak "face to face" with God through the everlasting Word, so that we may be "conformed to the image of his Son."[86] Being made in His image is the very language of Creation.

God's purpose for Creation has been fulfilled in the here and now. It is not an ancient myth. The new Jerusalem awaits only the general resurrection to be completed in matter as well as in time and space. The relationship between Creation and sanctified speech remains as vibrant and vital as it has been since the beginning of time. God continues to control the journey, and He has invited us as fellow workers in the process. He has left the everlasting Word to sustain us in our labors. What an honor and a blessing. Praise God!

85. Rom 8:26–27.

86. Rom 8:29.

# Conclusion

THE VERY STANDARDS BY which anthropologists and mythologists define and classify myths are sufficient to refute the idea that Creation is a myth. There should be no shame or hesitation in defending Creation as unique, unequaled by any other origin story. Creation is not a "cleverly devised myth," as St. Peter concluded more than two thousand years ago.

Creation is also not an event. It is a journey of re-creation, redemption, and salvation. It will be completed when the new kingdom is established "on earth as it is in heaven." At that time, the universe will have cast off the chaos of sin. Order will be restored, all things will be re-centered in the moral and ethical image of God, and humanity will once again live in a perfected relationship with the Creator. Myths only offer curious beginnings; Creation offers a dynamic finale.

Eschatology, simply stated, is the study of the end of human history. Implicit in such a thought process is the question of what happens when history ends. Humans, uniquely, have been afforded the opportunity to choose their ending. That choice is based on whether one believes there is a purpose behind Creation or that it is simply a series of random accidents.

Purpose infers intention, an intention to achieve something. If there is an underlying purpose in God's Creation of the universe, then it must be logical, cohesive, and sustained by some force or forces greater than ourselves. That purpose can only be positive, good, or utopian. It cannot be negative, evil, or dystopian. It would be illogical to imagine a force that creates only for the purposes of destroying itself.

The other option is an existence without purpose. If there is no purpose behind the beginning of the universe, then there can be no purpose to anything created thereby. It has no meaning. There is certainly nothing noble about humanity emerging under such circumstances. If human history demonstrates any consistent theme, it is humanity's desire for purpose and meaning. Aside from a few sociopaths, humans have sought to replace the chaos of wars, plagues, and natural disasters with some semblance of order. In short, people want to be happy, free from pain and sorrow. They want to opt for a purposeful, meaningful existence. Whether the skeptics want to admit it or not, people seek purpose because the prospect of this being all there is to life is hardly encouraging. Constantly seeking some purpose, some source of meaning, is the only antidote to a rather grim, hopeless existence otherwise. Existentialism is a theoretical philosophy, interesting to write about but impossible to live.

The question then remains: What path to follow? If one makes a choice logically, it will be a path that can be lived meaningfully and that offers some hope. It should be sustainable, with a narrative that has lasted and been tested over many thousands of years. It should be unchanged and unchanging, with a transcendent value proposition that serves both human and eternal needs. Its objectives must be transparent, clearly stated, and hopeful. It must have rules that support an achievable outcome.

Creation alone offers such a choice. There is no churning through various stages of existence. There are no contests among divinities for power or authority. There are no costly potions, crystals, or talismans. There is a clear and unambiguous promise of hope at the end of a carefully designed journey.

But a journey of hope and promise is only possible under a very specific set of circumstances. There can only be one divine creator, one value proposition, and one historical narrative. Neither multiple gods nor the absence of god can order a consistent, cohesive, eternal process. Gods moving in and out of history are the antithesis of consistency, as are a series of accidents that cannot support any narrative at all. A big bang may offer a suitable explanation for a physical beginning, but it cannot project any moral or ethical ending.

Myths offer narratives of chaotic and contentious emergence, ambivalent creators, erratic commitments, and doubtful conclusions. Beginnings and endings have, at best, a random relationship in mythology and offer nothing that spans the entire spectrum of time and space. No myth has the confidence to define the end of time, much less attract generations of believers across a broad cultural spectrum. They are guarded and provincial. A universe that is not structured according to a clear set of transcendent, unchanging principles cannot ever be completed. It can only expire without hope or promise.

Creation is the only explanation of the beginning of time where there is a supernatural being uniquely invested in the success of the enterprise, and whose commitment is immediate and evident at all times and in all places. God is never absent at any time or at any point in the Creation narrative, and at no point does He cede any measure of control to another god or demigod. His covenants call us to be partners. His intentions are irrefutable and unequivocal, wrapped in a consistent narrative.

There is an identifiable, logical, workable hierarchy in Creation, with definite responsibilities and a straightforward vision of defined expectations. The governing structures of other origin stories are vague. There are loose confederations of familial connections, frequently at odds with one another. No god has unambiguous authority. Human beings, to the extent that they may participate in myths at all, do so by negotiation or warfare, unlike Creation's plan, where mankind has been given the authority to manage the enterprise and the tools to deliver the results. God's plan has been accessible and evident since the beginning. Through the extraordinary gift of language and speech, the roles and responsibilities of mankind are made clear. The mechanism for recording and sustaining an authentic history has been provided. There is nothing this well-conceived in any other narrative or explanation of creation.

This is the uniqueness of Creation. The Scriptures outline the path forward and define the basis of the relationship between the Creator and Creation. They establish the pattern for properly ordering and governing the universe in accordance with God's moral and ethical standards. This imperative not only serves immediate human needs, with its insistence on care and compassion, but also offers an eternal partnership and fellowship in a perfected relationship with God. Even given the flaws of a fallen humanity, previous generations at least acknowledged the premise of Creation. But what has this become in a cynical, postmodern twenty-first century?

The underlying assumptions of Creation remain the same today as they have always been: one God, invested in our future, relying upon a careful and accurate rendition of the Creation narrative to move the process forward. The challenges also remain, although dressed up in a modern guise: idolatrous behaviors that supplant God as the animating force in our lives; the assumption of human understanding as the height of spiritual, intellectual, and emotional awareness; the seductive allure of alternate truths and realities, and those who champion them; and a feckless willingness to abandon our values to accommodate culturally derived concepts of peace and stability. The result is undeniable: chaos reigns, but we continue to dip into the same poisoned well searching for answers.

The characteristics that distinguish Creation from myth are not simply evidentiary. They are not prominent throughout Scripture simply to make a case. God does not need to prove anything. These distinctions exist and are constantly reinforced throughout Scripture for the purposes of defining human behavior. The underlying components of the journey to redemption and salvation are clear, not only in the Scriptures but also in the lives of patriarchs and saints: acknowledging the obligation to obey a monotheistic God, honoring the covenants that shape our faith, guarding the integrity of the authentic narrative of Creation, and accepting the responsibilities of building the new kingdom. They are the operating guidelines for our lives, guard rails that shaped the modern world for thousands of years but have been allowed to erode over the past six decades or so.

In practical terms, how should the faithful respond? Once again, the unique characteristics of Creation bracket the options. First of all, it is not sufficient to simply state there is only one true God and then move on. One must embrace the entirety of monotheism and all that it portends. Monotheism is the bedrock of our faith. Without it, there can be no covenants, no consistent narrative, no Word made flesh, no forgiveness, salvation, or redemption. For someone living the faith of godly monotheism, it cannot be merely acknowledged intellectually. It must be lived practically. Adopting a godly, monotheistic view of the world requires two profound intellectual and spiritual adjustments to contemporary thought.

The first is a willingness to confront the great contest between good and evil, the temptations that occasioned the first acts of disobedience. A wholehearted, spiritual commitment to the existence of an omnipotent and omniscient God requires acknowledgment of a God that is responsible for all that occurs, both good and evil. Everything falls at God's metaphoric feet.

This tension is the most commonly stated reason for rejecting the divinity of God. How can bad things happen to good people? This question is an excuse for idolatry, the willingness to look elsewhere for answers to the inexplicable mysteries of life. The coexistence of good and evil in a loving God is the source of the most complex and impactful choices at the core of human existence. It fashions the moral code of life, the ethics of human relationships. In fact, it is impossible to live within the fullness of God without understanding that He is the authority behind both good and evil. The theodical nature of the universe is necessary if there is to be a completed Creation at the end of time. Only under those circumstances can we see clearly that the center of the universe is God and not humanity.

The other option is simply dismissing or ignoring the complexities that lead to and flow from the coexistence of good and evil. It forces one to accept a universe with multiple spiritual authorities, or no spiritual authority, so that accountability for positive and negative outcomes can be assigned without ambiguity. The absence of a fully accountable creator in that sort of environment leads to the second adjustment in contemporary thinking: the recognition of sin.

The essence of sin is the rejection of God's authority. Outside of a monotheistic structure, other spiritual authorities, whether found in nature, the mysterious cosmos, or deep-seated psychological theories, can be defined, identified, and adopted as legitimate. When there are multiple authorities, nothing can deviate from authority. The result is a condition of moral anarchy. Sin, in the Creation context, has been virtually eliminated from the modern vocabulary, replaced by culturally derived definitions of right and wrong.

The matter of sin is highly charged with questions of power and authority, concepts which drive modern thinking. Who has power and how is it exercised? Under what authority can power be employed? The introduction of the idea of sin skews the argument. It suggests a failure of human authority to control its environment. It concedes power and authority to another, more powerful being. It also suggests the failure or unwillingness of that supernatural being to govern.

Understanding the defining characteristics of power and authority will help navigate the apparent conundrum. Power is the ability to affect real, substantive change in another person's life, whether permission to affect such change has been granted or not. Autocrats, whether political, social, or economic, are constantly exerting power over others. Authority, on the other hand, is the ability to affect change because it is both perceived and accepted as grounded in a greater authority than oneself, such as ethics or the law. If I accede to the decisions of duly elected officials, intellectuals of proven standing, or social figures who have earned respect, that is not a matter of succumbing to power. It is acknowledging authority.

Power flows from authority. It can be a legitimate, vested authority or one merely assumed by virtue of circumstances. Authority can also be complete or limited. Those seeking to exercise power always try to validate the source of authority from whence their power flows. It can be the divine right of kings, the power of the people, or the protection of the weak and powerless. The examples are profuse and imaginative, but everyone in a position of power goes to great lengths to justify exercising power. They also go to great lengths to shift blame for failure to those appealing to other sources of authority. This relationship of power and authority seems ingrained in human nature. In a purely secular context, sources of authority can be relatively stable, but, as history demonstrates, they are subject to change. These changes can be beneficial or malignant, but secular sources of authority are unstable and often unjust.

From the standpoint of Creation, God is the source of ultimate authority. Ultimate authority means that the existence of both good and evil flows from the same source with no excuses. This recognition forces mankind to confront the reality of evil, the existence of sin, as something that operates subject to godly authority. It cannot be accidental or unintended in a purposeful Creation. At some point, humanity began to distance itself from the idea of Satan (the devil, the enemy, the evil one, the accuser, Lucifer, or whatever it might be called) as an embodiment of evil that materially impacts our lives. There has been nothing more convenient for the author of sin than to be dismissed as irrelevant. Certainly, any sense that Satan might exist, let alone exercise power and authority, has been ridiculed even in many circles claiming to be Christian.

There are two important points to consider in this regard. First, refusing to acknowledge the author of evil and sin diminishes the significance of the author of goodness and forgiveness. This is precisely where the secularists want us to be. Satan must be recognized as a real force in this world, disrupting the heavenly order and creating chaos. Satan influences thoughts and minds, sowing discontent, outrage, disrespect, pettiness, lies, and ultimately, eternal damnation. If a force such as this is dismissed, then the balancing forces of life-giving peace and unqualified love have no meaning. Their impacts are insignificant because the challenge has been nullified. What fills the vacuum is the unreliability of human wisdom, a dystopian god without hope or promise. We see this on daily display in art, literature, movies, politics, education, and the media.

Secondly, the nature of the power and authority that resides in Satan has increasingly been ignored or co-opted by cultural imagery, moving

Satan from reality to fiction. The conceit that humanity is the center of the universe has pushed every other consideration aside, which explains the unwillingness to accept the existence of a material force of evil that cannot be overcome by human endeavor alone. Better to make such a concept a fictional device than come to grips with the inability of mankind to confront such a creature on its own. Surrender is preferable to an admission of inadequacy in a human-centered worldview.

Both the Old and New Testaments provide the proper perspective, clarifying the existence of Satan, the source of his authority, and the limitations of his power. Through the Scriptures, Satan becomes comprehensible. When this is understood and fully appreciated, the weaknesses of the enemy are exposed, and we can take comfort that we do not face spiritual warfare alone. The apparent contradictions of theodicy disappear.

The boundaries and constraints of evil can be best seen in both Matthew and Luke, which contain an account of Satan tempting Christ.[1] In both instances, Satan told Jesus that he had the authority to give Him all the kingdoms of the world if Jesus would worship him. "To you I will give all this authority and their glory, for it has been delivered to me, and I give it to whom I will."[2] What Satan is referring to in this passage as "it has been delivered to me" is his authority to operate, not the possession of the kingdoms of the world. Satan's authority was not, by his own admission, organic. This power and authority did not originate in Satan but was "delivered" to him by something or someone far more powerful and possessing even greater authority.

This grant of limited authority to Satan was the direct result of humanity's fall from grace. Part of God's punishment for the original sins of disobedience was giving Satan temporary, albeit limited, authority in the world. If mankind was presumptuous enough to assume godly authority over life and death, then it would live with those consequences. This limited authority was revealed in Job, when God granted Satan the right to strip Job of all he had. "Only against him do not stretch out your hand."[3] Similarly, it was God who gave the devil the power and authority to tempt Jesus, as corroborated in the first letter of John and Paul's second letter to the Corinthians.[4]

1. Matt 4:8–9; Luke 4:5–7.
2. Luke 4:6.
3. Job 1:12.
4. 1 John 5:19; 2 Cor 4:4. The recognition of God's greater spiritual authority is

The point here is that by rejecting the real manifestation of evil, the entire idea of sin has been vitiated. In our current cultural climate, there is really no such thing as sin. There are only departures or deviations from accepted cultural norms or governing interpretations of law. As is readily evident, cultural norms and legal interpretations are overturned regularly, generally creating confusion and anxiety.

The reality is, as strange as it may seem, that accepting the existence of sin and evil properly realigns relationships. The definition of sin is derived not from human convention but from God's moral and ethical standards, His value proposition. Our responsibility to order Creation according to these standards does not allow human convention to supersede God's control over good and evil.

There is no list in the Bible that establishes a hierarchy of sin. Like it or not, we are all equal in our sinfulness. In ordering Creation, we have been given the authority to identify certain social behaviors as more onerous than others, which clearly makes possible the ability to distinguish bad behavior from acceptable behavior. But it has not given us the authority to condemn one another as more sinful. The flip side of the biblical call to love one another is the commandment not to judge one another. These two principles go hand in hand. They cannot be separated. You cannot truly love your brother if, at the same time, you are consigning him to a place of eternal damnation. Unfortunately, when morality becomes a purely human convention, these boundaries do not exist.

Jesus made this point quite forcefully:

> Judge not, that you be not judged. For with the judgment you pronounce you will be judged, and with the measure you use it will be measured to you. Why do you see the speck that is in your brother's eye, but do not notice the log that is in your own eye? Or how can you say to your brother, "Let me take the speck out of your eye," when there is the log in your own eye. You hypocrite, first take the log out of your own eye, and then you will see clearly to take the speck out of your brother's eye.[5]

This is the only possible basis for developing and sustaining a common, shared human experience. Acknowledging our sin and disobedience and seeking redemption and salvation from the same loving God

---

confirmed in Zech 3:2 and Jude 9, where godly authority rebukes Satan. St. Peter's discussion of false prophets and teachers in his second letter (2 Pet 2:1–16) makes the same point.

5. Matt 7:1–5.

creates a bond between humans that is superior to any other. It focuses attention away from the clumsy and destructive attempts at judgment and reconciliation that define our current culture. It places all people on the same eternal plane. Whatever the time frame, a human life is nothing in the span of eternity. The fundamental similarities of having been created equal in the image of God, sharing a fallen nature, and seeking forgiveness should be the basis for human relationships, not unwarranted superiority or self-affirming judgment. This is what fully accepting the responsibilities of godly monotheism calls us to be: non-judgmental, caring, and compassionate people. People who reject hatred and violence, bitterness and deceit, strife and enmity, and instead really understand what Jesus meant by the simple statement of "love thy neighbor."

Denying scriptural monotheism is the source of idolatry in the twenty-first century. Worshiping a small token or figurine is obvious, and humans continue to worship things, but the real issue of idolatry is placing something else, material or otherwise, ahead of God, stripping Him of power and authority. The sense of moral superiority that has come to be the axis of human interaction has become a consuming, unhealthy focus. It is the center of our lives, the defining standard for all our thoughts and actions. Increasingly, we seek wisdom anywhere but God. It may be a horoscope, a television doctor, an internet influencer, or a self-help practitioner. In other instances, a fixation on fame, money, cultural superiority, or physical beauty. Notwithstanding, it is idolatry. It is the substitution of god as a human contrivance for the God of Creation. Embracing one true God and acknowledging the nature of evil in our lives centers the source of wisdom. It is not a whim or fancy that floats in and out of fashion; it is the wellspring of genuine worship.

The logic of Creation monotheism leads directly to personal, moral accountability and responsibility. In an atheistic, agnostic, or polytheistic environment, the existence of many gods or no gods diffuses moral authority and transfers the power to define ethical standards to whatever one chooses to worship. Those worshiping something other than the God of Creation recognize only that which they worship as the source of morality. When everything has moral standing, nothing has moral standing. There is no need to confront an existential evil or accept personal responsibility. One simply selects from a menu of alternate moral authorities and moves on. It does not matter if it is hurtful to others as long as it is consoling to me. It is this lack of moral responsibility and accountability that facilitates chaos. We all carry seeds of idolatry. We are all tempted by the allure of other gods. The late author David Foster Wallace, in a commencement address to the 2005 graduating class at Kenyon College, acknowledged as much when he said, "You get to decide what to worship. . . . Because here's something else that's true. In the day-to-day trenches of adult life, there is actually no such thing as atheism. There is no such thing as worshiping. Everybody worships. The only choice we get is *what* to worship."[6]

And this did not come from a place of faith. But it is a secular affirmation of the earlier observation that we get to choose. God gives us the opportunity to choose to worship Him or worship something else. And He gives Satan temporary power to work evil in this world. We all experience those moments when Satan takes us to the mountain top and offers the kingdoms of the world. Recognizing the personal responsibility of being created in the image of God and choosing that path is the beginning of true wisdom. "But now you must put them all away: anger, wrath, malice, slander and obscene talk from your mouth. Do not lie to one another, seeing that you have put off the old self with its practices and have put on the new self, which is being renewed in knowledge after the image of its creator."[7]

Moving to the matter of godly covenants, a monotheistic belief system provides substance and vitality to the covenants. It is easy, when broaching the question of covenants, to treat them as something important at the time but archaic now. But when asking ourselves how a Christian should respond to a postmodern, increasingly secular and dominant culture, the matter of Old Testament covenants is as important as understanding the obligations inherent in a monotheistic worldview. The covenant characteristics of Creation are one of the distinctions separating Creation from myth. Honoring the covenants that God made with the Old Testament patriarchs, and the covenant that took on the form of a man who was the living image of God, is a requirement of the Creation experience.

In the first place, it clearly establishes the primacy of one God over all other pretenders. A covenant is an agreement with deliverables. Such an agreement could not be made without acknowledging the standing of two parties. A contract is not enforceable if it was entered into as a result of pressure or if one of the two parties cannot be held accountable for his

6. Wallace, "David Foster Wallace on Life."

7. Col 3:8–11.

or her actions. There is no evidence that God pressured Abraham, Noah, Moses, or David to sign on the dotted line, and sacrificing His own flesh to offer a covenant of eternal reconciliation was certainly not a power play. Furthermore, the fact that God was willing to enter into agreements with mankind is an incredible confirmation of how much He values us. In order to honor an agreement, one must accept the legitimacy of the other party and expect compliance. From a human standpoint, this is an acknowledgment of one true God, with the power and authority to deliver as promised. From God's standpoint, it is a measure of His mercy and grace.

Secondly, in a world of many gods, covenants are impossible. In buying a house, one signs a contract with the seller for the whole house. The buyer does not negotiate for the sale of the bathrooms from one source, the kitchen from another, and so on. No one would be responsible for the whole. God is responsible for all the universe. It is not necessary to chase down one god for the rain, another for healing, or a third for success in business. His covenants are all inclusive, especially His last covenant of reconciliation, finalized by the crucifixion, resurrection, and ascension of Jesus Christ. This covenant has already come to fruition in the hearts of believers and will come to material fruition in the new kingdom.

Covenant agreements speak to partnership. God made Abraham, Noah, Moses, and David partners in rescuing a fallen people and reenergizing their faith. That tradition continued when Jesus became the embodiment of the Old Testament covenants and called us to partner with Him in the building of the new kingdom. A Christian today must recognize that the task before him or her is to be as diligent in establishing covenants with the community and one another as the earlier patriarchs were. We must see ourselves as inheritors of living covenants that are immediate and binding. The Scriptures are full of agreements between God and man. They are covenants and an ingredient of a faithful life. Fulfilling covenant obligations is key to the partnership trust.

The Old and New Testament covenants are what bind the history of Creation. An appendix entitled "Who Owns History?" is a part of this volume. The recognition that God is in charge of history, and that, in fact, He owns human history, brings with it the understanding that part of our responsibility is to defend that history, to assure that the authentic narrative of history is accurately preserved and passed on to future generations. That obligation is restated time and time again throughout the biblical text.

Accurately guarding the narrative and defending history requires knowledge and a diligent commitment to scriptural truth. Success in any endeavor demands discipline and repetitive behaviors that reinforce that discipline. We applaud the professional golfer who hits hundreds of balls each day on the range, the chef who consistently tests new recipes, the engineer who stays current with the latest practices and materials, the medical practitioner who gives up free time to read the most recent juried articles, or the corporate executive who constantly finds ways to improve the workplace and the quality of the company's goods or services. Repetition hones the skills and perfects the outcomes.

Many Christians, in their secular roles, willingly adopt these routines. Yet we are often not as rigorous in the practice of our faith. We talk about practicing faith, but that has become more of a euphemism for going to church. Practicing *for* faith might be a better way to put it. Every day should have time for Scripture, prayer, and a search for wisdom. "And this is the confidence that we have toward him, that if we ask anything according to his will he hears us."[8] We need to mature as Christians as we seek to mature in our secular roles. A mature faith leads to a greater understanding of the Creation narrative and the strength to live it out in our personal lives.

Paul recognized the importance of being steeped in the knowledge and wisdom of God. The purpose was:

> for building up the body of Christ, until we all attain to the unity of the faith and of the knowledge of the Son of God, to mature manhood, to the measure of the stature of the fullness of Christ, so that we may no longer be children, tossed to and fro by the waves and carried about by every wind of doctrine, by human cunning, by craftiness in deceitful schemes.[9]

It is Paul's last phrase that is the crux of the matter. Human cunning and craftiness in deceitful schemes represent the replacement of God's understanding with human understanding. False teachers, prophets, and prophesying are rather old-fashioned concepts, easy to dismiss. But a corrupted and distorted version of prophets can be seen everywhere. They are the experts who presume to have a special knowledge not available to others. Their knowledge is frequently accompanied by dire warnings. Those rejecting their warnings are classified as irredeemable fools, or

8. 1 John 5:14.

9. Eph 4:12–14.

worse, worthless creatures that need to be condemned and driven from our midst. We see them every day. Zealots on all sides of every issue. They do not speak from a place of care and consideration. They do not plead for salvation or redemption. They supplant wisdom with a human understanding of their own provenance. They do not acknowledge an authority greater than themselves. Unfortunately, they have created a model for human behavior that is arrogant, suspicious, selfish, and ignorant.

Peddling falsehoods has become the norm in politics, the media, science, education, and public policy. Even in the modern Christian community, it is not uncommon for those in authority to selectively cull out sections of the Bible convenient for their purposes and reject those that are inconvenient. They reject sin and replace it with social consciousness, whatever that means. They are not guarding the narrative or passing on the authentic truths of God's history. They are not protecting the semiotics, the symbolism of faith that passes all understanding, which has provided comfort and peace to generations of believers. Under these circumstances, it is little wonder that churches are losing their members and their relevance. Social clubs and political action committees are more appealing. At least in those circumstances, one can find a place where one's own conceits are not challenged. The cultural surrender that Joshua so forcefully condemned is on full display in our time.

Joshua spoke about building a kingdom. It was the earthly kingdom that God had promised Abraham. But with the new covenant of resurrection and ascension, a new kingdom has been inaugurated, one that calls us to be the stewards we were created to be. The idea of being created in the image of God needs to be reclaimed and reenergized. It is a profound responsibility, not to be disregarded or taken lightly. We have forgotten what it means to be created in His image.

It would seem obvious that at the Creation, Adam and Eve were the perfect image of God, perhaps not physically but certainly intellectually, ethically, and spiritually. That did not confer equality with God, but if the initial Creation existed in a perfected state, then Adam and Eve could only have been perfected to some degree themselves. It is after the original acts of sin that the issue becomes more complex. Fallen humanity was not capable of any degree of perfection.

However, as we know, God did not abandon His Creation but set in motion a process for the ultimate redemption and salvation of humanity. The new kingdom is promised as a re-creation of the initial, perfected relationship between God and humanity. Thus, it follows logically that with the inauguration of the new kingdom, humanity will once again assume the perfected image of God. There is a great gap between sharing the image of God in the beginning and sharing His image at the end, leaving the question of what being created in the image of God means in the interim.

There is a vast body of literature and scholarship demonstrating an evolving view of what this means. Jewish writings in the Second Temple period, wisdom literature, and Paul's epistles present the idea in a number of different shades, encompassing physical, intellectual, and moral imagery.[10] The importance, from our standpoint, is that it is part of the journey of Creation, a journey in which we are invited to participate. In order to participate, there must be some remnant of God's image still active within us.

What remains, and what can be seen throughout all of Paul's writings, is an imperfect spark of God's omniscient and omnipresent moral and ethical nature. Although the chosen stewards of this value proposition were corrupted by sin, the proposition itself remained pure and unadulterated. It was not adjusted to conform to human weakness and conceit but continued steadfast and true. It is part of our responsibility to tap into this reservoir. Working this mandate out under real circumstances can put Christians in a particularly difficult position. Either we follow the script as a responsible people set apart, or we adjust the narrative so it becomes more manageable and comfortable.

Unfortunately, in rejecting the Creation narrative, we have tossed aside what it means to be created in the image of God. It has become fashionable in political, academic, and media circles particularly to rely on an identification model to evaluate one's probability of success. Unless an individual can identify with someone "who looks like me," they are handicapped in their ability to achieve. Validation is impossible unless it comes through an identification lens.

There is no question that role models are important and that chances for success are improved by role models and mentors. But selecting racial or gender characteristics as determinants of success actually reduces chances for success. It can become an excuse for failure. It forces opportunity through a narrow funnel that continues to dissect society into even smaller and more parochial camps. It ignores qualities such as moral fiber, courage, intellectual ability, curiosity, or experience. These are qualities that transcend physical images, images that can be distorted

10. See, for example, Montgomery, "Image of God."

and manipulated into destructive behaviors by cultural pressure or the internet. Eating disorders, drug use, unhealthy lifestyles, and healthcare charlatans abound on social media. There are studies in the fields of advertising and marketing, for example, that suggest how ethnicity modeling has a limited, and in some cases, negative impact on purchasing behavior.[11] The only real, sustainable models are found in the image of God.

A good measure of whether the characteristics of Creation and the image of God are meaningful is the way in which any given audience chooses to relate to the past (history), to view physical reality (science), and how it defines and values humanity (social justice).

Creation is history. It is the history of salvation, the history of God's ceaseless efforts to replace chaos with order, the history of redeeming Creation, and the history of the new kingdom. Increasingly, we have chosen to reject history rather than deal with truths, both uplifting and ugly. Instead, the study of history has become a process of self-affirmation. Popular historical narratives are being crafted to reinforce competing prejudices and biases and to prove the legitimacy of one's own conceits. Cultural patterns and beliefs, which served to inform the past, present, and future, and which provided social and psychological stability, have been ridiculed and rebuked, pitting segments of society against one another. What remains is schizophrenic cultural immolation.

We reshape and distort the past to avoid confronting truths about human nature, and in doing so, seek to absolve ourselves from any suggestion that we may be just as flawed. The 1619 project, sponsored by *The New York Times*, is an example of recreating an alternate narrative to excuse contemporary behavior and support arguments for bias and prejudice. It has been roundly, and quite properly, criticized by historians and academics across the entire spectrum of political opinion. The theory of settler colonialism, another modern conceit, condemns western civilization for dispossessing indigent populations and demands that anyone not a direct descendant from an indigenous population acknowledge their guilt and apologize for their crimes. The suggestion that Western development is illegitimate and its successes should be surrendered to more legitimate authorities permeates the entire conversation. Northwestern University offers one of many examples of how this plays out. It has posted a land acknowledgment on the internet that "recognizes

11. For example, see Raphael, *Gospel of Wellness*; Rosner and Eisend, "Ethnic Minorities in Advertising"; and Overgoor et al., "From Representation to Reception."

and respects Indigenous Peoples as traditional stewards of this land" that the campus occupies. "Land acknowledgements do not exist in a past tense, or historical context: colonialism is a current ongoing process, and we need to build our mindfulness of our present participation."[12] Aside from the fact that this is a pointless, self-serving statement, it does no justice to indigenous peoples themselves. It provides them with nothing of meaning or substance. It exploits indigenous peoples for the purposes of making the leadership of Northwestern feel better about their own cosseted positions. It also conveniently ignores the fact that many indigenous populations prospered by conquest and the subjugation of other indigenous populations. The Aztecs did not create a vibrant culture or a powerful empire by issuing land acknowledgments.

In fairness, this is not an entirely new phenomenon. The popular notion that the Puritans traveled to North America to seek religious freedom is belied by the fact that the Puritans wanted nothing to do with any religion that did not conform to their unique brand of faith. They were as aggressive in rooting out heretics and apostates as the countries they left. Another example is the Myth of the Lost Cause that emerged after the Civil War, recasting the conflict as one pitting a noble, chivalric class defending its rights and honor from a rabble of avaricious, industrial barbarians who finally prevailed on the basis of their economic might. Misrepresentations of Union buffoonery versus Confederate gallantry were invented and perpetuated by the Southern Historical Society, founded in part by Confederate Gen. Jubal T. Early. "For instance, to explain defeat, they asserted that Johnny Reb was actually the superior combatant, but the North's endless population and the willingness of boorish Union commanders to win by attrition eventually turned the conflict."[13] Similarly, many murderers, thieves, and social misfits of the late nineteenth century emerge as heroes of the "Old West," while Bonnie and Clyde are merely misunderstood, modern-day Robin Hoods.

Whether revisionist histories, which become part of history themselves, should be eradicated by equally tenuous revisions of history is an entirely different matter. By defaulting to an arrogant presumption of tribal righteousness, however, we end up exploiting our differences and being dismissive of others. Selectively restating the past makes it impossible to envision the future. I would hope that historians hundreds of

12. Northwestern University, "Native American and Indigenous Initiatives," cited from LSPIRG, "Know the Land Territories Campaign," para. 2.

13. Hulbert, *Oracle of Lost Causes*, 210.

years from now are more intellectually honest and gracious to us than we have been to those who preceded us. But denying history is to ignore the message of Creation. The past is meant to be instructive. The entire message of redemption and salvation calls us to honestly confront our own fallen natures. It is deemed critical to maturing in divine wisdom and understanding. Only through a willingness to view history through a lens broad in its perspectives and painfully honest can individuals experience sustained growth and development. The same is true for societies. Crafting accounts of the past that force contrived binary choices destroys the cohesiveness and completeness of society, which is meant to reflect God's order.

A dangerous and systemic issue behind all these efforts to rewrite history through the lens of "my truth" (as though personal truth exists on a higher plane than any other truth) is the matter of victimhood. In the absence of a stable, transcendent ethos, we wallow in a pig stye of victimization. To be relevant in many circles today, one must be able to claim a victim status of some sort. This is not what God intended when He created man and woman in His own image.[14] Nothing that God created is meant to be denigrated as being a victim. There are genuine victims out there, and they deserve all the compassion and assistance a thoughtful society can provide. They do not deserve to have real, compelling needs sidetracked by false claims. Purposely choosing to be a victim is not godly. In Kant's *The Metaphysics of Morals*, he establishes, within his doctrine of virtue, a division of ethics. One of the specific ethical duties to oneself is to avoid false humility, which diminishes the nobility of one's humanity.[15] When issues are structured around culturally defined guilt, they create two classes: one of inherited and enduring superiority and another of ceaseless and inescapable inferiority. The first can't help themselves and are therefore condemned to eternal shame, and the other can't help themselves and are condemned to eternal failure.

Science suffers from the same sort of social appropriation. Science is no longer viewed within the context of discovery and examination; it is cherry-picked for single points of argument, without context, in order to defend a predetermined bias. Taking, for example, the matter of what

14. A new book, just released at the time of this writing, takes the idea of the image of God much further. The author persuasively argues that the image of God is central to the development and promulgation of the value structure of Western civilization. Persico, *In God's Image.*

15. Kant, *Metaphysics of Morals*, 181, 201–12.

is safe to eat or breathe, an ingredient may be classified by regulators as toxic, and therefore as a clear and present danger. But if it requires fifty times an average body weight, consumed twice a day, its toxicity is irrelevant. Health and safety zealots are willing to sacrifice reality-based science for their own causes. Science is not an answer; it is a process—a process of greater understanding that is ordained by God as a legitimate path to wisdom. Time and again, we have shown disdain for the process, opting for answers that are convenient, reinforce our prejudices, and do not demand discipline or honesty. In this current age, we look to the latest internet solutions to see what the members of our tribe currently embrace. We mock the snake oil salesmen and patent medicine peddlers of the past but are willing to inject or ingest some of the oddest things because a TikTok influencer has endorsed it or it has a huge Facebook following. We largely ignore scientists but will eagerly embrace the wackiest theory if it has millions of followers. We explore the great expanses of the cosmos but cannot see its mystery and majesty.

The drive for market share has propelled marketing and advertising as the first order of business for most corporations, not product reliability, cost effectiveness, or safety. The practice of wellness, "the pursuit of well-being outside the realm of medicine" (and I would add science in general), is now a $4.4 trillion industry, created in large measure by charlatans and championed by corporate greed.[16] An excellent study of the wellness industry includes a chapter entitled "Gym as Church."[17] In a rush to be first with the latest, journalism sacrifices thorough and thoughtful analysis for dramatic headlines. Every morning television show has a house doctor who breathlessly announces the preliminary results of some study, which, after further study, is incomplete at best if not actually wrong. By putting greater emphasis on ratings or followers, for example, credibility has been ceded to crackpots such as those who claim that vaccines cause autism. Meanwhile, suspicions of vaccines gave rise to diseases that were virtually eliminated generations earlier, and serious study of autism is derailed by the need to refute false claims. Eggs were the devil's handiwork a few years back but are now considered a near-perfect food. Better fry a couple quickly because they are likely to be consigned once again to the culinary dustbin in the future.

16. Raphael, *Gospel of Wellness*, 4.

17. Raphael, *Gospel of Wellness*, 93–120.

We ignore the physical realities of biology and, in the process, destroy the very people we claim to protect. We demand, as we should, the end of sexual predation and exploitation, but we erase the very distinctions that make such efforts meaningful. Women, who have struggled so courageously for their rights and identities over the past hundred years, are now being denigrated as mere "birthing parents" or "people with a capacity for pregnancy." One law professor is quoted as saying, "There are also trans men who are capable of pregnancy as well as nonbinary people who are capable of pregnancy."[18] The profundity of Creation's gender distinctions and the perfect model of gender relationships are impossible to discern or protect when there are no identifiable sexes. It now becomes a matter of finding a label along some contrived and fluid spectrum that can be used to leverage one's personal rage. The very act of constantly labeling and relabeling disengages one individual from another. These are false choices between flawed narratives. Torturously reshaping and redefining gender in an effort to overcome biological realities is exhaustive and has become an end in itself. When causality is separated from its roots, solutions cannot exist.

Human sexuality is complex and at times difficult to comprehend. Sexual behavior can be stressful and confusing. Choices are made, sometimes painfully, and sometimes under social pressures to conform. But genuine care, compassion, and understanding are impossible in the race to endlessly vivisect gender. We were not created simply to exist, in whatever form we choose, but to exist for others through the never-ending grace of God.

Living outside the sexual structure of Creation is sinful, but it is no more sinful in the eyes of God than any of the other myriad sins identified in the Bible. Again, it is worth repeating, there is no hierarchy of sin anywhere in the Scriptures. The never-ending grace of God demands that we approach one another from the shared standpoint of a fallen human nature, neither through judgment nor condemnation. It also means that we do not apologize for sin but profess the truths of the authentic narrative of Creation.

There is only one unforgivable sin, and that is denying the power of the Holy Spirit to affect real and immediate change in a person's life. When liberal theologians forsake their duty to teach and live the authentic narrative of redemption and salvation by treating sinful behavior as

18. US Senate testimony from Khiara Bridges, Senate Judiciary Committee, July 12, 2022.

acceptable in order to address a social issue, they are denying the power of the Holy Spirit to change the lives of sinners. They are further rejecting the argument that we are all sinners and should stand before God, begging forgiveness. That sets up two classes of people, which is contrary to God's sense of social justice. Liberal theology is not doing anyone any favors by rejecting Creation realities. It is merely prolonging pain and suffering by denying undeniable truths of biology and letting others suffer for their indifference to Creation truths and Christian responsibility.

Science should be a revelation of the Creation process. "I praise you, for I am fearfully and wonderfully made. Wonderful are your works; my soul knows it very well."[19] We idolize the physical component of mankind as the centerpiece of Creation, despite its imminent and observable decline, but deny all evidence of the eternal nature of the whole, comprehensive, created being.

To those who would ridicule this perspective as stupid or naïve, I would challenge them to look at the current state of affairs. Social justice suffers as warped and distorted messaging creeps into every aspect of our lives and our children's lives through advanced algorithms and artificial intelligence. Television doctors purporting to enlighten and heal instead become platforms for tortured and benighted souls to expose themselves to ridicule in front of millions of viewers. At some point, a prophet arises, utters his or her edicts, and proclaims the matter resolved. This is usually followed by triumphant tours of stage and screen, massive contract negotiations, and various books and podcasts promising fulfillment and a better life. Television judges cynically dispense justice to those willing to accept remuneration for celebrating their bad behavior through endless cycles of syndication. "And in their greed they will exploit you with false words."[20] Hypocrisy and logical incongruities are impossible to defend or ignore. They are either challenged or they fuel false narratives.

Meanwhile, millions of people who suffer real pain have little access to doctors and hospitals, and those seeking legal justice often have no recourse to swift and unbiased adjudication. This is precisely the problem Amos identified when prophesying to Israel. Social justice is part and parcel of the Lord's value proposition. "But let justice roll down like waters, and righteousness like an ever-flowing stream," later adding, "Hear this, you who trample on the needy and bring the poor of the land to an

19. Ps 139:14.
20. 2 Pet 2:3.

end."[21] As in Amos's time, those seeking answers for their broken spirits frequently find places of worship that are more interested in becoming political action committees.

A novel titled *Everything We Never Knew*, coauthored by a popular television personality, encourages us to identify our elemental makeup by exploring the four elements of nature—earth, air, water, and fire—and determining which best explains our unique elemental make up. Once discovered, the process for psychic self-examination can begin, where we de-layer by stripping away all prior beliefs and experiences to find real healing.[22] These are elements first proposed by the Greek philosopher Empedocles in 450 BCE, although there are serious doubts that he did any de-layering. Television shows such as *Big Brother* and *Survivor* reward people for deceit and manipulation. The popular series *The Bachelor* and *The Bachelorette* celebrate each act of distrust and betrayal with the straight-faced promise that each journey is a legitimate path to true love. All these productions are popular, with millions of viewers enjoying intimate details of individual lives eagerly displayed by the participants. Our lives have become carnival side shows, where everyone pays a dime to see a bearded lady or a human unicorn and walks away relieved that there is someone more pitiful than themselves. This is not the state of affairs that God ordained at the Creation, and it certainly does not reflect His image.

One of the Collects in the Book of Common Prayer opens with "Grant, O Lord, we beseech thee, that the course of this world may be so peaceably ordered by thy governance."[23] That is the task before us. To joyfully embrace the call to build the new kingdom. Myths do not call us to do anything. Apologists may find myths to be a storehouse of unconscious reactions to the world around us, but they do not motivate us to do good. One of the great canards is elevating the unconscious above the conscious. Unconscious behavior is now used to justify all manner of abhorrent thoughts and actions. But the strength and joy of the Creation narrative is that we have been empowered by the Creator to choose. We are measured by that which we consciously choose precisely because that is what we were created to do. The image of God, the covenant of reconciliation made manifest in the King of Kings, and the personal

21. Amos 5:24, 8:4.

22. Julianne Hough discussed the book in a *Good Morning America* interview on Aug. 13, 2024.

23. BCP, 616.

responsibilities of stewardship all culminate in eternal salvation. That is a narrative no subconscious urge can satisfy. The world can be a tough and ugly place. That is part of its reality. But it must be met with eyes wide open. Fortunately, through the power, mercy, and grace of God alone can we become forces of goodness and order. He has given us the strength and tools to do so. He has offered us real choices. It is up to us to make them.

# Appendix: Who Owns History?

The term history has two connotations. It can refer to all that has preceded the immediate present. This includes events, people, physical artifacts and even periods of great intellectual, scientific, political, or economic change. History can also refer to the art of recording and interpreting all that has occurred in the past. Both are subject to widely varying opinions and tend to elicit passionate reactions.

Until the late nineteenth and early twentieth centuries, people, events, and "things" were identified, debated, classified, and ultimately accepted as facts. These facts were dutifully recorded. The extent to which something was accepted as factual was, in many respects, considered to be of greater importance than any interpretation of the fact. Thus, a historical canon emerged that was generally and widely accepted as a baseline for the past.

The explosion of scientific discovery during the late eighteenth through the nineteenth centuries challenged the prism through which the natural world was viewed, and that shift gradually crept into the study of history. What became known as the scientific method supplanted earlier approaches to the physical world, based, as they were, on a general acceptance that there was an objective certainty behind known truths. The new approach began with hypotheses, built around what were perceived as known facts. Others, looking at the same fact pattern from different perspectives, tested and, if necessary, restated the initial proposition. The process was repeated as interest in the subject grew and, in its course, various, often competing, theories emerged. The recognition of the subjective quality of facts and fact patterns created an environment within which scientific knowledge increased, was enhanced and matured.

As this intellectual approach gained increasing acceptance, historians began to understand facts not as definitive truths but as dependent upon those interpreting the fact and the unique perspectives they brought to the process. The idea that there was a body of facts around which all of history could be packaged gave way to a more reasoned understanding that no one can approach a fact without the baggage of his or her own past. The mere thought that a fact, approached from different perspectives, could be seen and evaluated in surprisingly different ways was a shocking development for anyone steeped in nineteenth-century dogma. The foundational understanding of history up to that point assumed that a fact, once identified, was indisputable. The nineteenth-century approach to history was premised on the expectation that, eventually, all facts could be discovered and recorded. Through an increasingly enlightened knowledge of history, with all known facts available for review, the premise was that humanity would progressively benefit and could be improved even to the point of perfection.[1]

This illusion was shattered by two world wars in the early twentieth century. With the demise of nineteenth-century optimism and waning confidence in the absolute certainty of facts, a new approach began to take shape. Everything that was not physical science but involved the study of humans in their relationships with one another gradually morphed into the social sciences. The thought was that the scientific process could be applied to existing disciplines such as history, economics, literature, and the arts, and new areas of academic interest employing a scientific process would emerge which would be beneficial for improving human understanding. Sociology, political science, and anthropology, to name just a few, were no longer subsets of the older, core disciplines of classical liberal education but subject matters unto themselves. The result was that any school of thought that did not employ the hard calculus of scientific analyses was dismissed as out of touch.

The pivot to a more scientific approach put pressure on any hypothesis that did not display properties similar to those of the physical sciences. This would prove particularly problematic for something like theology. Since God, or any idea of an immediate and discernible divinity, was not accessible through hard facts, a void in long-standing cultural assumptions now appeared. The void of the unknowable had been removed from history except to the extent that the unknowable itself was viewed

1. Carr, *What Is History?*, 70–78.

as a fact pattern to be studied in terms of its social impact. That which was inexplicable and miraculous had to be replaced by something. One such approach was to reduce the miraculous to a deep-seated psychological reaction that could be explained as a repeatable pattern of responses to environmental stimuli common to all of humanity. Functionalism and structuralism offered one avenue of approach, mythology another, or simple agnostic rejection of anything divine, a third.

Not surprisingly, from a historical standpoint, these developments led to a certain hierarchy of factuality. There are, indeed, some points of the past that are unassailable truths, not subject to interpretation. Tutankhamun was a pharaoh, King Charles I was beheaded, the *Titanic* sank. These are what E. H. Carr called the "raw materials of the historian rather than of history itself."[2] But how King Tut died, why Charles I was beheaded, and who was at fault for the sinking of the *Titanic* are not quite so clear. And at the risk of beating the subject to death, the decision on which facts to apply can dramatically alter someone's recording and interpretation of the past. One can write a history of Egypt under the pharaohs, for example, and choose not to spend time on how and why Tut met his demise or its impact on Egyptian history. Until his tomb was uncovered, Tut may not have even shown up. Whether that is considered "good history" or not is in the mind of the beholder.

When the nature of factuality is recognized, a record of the past may very well be simply a reflection on what was important to the one doing the recording. The historian is an individual, with a past, and who is herself part of history. She interacts constantly with the elements of her own background and chooses what to include in her own reflections on the past. Again, citing Carr, "The dialogue between present and past, is a dialogue not between abstract and isolated individuals, but between the society of today and the society of yesterday."[3] Another noted historian of the art of history, Marc Bloch, put it this way: "A good half of all we see is seen through the eyes of others."[4] "Every age has its own outlook," C. S. Lewis wrote. "It is specially good at seeing certain truths and specially liable to make certain mistakes. . . . All contemporary writers share to some extent the contemporary outlook."[5]

2. Carr, *What Is History?*, 8.

3. Carr, *What Is History?*, 69.

4. Bloch, *Historian's Craft*, 49.

5. Athanasius, *On the Incarnation*, 6.

The question of right or wrong in history is equally nuanced. No human comes to the table without some sense of morality. Even one claiming to be neutral on questions of morality has already made a moral pronouncement. If history is indeed the reactions of individuals and society and between societies of different generations, then moral judgments will be colored by those experiences. Since historians get to choose what they wish to include as facts and will maintain a moral posture to some extent shaped by their environment, the reader of history has every right, if not obligation, to spend as much time studying the historian as they do the historian's output. That does not automatically validate or discredit the historian or his or her observations, but it does add an additional layer of understanding to history itself. It is important to understand that a historian, writing about the Great Depression, having seen his parents financially ruined, will have a unique take on financial institutions, the New Deal, and President Roosevelt. His granddaughter, writing two generations later, may have an entirely different view, particularly if her parents prospered during the 1950s and '60s. The one will excoriate banks and financiers, considering them both evil and malicious, while the other may well have celebrated the gains on bank investments in her IRA portfolio.

To the question, "Who owns history?" the glib answer is, whoever writes it. To a very large extent, that is correct, except that the intellectually honest historian will acknowledge biases and will give competing theories their due. However, in the current climate of celebratory victimhood and intersectionality, the glib is ascendent. As a result, history is being rewritten, slanted towards erasing the past and replacing it with a new version that sacrifices accuracy for ideology. Representations of figures and events of the past are no longer discussed within a classically liberal framework but are instead simply eliminated. The vacuum is filled with indoctrination and censorship. But the joy of history is that truths always find an inconvenient way to unsettle demagoguery. Time is the agent of truth and the enemy of the doctrinaire. As one author put it, "History is a merciless judge. It lays bare our tragic blunders and foolish missteps and exposes our most intimate secrets, wielding the power of hindsight like an arrogant detective who seems to know the end of the mystery from the outset."[6]

6. Grann, *Killers of the Flower Moon*, 256.

But there is another, common-sense aspect to historicity that is often overlooked in the effort to knit together a useful perspective on the past, one that is particularly true the older the subject. Understandably, the more distant the narrative, the more difficult it is to access the raw materials of history with any real certainty. The historian is increasingly reliant on primary documentation that is difficult to verify. We trust Thucydides, Tacitus, Eusebius, and Josephus, even though it is a challenge to verify or test their fact patterns. The older the account, the greater the gaps. Hence, we tend to have a broader tolerance and accept a wider latitude of interpretation for accounts thousands of years old than we do for those only a hundred years removed from the moment.

Equally valuable as the sources, however, all historical analyses, including ancient accounts, should be able to validate their accuracy by virtue of their linear connections with the present. Blocks of data that seem to be outliers in the narrative, and which may require intellectual gymnastics to make fit, are probably suspect. While we may vigorously dispute the outcomes, we must still acknowledge the value of such a process. Historical linearity adds to credibility, even though the tensions of interpretation remain.

A simple example from my own area of graduate research, colonial and revolutionary America, may be helpful. The lost colony of Roanoke has become the grist for many an academic mill, but four hundred fifty years later, there is still no definitive explanation for its significance or disappearance. Yet we do not doubt that its existence adds to a much larger pattern of understanding what followed: the European founding of the colonies, their subsequent development, and the emergence of the United States. Furthermore, it does not fall outside of the pattern preceding the Roanoke settlement. It is not an outlier; it is not unique despite its opaqueness. The point is that it really does not matter for the larger purposes of understanding colonial, English, or American history precisely what happened to the lost colony because the broad strokes of history before and after 1587 are patently evident. The present does not deny the certainty that something happened in the sixteenth century that we cannot explain, nor does the fact that the exact circumstances of that event are as yet unknown undermine, in any meaningful way, the present. We know something happened in 1587, in part, because the narrative that precedes and follows is cohesive. Present realities are completely consistent with the lost colony, and the story of the lost colony supports and reinforces these present realities.

The requirement that history demonstrate linear logic and cohesiveness is an important part of understanding the historical credentials of the Creation narrative. Archeologists and anthropologists have brought to light some exciting and fascinating finds over the past two or three centuries. As their tools continue to become more sophisticated, we can expect even more information to be uncovered in the future. Much of this has taken place in territories covered by the biblical narrative. Without getting sidetracked on questions of whether there was a real Noah or an actual ark, the evidence makes clear, and continues to make clear, that something real did exist and that it has informed generations for thousands of years. The fact that Abraham, Moses, and the patriarchs are essential to Judaism, Christianity, and Islam up to the present provides that linear connection with the past. We are not allowed to bypass the logical in order to form the past in our own image.

While America and the lost colony are geopolitical narratives, the same rules of evidence should apply to religious narratives. Judaism, Christianity, and Islam have been at one another's throats, in one shape or another, since the third or fourth centuries, but each faith tradition holds tight to the reality of the Creation narrative. Something happened thousands of years ago that gave rise to Abraham, Moses, and the patriarchs, and what happened has been memorialized in the Torah, the first five books of the modern Bible. And it is real because it has a cohesive linearity with present realities.

We accord some tangible reality to the lost colony because there is a tangible reality to the American colonies, the United States, and their recorded histories, even if the interpretations of those histories vary widely. This despite the fact that many individual details have been rethought or rejected over time. The raw materials line up with what we know and experience. We must accord the same tangible realities to the first five books of the Bible because there continues to be a tangible reality to the faith narratives that grew out of a documented tradition dating back to Abraham. Judaism is a historical reality that can be documented, as can Christianity and Islam. The fact that intense disagreements continue to divide the faiths only reinforces the reality of those faiths to their adherents. The present is real, and its realities are logically and linearly connected with the past.

Those who wrote the Bible were not historians in any modern sense in that they did not utilize anything closely approximating a scientific method. They did consult the concrete, raw materials of history available to them in order to form a narrative of their past and the past of the region they inhabited. They were scrupulous enough to record details that would be recognizable for the generations that followed. And they were sufficiently successful as evidenced by the impact their narratives have had on that which followed.

This despite the fact that they recorded events that were absolutely contrary to, or in defiance of, normative individual or social patterns. Take the case of Abram, who was called to sacrifice his son. That was not an uncommon practice at the time, particularly in the pagan culture Abram and his family inhabited. Often, sacrifices of this nature, as abhorrent as they appear to the modern reader, were part of the process of appeasing the gods. The horrific evidence of child sacrifice has been uncovered in what was ancient Carthage, even after the practice had been harshly criticized and abandoned throughout the Roman Empire.[7] What was uncommon was Abram's decision to interrupt the sacrifice, something that would have been considered dangerously offensive to the gods. It was outside of normative cultural expectations. In other words, if the Scriptures were developed to further an existing agenda, why would such emphasis have been put on something that deviated so far from the norm?

Furthermore, Abram named the place. The one writing the account thousands of years later notes that it is still known "to this day."[8] That observation would be illogical and would undermine the credibility of the account, if readers could not find and identify the place. And there would have been no value in recording Abram's decision to deviate from existing norms, had Abram and that event not remained relevant and impactful for millions of people in the future. There can be little doubt that others deviated from cultural norms in the past, but Abram's behavior informed the future in ways others' behaviors have not.

The lineage of Abram/Abraham is confirmed in a variety of ways, and documentation leads to kings whose existence can be independently verified. These kings, including David and Solomon and the kings of Israel and Judah who followed, left increasingly accessible artifacts of their reigns and their interactions with kingdoms and empires around them. As more archeological data has been discovered, nothing has appeared to invalidate their existence or the general outlines of their societies and

7. Hanson, *End of Everything*, 72–73.

8. Gen 22:14. These sorts of references can be found throughout the Old Testament.

cultures. Despite redaction analyses that question who may have written what and when, or even suggest that some elements of scriptural history were invented to fit the narrative, both the Old and New Testaments have an indisputable linear relationship with the broad strokes of the last two thousand or so years of world history. To deny this truth defies both logic and common sense.

Source materials and motivations are part of the fabric of all historians. In the case of the Bible, many of its writers were trying to simply record what was going on around them. There is ample evidence to document Israelis in Egypt at the time of the pharaohs, and the migration of a group of Jews from Egypt. The same can be said for their arrival in Canaan, exile in Babylon, and the rebuilding of Jerusalem. Historians both sacred and secular acknowledge the person of Jesus, as well as the life, death, and writings of the apostles. Clearly, the world is radically different in the decades following Jesus' life on this earth from life before Jesus. People observed what was around them, did their best to make sense of it, and recorded why and how things came to be. It is a cohesive and linear story, and there is no reason to dismiss the narrative simply because it seems miraculous to some today. There are myriad examples of fortuitous occurrences in many historical accounts that cannot be easily explained, yet these events are not dismissed out of hand as the miraculous is in Scripture.

What too many today are afraid to do is acknowledge the word of God as a reliable source. If someone avoids a fatal accident, it is good fortune. If a decision is made in the moment that turns out to be the right one, it is intuition. Those writing the Bible were divinely inspired. They moved beyond history as participants in a divine narrative. God is the historian, which does not make this any more suspect than some of the questionable historical theories recounted on popular television, film, or literary outlets. Furthermore, unlike many of these documentaries, the biblical accounts are part of a linear narrative that is internally cohesive and logical from Genesis to the Revelation.

Creation is the beginning of history. Creation is history; it is the history of salvation. It is the story of a Creator who has such love for His creation that he does not abandon it when it fails but sustains it through time. The creation of the universe, moving through the patriarchs, recorded in the Torah, and documented in the lives and artifacts of prophets and apostles, is a living, ongoing history. It is believable because it is real, a reality reflected in the thoughts and actions of its followers from the beginning of time. Thoughts and actions that have had profound, meaningful, and irrefutable impacts on human society. There can be no greater reality.

No serious scholar would deny the impact Christianity has had on Western civilization, and the emergence of a powerful intellectual, political, social, and economic impulse that drove the development of the modern world. For thousands of years, that guiding impulse was, and can still be, traced back through the scriptural narrative straight to the idea of Creation by an omnipotent and omniscient Creator. All of that came under assault from a mid-twentieth century postmodernism, which derived its energy from a secularism divorced from any of the Abrahamic faith traditions. Whether coherently articulated or not, the purpose was to undermine Creation as a legitimate, documented historical narrative. When Creation as a history of salvation and redemption, in the truest sense of history, is allowed to be discredited, then it can be disconnected from the truth and allowed to languish as a distant artifact of an unsophisticated past.

Secular history is being written; God's history is already written. The gift of being made in His image, of being offered language and speech as instruments of governance and social responsibility, is the gift of participating in both histories simultaneously. Paul's call to be workers in the new kingdom is the opportunity to identify and share God's history. The threads of language and speech that bind all of Scripture are evidences of the living history of Creation. Monotheism and the covenantal nature of our enduring relationship with God are certainly traits that distinguish Creation from myth, as does the power of language and speech. But it is through the latter that we are uniquely invited to immediately and materially act on His behalf. To the question, who owns history? God owns history, and we are called to be His curators.

# Bibliography


Arnold, Bill T., and Bryan E. Beyer. *Readings from the Ancient Near East.* Grand Rapids: Baker Academic, 2002.

Athanasius. *On the Incarnation.* Translated by Sister Penelope Lawson. N.p.: Pantianos Classics, 1944.

Barker, Kenneth, ed. *KJV Study Bible.* Grand Rapids: Zondervan, 2002.

Barton, John, and John Muddiman, eds. *The Oxford Bible Commentary.* New York: Oxford University Press, 2000.

Bloch, Marc. *The Historian's Craft.* New York: Vintage, 1953.

*Book of Common Prayer.* Huntington Beach, CA: Anglican Liturgy, 2019.

Campbell, Joseph. *The Hero with a Thousand Faces.* 3rd ed. Novato, CA: New World Library, 2008.

———. *Pathways to Bliss: Mythology and Personal Transformation.* Novato, CA: New World Library, 2004.

———. *Thou Art That: Transforming Religious Metaphor.* Novato, CA: New World Library, 1991.

Campbell, Joseph, and Bill Moyers. *The Power of Myth.* Edited by Betty Sue Flowers. New York: Anchor, 1991.

Cargill, Robert R. *The Cities That Built the Bible.* New York: HarperCollins, 2016.

Carr, Edward Hallett. *What Is History?* New York: Vintage, 1961.

Dennis, Lane T., et al., eds. *ESV Study Bible.* Wheaton, IL: Crossway, 2008.

Foster, Gaines M. *Ghosts of the Confederacy: Defeat, the Lost Cause, and the Emergence of the New South, 1865–1913.* New York: Oxford University Press, 1987.

Gathercole, Simon, ed. *The Apocryphal Gospels.* London: Penguin Classics, 2021.

Gordon, Cyrus H., and Gary A. Rendsburg. *The Bible and the Ancient Near East.* New York: W. W. Norton, 1997.

Grann, David. *Killers of the Flower Moon.* New York: Doubleday, 2017.

Hanson, Victor Davis. *The End of Everything: How Wars Descend into Annihilation.* New York: Basic, 2024.

Hawkes, Terence. *Structuralism and Semiotics.* 2nd ed. New York: Routledge, 2003.

Honderich, Ted, ed. *The Oxford Companion to Philosophy.* New York: Oxford University Press, 1995.

Hulbert, Matthew Christopher. *Oracle of Lost Causes: John Newman Edwards and His Never-Ending Civil War.* Lincoln: University of Nebraska Press, 2023.

Kant, Immanuel. *The Critique of Practical Reason.* Translated by Thomas Kingsmill Abbott. Orlando: Value, 2024.

———. *Critique of Pure Reason*. Translated by J. M. D. Meiklejohn. Orlando: Reprinted from the public domain, 2024.

———. *Groundwork of the Metaphysics of Morals*. Translated by H. J. Paton. New York: HarperCollins, 2009.

———. *The Metaphysics of Morals*. Edited by Lara Denis. Translated by Mary Gregor. Cambridge: Cambridge University Press, 2017.

King, Charles. *Gods of the Upper Air: How a Circle of Renegade Anthropologists Reinvented Race, Sex, and Gender in the Twentieth Century*. New York: Doubleday, 2019.

Laurier Students' Public Interest Research Group (LSPIRG). "Know the Land Territories Campaign." https://www.lspirg.org/knowtheland.

Levi-Strauss, Claude. *Myth and Meaning: Cracking the Code of Culture*. New York: Schocken, 1979.

Lewis, C. S. *The Lion, the Witch, and the Wardrobe*. The Chronicles of Narnia 2. London: HarperCollins, 2023.

———. *The Magician's Nephew*. The Chronicles of Narnia 1. London: HarperCollins, 2023.

*Life Application Bible*. Wheaton, IL: Tyndale House, 1988.

Long, Charles. *Alpha: The Myths of Creation*. New York: George Braziller, 1963.

May, Herbert G., and Bruce M. Metzger, eds. *The New Oxford Annotated Bible with the Apocrypha*. New York: Oxford University Press, 1977.

McGrath, Alister. *Heresy: A History of Defending the Truth*. New York: HarperCollins, 2009.

Metzger, Bruce M., and Michael D. Coogan, eds. *The Oxford Companion to the Bible*. New York: Oxford University Press, 1993.

Mittelmeier, Martin. *Naples 1925: Adorno, Benjamin, and the Summer That Made Critical Theory*. Translated by Shelly Frisch. New Haven, CT: Yale University Press, 2024.

Montgomery, Eric R. "The Image of God as the Resurrected State in Pauline Thought." Presented at ETS Southwest Regional Conference, New Orleans Baptist Theological Seminary, Mar. 11, 2005.

Morrow, Lance. "America's Political Story Lines Need a Reboot." *Wall Street Journal*, Aug. 15, 2022.

Northwestern University. "Native American and Indigenous Initiatives." https://www.northwestern.edu/native-american-and-indigenous-peoples/.

Otto, Rudolf. *The Idea of the Holy*. Translated by John Harvey. N.p.: Pantianos Classics, 1923.

Owens, D. Alfred, and Mark Wagner, eds. *Progress in Modern Psychology: The Legacy of American Functionalism*. Westport, CT: Praeger, 1992.

Overgoor, Gijs, et al. "From Representation to Reception: Evaluating the Impact of Diversity in TV Advertising on Consumer Purchase Intention." Research paper no. 4471248, Northeastern University D'Amore-McKim School of Business, June 2023.

Persico, Tomer. *In God's Image: How Western Civilization Was Shaped by a Revolutionary Idea*. New York: New York University Press, 2025.

Peters, F. E. *Judaism, Christianity, and Islam: The Monotheists*. Prince Frederick, MD: Recorded, 2003.

Podhoretz, Norman. *The Prophets: Who They Were, What They Are.* New York: Free, 2002.

Raphael, Rina. *The Gospel of Wellness: Gyms, Gurus, Goop, and the False Promise of Self-Care.* New York: Henry Holt, 2022.

Rendsburg, Gary A. *The Redaction of Genesis.* Winona Lake, IN: Eisenbrauns, 2014.

Roper, Lyndal. *Martin Luther: Renegade and Prophet.* New York: Random House, 2016.

Rosner, Anna, and Martin Eisend. "Ethnic Minorities in Advertising." *Journal of Advertising* 52.5 (2023) 774–84. https://doi.org/10.1080/00913367.2023.2255247.

Singer, Peter, ed. *A Companion to Ethics.* Malden, MA: Blackwell, 2001.

Slotkin, Richard. *A Great Disorder: National Myth and the Battle for America.* Boston: Belknap, 2024.

Smith, Mark. *The Origins of Biblical Monotheism.* New York: Oxford University Press, 2001.

Sproul, Barbara C. *Primal Myths: Creation Myths Around the World.* New York: HarperCollins, 1979.

Strong, James. *The New Strong's Expanded Exhaustive Concordance of the Bible.* Nashville: Thomas Nelson, 2010.

Sturrock, John. *Structuralism.* 2nd ed. Hoboken, NJ: Blackwell, 2003.

Swaim, Barton. "Like Pharaoh, Putin's Heart 'Was Hardened.'" *Wall Street Journal*, July 17, 2025.

Wainwright, William. "Monotheism." *Stanford Encyclopedia of Philosophy*, edited by Edward N. Zalta. https://plato.stanford.edu/entries/monotheism/.

Wallace, David Foster. "David Foster Wallace on Life and Work." *Wall Street Journal*, Sept. 19, 2008. https://www.wsj.com/articles/SB122178211966454607.

Wright, N. T. *The Day the Revolution Began.* New York: HarperCollins, 2016.

———. *Surprised by Hope.* New York: HarperCollins, 2008.

Young, Edward Joseph. *Old Testament Prophecy: Lectures Delivered in Toronto Baptist Seminary.* Toronto: Gospel Witness, 1965.

www.ingramcontent.com/pod-product-compliance
Lightning Source LLC
LaVergne TN
LVHW050625100826
845148LV00011B/1738

* 9 7 9 8 3 8 5 2 7 5 6 2 5 *